∾ ∾

HORS D'OEUVRE VARIE

CELERY   OLIVES   NUTS   ROLLS

CONSOMME CELESTINE

FILET OF SOLE SAUTE AU BEURRE

HALF BROILED CHICKEN ON TOAST

NEW STRING BEANS   LONG BRANCH POTATOES

LETTUCE AND TOMATOES WITH FRENCH DRESSING

VANILLA AND CHOCOLATE ICE CREAM

CAKES

DEMI TASSE

ADD A PINCH OF PIZAZZ

The proceeds realized from the sale of ADD A PINCH OF
PIZAZZ will return to the community through the ten
services supported, sponsored and provided by
Assistance League of Southern California:
Children's Theatre
Day Nursery
Family Service Agency
Girls' Club of Hollywood
Operation School Bell®
Over-Fifty Club
Hollywood Senior Citizens Multipurpose Center
Toy Loan
San Fernando Valley Volunteer Bureau
Valley Child Care Centers

Published By
Assistance League of Southern California
1370 North St. Andrews Place
Los Angeles, California 90028

First Edition
First Printing 1979

Library of Congress Catalog Card Number: 79-67240

Produced By
Kenneth Davidson

Composition by
Toby Weston
Woodland Hills, CA

Printed in the United States of America

ADD A PINCH OF PIZAZZ

WITH RECIPES
FROM MEMBERS AND FRIENDS
OF
ASSISTANCE LEAGUE OF SOUTHERN CALIFORNIA
INCLUDING
INTERNATIONAL LEADERS IN THE
ARTS AND PROFESSIONS

*Special Material
Written and Compiled By
Lorraine Wood*

ASSISTANCE LEAGUE OF SOUTHERN CALIFORNIA

INTRODUCTION

"All For Service And Service For All"

Situated in the heart of Hollywood, Assistance League of Southern California has been serving the community since 1919.

In 1924, as a means of aiding mothers working in the new motion picture studios as "extras," the League opened the first licensed Day Nursery in Los Angeles. For many years the large private estates in the Los Angeles area could be obtained for film sites only through the League's Film Location Bureau, hailed as an indispensable boon by all production executives.

In addition to the many philanthropies begun since that time, our Tearoom has been well known as a charming oasis of simple elegance, good food, and a relaxing atmosphere. Performers and executives working in the nearby movie and radio studios have made it their favorite spot for luncheon since the heydays of the 20's, 30's and 40's. Since the 50's, television and recording artists have added their charisma to carry on the tradition.

Our first cookbook, "THE PALATISTS", was published in 1933 with many of Hollywood's most distinguished and talented citizens joining in. Our sixtieth anniversary will be celebrated by bringing you "ADD A PINCH OF PIZAZZ" and we are, again, proud of the enthusiastic cooperation we have received.

Barbara Harris

MRS. CHANDLER HARRIS
President
Assistance League of
Southern California

FOREWORD

Creating and assembling "ADD A PINCH OF PIZZAZ" has been a labor of love, and an opportunity for an exceptional group of women to work together in the interests of their community. Volunteers rarely receive the recognition they deserve so we give a special word of appreciation for some extraordinary contributions to the publication of this book. Patricia Alcantara is responsible for the outstanding collection of recipes you will find here and had to make some difficult decisions in selecting about five hundred recipes from over one thousand four hundred submitted. Helena Smith received, collated, converted and distributed countless copies of those fourteen hundred recipes. For over a year Mary Melone and Kathleen Parker supervised and coordinated sixty-eight evaluators who had agreed to spend considerable time, effort and money in personally testing all of these recipes. Fran Armstrong was given the thankless job of formulating an "absolutely perfect" index and we think she succeeded admirably.

Each member of the Cookbook Committee was perceptive and productive. In particular, Sylvie Mast, Edna Benoit and Kathleen Ramos gave countless hours and months of dedication to their tasks. In the land of the super-colossal, the super-fantastic, and the "supercallifragilisticexpialadocius," this Committee was Super-Everything! Hope you enjoy reading and using this book as much as we enjoyed preparing it for you.

LORRAINE WOOD

COOKBOOK COMMITTEE

Lorraine Wood
Chairman

RECIPES

Patricia Alcantara
Chairman

Frances Armstrong
Glenda Gribben
Nancy Kemp
Kathleen Ramos
Helena Smith
Marilyn Smith

EDITORS

Gretchen Adamson
Gloria Arnett
Edna Benoit
Patricia Brander
Jean Maloney
Sylvie Mast
Helen Ostengaard
Catherine Rea
Adrienne Underwood

EVALUATION

Mary Melone
Kathleen Parker
Veronica Plested

DISTRIBUTION

Patricia Brander
M. Evelyn Field
Marty Morin

ART

Patricia Spears

EX OFFICIO

Barbara Harris
President

PROMOTION

Shirley Uhler
Esther Wachtell

Barbara Ryan
*Vice President,
Ways and Means*

Assistance League of Southern California
EXECUTIVE COMMITTEE

Barbara Harris
President

Evaluation Committee

Mary Melone, Kathleen Parker, Veronica Plested

Co-Chairmen

Frances Ach
Patricia Alcantara
Barbara Amstadter
Edith Anderson
Gloria Arnett
Frances Armstrong
Carol Baum
Claire Baumen
Barbara Baumgartner
Judy Brown
Tenita Christensen
Helen Clark
Roberta Copas
Lorrie Edelbrock
Susan Ehlers
Christina Emerson
Martha Farrell
Dorothy Gattman
Catherine Graw
Katherine Gray
June Griffen
Elizabeth Haberman
Kirsten Hall
Millicent Hardinge
Pauline Harris
Jeanne Hayes
Ingrid Hedberg
Mimi Hodge
Beth Howell
Rose Huff
Helen Johnston
Lea Ann King
Andrea Klausen

Hazel Lane
Louise Larsen
Adrienne Lee
Rita Livingston
Muriel Lowther
Vicki Mazzei
Eileen McConnell
Ann McGeary
Grace Hester McKnight
Sally Mitchell
Katherine Morris
Kathryn Murphy
Helen Mynatt
Diane Newhouse
Helen Ostengaard
Carolyn Padden
Roberta Pollack
Ingrid Pollakoff
Linda Prinn
Louise Reich
Jean Rousselot
Barbara Ryan
Evelyn Sampson
Diane Saunders
Roberta Skovo
Patricia Spears
Janet Steiger
Mary Anne Thomas
Beverly Thrall
Jewell Waters
Sally Williams
Lorraine Wood
Karen Young

Marjorie Kolliner

ACKNOWLEDGEMENT

of our grateful appreciation to
the gracious and cooperative chefs, directors of public relations, managers and owners
who so generously gave of their assistance, their knowledge and their time.

HOTELS

Ambassador	Beverly Hills	Beverly Wilshire
Bel-Air	Beverly Hilton	Biltmore

RESTAURANTS

Assistance League of Southern California Tearoom

Bernard's	Ma Maison
The Bistro	The Music Center Pavilion
Bullocks Wilshire Tea Room	NBC Commissary
Clifton's Cafeterias	Perino's Restaurant
Cock 'n' Bull Restaurant	Rangoon Racquet Club
L'Ermitage	Ruffage Restaurant
Jimmy's Restaurant	Scandia
Madame Wu's Garden	The Windsor Restaurant

CATERERS

Catering by Milton, Inc.
The Moveable Feast
Rócoco, Custom Catering Service

The Academy of Motion Picture Arts and Sciences; Les Amis d' Escoffier; Hernando
Courtright; The Greater Los Angeles Zoo Association; Junior League of Los Angeles; Bee
Lavery, Protocol, Office of the Mayor; Los Angeles County Museum of Art; and Variety
Clubs International for allowing us to share the memories of their events.

Lindsley Parsons, Jr., Paramount Pictures Corp., for permission to use the "Western
Street" for the photograph on the jacket cover, and to Jerry Smith, International
Photographers, Local #659, I.A.T.S.E. for the waiver to photograph on the studio
premises.

George B. Spears, an amateur photographer with professional skill, for the photograph on
the jacket cover.

Kenneth Davidson, of the Times Mirror Press, Los Angeles, California, for his support
and guidance.

Accent on Seasoning, Irma G. Mazza (Little, Brown and Company); *American Popular Songs,* edited by David Ewen (Random House); *American Society of Composers, Authors, and Publishers Biographical Dictionary,* compiled and edited by The Lynn Farnol Group, Inc.; *The Art of Eating,* M.F.K. Fisher (Vintage Books); *Astrology, Nutrition and Health,* Robert Carl Jansky (Para Research, Inc.); *The Complete Astrologer,* Derek and Julia Parker (McGraw-Hill Book Company); *Encyclopedia of Medical Astrology,* Howard Leslie Cornell, M.D., L1.D. (Llewellyn Publications); *Herbs, Health and Astrology,* Leon Petulengro (Keats Publishing, Inc.); *The Literary Gourmet,* written and edited by Linda Wolfe; *Oxford Dictionary of Quotations* (Oxford University Press); Brillat-Severin's *The Physiology of Taste,* translated by M.F.K. Fisher (Alfred A. Knopf); *Popular Music,* edited by Nat Shapiro (Adrian Press); *Variety Music Cavalcade,* Julius Mattfelt (Prentice Hall, Inc.); Academy of Motion Picture Arts and Sciences Library; *Los Angeles Examiner; Los Angeles Herald Examiner; Los Angeles Times;* Ichiro Kawamoto and Tom Martin.

the "stars" who took the time and effort to join us in presenting this star-studded culinary picture of our community.

all members and friends of Assistance League of Southern California who gave so generously of their recipes, and who will be understanding and forgiving if their special favorites didn't make it into print.

CONTENTS

MEMORABLE
MENUS

"LIGHTS! CAMERA! ACTION!!"

The first Oscars had been presented the year before when the Academy of Motion Pictures Arts and Sciences gave its first Awards Banquet on Thursday, May 16, 1929, in the popular Hollywood Roosevelt Hotel on Hollywood Boulevard, across the street from the famous Grauman's Chinese Theatre.

William DeMille presided over 250 guests also celebrating the fiftieth anniversary of the first motion picture. A host of notables, including Al Jolson and Ruby Keeler with Norma Shearer and Irving Thalberg were there to see who would win the awards for outstanding achievement in the motion picture field during 1928.

The winners included Emil Jannings, best actor in "The Way Of All Flesh" and "The Last Command"; Janet Gaynor, best actress in "Seventh Heaven", "Sunrise", and "The Sweet Angel"; and Ben Hecht, best writer of an original story, "Underworld". The most outstanding picture was "Wings" by Paramount Famous-Lasky Corp., and a special first award went to Warner Bros. for producing "The Jazz Singer", the pioneer outstanding talking picture.

DINNER

Hors d'oeuvres Varie
Celery   Olives   Nuts   Rolls
Consomme Celestine
Filet of Sole Saute au Buerre
Half Broiled Chicken on Toast
New String Beans   Long Branch Potatoes
Lettuce and Tomatoes with French Dressing
Vanilla and Chocolate Icecream
Cakes
Demi Tasse

"MAY I HAVE THE ENVELOPE, PLEASE?"

On the golden anniversary of the Academy of Motion Picture Arts and Sciences, April 3, 1978, a golden assemblage of the top screen personalities and executives met at the Beverly Hilton Hotel for the traditional Governor's Ball following the presentation of Oscars at the Music Center.

The applause was sincere as the winners approached their tables...Woody Allen's "Annie Hall" had won for Best Picture, Richard Dreyfuss was the Best Actor, and Diane Keaton was Best Actress. The Jean Hersholt Humanitarian Award had been given to actor Charlton Heston and producer Walter Mirisch had earned the coveted Irving Thalberg Memorial Award for Outstanding Achievement.

Bob Hope had been the master of ceremonies for the fourteenth time (including the first televised Academy Awards ceremonies from the stage of the Pantages Theatre in 1953). Everyone was talking about "Close Encounters of the Third Kind," winner for Best Cinematography, and John Williams' winning score for "Star Wars."

The walls of the International Ballroom were covered with yellow silk, the mirrored epergnes on each table reflected the chrysanthemums, iris, roses, and acacia in many shades of yellow. The ceiling was hung with Southern smilax and baskets of more yellow flowers. Even the caviar was served to each guest in a giant yellow chrysanthemum.

Huge Oscars stood in front of black velvet shadow boxes around the edges of the room and were repeated in 5" miniature Oscars on the individual two-tiered Anniversary cakes brought to each table. Among the diners rising to light candles in the dimmed Ballroom and singing "Happy Birthday, dear Oscar," were Fred Astair, Richard Burton, Frank Capra, Bette Davis, Olivia de Havilland, William Holden, Neil Simon and Marsha Mason, Barbara Stanwyck, John Travolta, Henry Winkler and Robert Wise.

SUPPER

Russian Beluga Caviar

Chilled   Eggs Mimosa with Chopped Onions

Stolichnaya Vodka Melba Rounds with Rosettes of Sour Cream

in Ice Block   Canapes of Smoked Salmon

with Onion Rings and Capers

Puilly Fuisse

Les Crays   Crab Legs with Mustard Dill Sauce

1976   Broiled Lobster Tail

with Drawn Butter

Nest of Pommes Alumette aux Champignons

Artichoke Hearts Florentine

Anniversary Cake

Chocolate Mousse, White Icing, Gold Trimming

"50" Inscribed on Each Bottom Tier

"GUESS WHO'S COMING TO DINNER, DEAR?... THE BRITISH HEIR TO THE THRONE, HIS ROYAL HIGHNESS THE PRINCE CHARLES, PRINCE OF WALES."

After a strenuous day of sightseeing and attending a reception given by the British Consul General, the Prince relaxed in the Hancock Park mansion of Los Angeles Mayor and Mrs. Tom Bradley one evening in October, 1977. About eighty dinner guests gathered to greet him, including Olivia Newton-John; Mr. and Mrs. Peter O'Malley, owners of the Los Angeles Dodgers; Helen Reddy; and the Lew Wassermans of the MCA entertainment empire.

The next night a charity benefit at the Beverly Hilton Hotel jointly hosted by St. John's Hospital Health Care Center and Variety Clubs, International, sparkled with more of Hollywood's big names. Cary Grant, chairman of the event, led the guests rising to honor His Highness' entrance.

Tasting hors d'oeuvres at the Jubilee Reception in the Versailles Ballroom, guests admired the two impressive ice sculptures on the long buffet table, then entered the International Ballroom for dinner and dancing. The perfect ending to a perfect evening was Dean Martin as master of ceremonies, presenting a program featuring Bob Newhart with some hilarious monologues and, of course, Dino himself in full voice, witty and charming.

Later, among those waiting for their cars and limousines under the marquee at the U-shaped drive, Farrah Fawcett-Majors with Lee Majors, the Charlton Hestons, Sophia Loren and Carlo Ponti, the Gregory Pecks, the Sidney Poitiers, Governor and Mrs. Ronald Reagan, and the Jimmy Stewarts could be seen.

RECEPTION

Whole Smoked Salmon Garni on Wooden Board

Tartines of Rye and Pumpernickel Bread

Lemon Wedges and Capers

California Crab on Ice

Fresh Jumbo Shrimps in giant sea shells and Cocktail Sauce

Blue Point Oysters on Half-Shell

Cherrystone Clams on Ice

California Raw Vegetable Tray with Fresh Parsley Yogurt Dip

Hot Hors d'Oeuvres Will be Passed Butler-style During the Reception:

French Quiche Lorraine

Mushroom Caps Dante with Crab

Hawaiian Teriyaki with Cho-Chos

Chinese Eggroll

Polynesian Rumaki

Susu Curry Puffs

Russian Meat Piroshkis

DINNER

California
Vintage
White Wine

California
Vintage
Red Wine

Grand
Marnier

California Avocado with Seafood Remoulade

Half Avocado filled with Seafood served in Silver Supreme

Roast New York Sirloin of Beef

Sauce Perigourdine

Baked Tomato Florentine

Broccoli Hearts Polonaise

San Bernardino Biscuit Glacé

Orange Sherbet and Vanilla Ice Cream between Pastry Layers decorated with miniature U.S. and British Flags, served with Apricotine Sauce

Bounty of Country Cheeses

with

Cornucopia of Fresh Fruit and Crackers

Coffee

"CONGRATULACIONES Y DESEOS!"

A highlight of the Summer Social Season in Beverly Hills was the August 18, 1978, wedding of Florence Falzone and Hernando Courtright.

Known affectionately as El Padrino of Los Angeles, an honorary title for a leading citizen held by only one other, Leo Carrillo, Mr. Courtright is the builder and owner of the Beverly Wilshire Hotel. Scion of one of California's earliest families, he claims his Spanish heritage as a direct descendant of the 15th-16th century conqueror of Mexico, Hernando Cortez.

No ancient Spanish garden ever looked more romantic than the Ballrooms in his hotel that evening. White lace over lace tablecloths in the Grand Trianon held centerpieces of crystal candlesticks and silver cylinders, 24", 30", and 36" tall with white candles, maidenhair fern, gardenias, and peach tuberous begonias arranged on mirror bases.

Topiary trees trimmed with gardenias and peach begonias provided a setting for strolling violinists during the Reception in the Petit Trianon. Murray Korda and his orchestra played for dancing later from a stage set with nine-foot crystal epergnes where white and peach roses towered above the musicians.

Among the close friends congratulating El Padrino and his bride were Mr. and Mrs. Miguel Aleman, Jr., the Edgar Bergens, Mrs. Clark Gable, Judge and Mrs. McIntyre Faries, Mr. and Mrs. Michael J. Fasman, Mrs. Irene Dunne Griffin, the Arthur Linkletters, Sheriff and Mrs. Peter J. Pitchess, and Mr. Jose Trujillo.

RECEPTION

1971 Taittinger
Blanc de Blanc Brut

Canapes
Smoked Sturgeon
Scottish Salmon
Pate de Foie de Gras Truffe

DINNER

1971 Taittinger
Blanc de Blanc Brut
1971 Batard-Montrachet
Raoul Clerget
1964 Grands-Echezeaux

Baked Potato with Caviar
Scampi au Vin Blanc de Bourgogne
Medallion of Veal Madere
Souffle Potatoes
Chinese Peas
Kentucky Limestone
Brie Cheese

1976 Schlor Johannisberg
Spatles
Cognac

Raspberries, Heavy Cream
Wedding Cake
Demi-Tasse
Zeste d'Orange

"AND-AH ONE, AND-AH TWO, AND-AH SEVENTY-FIVE!"

No one laughed louder nor danced longer than the Birthday Boy himself when Lawrence Welk celebrated his seventy-fifth birthday on March 11, 1978. As their gift, members of his musical family provided the entertainment with a tuneful "roast" of song parodies relating to Welk's seventy-five years. Other gifts included a giant video screen for his home and a life-size oil portrait. Capping this evening of polkas, parodies and portraits, was the three-tiered birthday cake, chocolate with mocha cream filling, white icing, pink highlights, and a large diamond-studded "75" on top! The Crystal Ballroom of the Beverly Hills Hotel was filled with 150 close friends and members of the Welk personal and musical families, including his wife and two daughters, Shirley and Donna; Larry, Jr. and his wife Tanya; Eddie Shipstad of the Shipstad and Johnson Ice Follies; singers Joe Feeney and Jim Roberts; dancers Bobby Burgess and Cissy King; clarinetist Henry Cuesta; dancer Arthur Duncan and singer Ana Cani with her new husband.

HORS D'OEUVRES

Polo Dip

Platters of Guacamole, Salmon, and Plain Cheese Dip

DINNER

Iced Relishes

Seafood Au Gratin En Coquille

Eastern Roast Sirloin of Beef, sauce Choron

Special Baked Potato

Broccoli Polonaise

Rolls And Butter

Spumoni Ice Cream Bombe

Kirsch Sauce

Coffee Tea Sanka

Birthday Cake

日 米 親 善 の 宴

Following a public appearance at the Music Center on October 8, 1975, Their Majesties, the Emperor and Empress of Japan, were escorted by Mayor and Mrs. Tom Bradley to the Grand Hall of the Dorothy Chandler Pavilion as the guests of honor at a luncheon attended by about 500 invited guests. The huge Bavarian crystal chandeliers shone down on a large portion of the Japanese-American community and the leaders of the civic, cultural and business sectors of Los Angeles.

It was truly an Affair of State. Keiichi Tachibana, Consul General of Japan in Los Angeles and Mrs. Tachibana; the Victor Carters, president of the local chapter of the Japan America Society; Mr. Kumanosuke Inadomi, president of Japanese Chamber of Commerce of Southern California; and Mr. Motosume Kobayashi, president of Japan Traders Club, were chatting with members of the official royal party from Japan.

Among the guests admiring his Majesty's Imperial Seal, reproduced in flowers hanging from the Pavilion balcony, were Mrs. Norman Chandler, John Wayne, the Charlton Hestons, Mrs. Francis Lederer, Dr. and Mrs. Thomas Noguchi, Iron Eyes Cody, the Eddie Alberts, and former California governor, the Honorable and Mrs. Edmund G. Brown.

The decor and menu featured the official colors of the City of Los Angeles. Donated by the Southern California Flower Growers, Inc. and the Japanese American Florists, centerpieces of yellow chrysanthemums and bird of paradise (the city's official flower) were set on orange tablecloths made especially by members of the West Los Angeles Japanese Citizens League Auxiliary.

The ceremonies opened with the stirring anthems of both countries..."Kimigayo" and "Star-Spangled Banner", played by the Japanese Philharmonic Orchestra of Los Angeles under the direction of Akira Kikukawa. Representing the Spanish and Mexican heritage of Los Angeles, "Los Trovadores", a Mexican-American mariachi band, played background music during the Reception and Luncheon.

LUNCHEON

California Salad

Almaden Special
Selection
Pinot Chardonnay

Bibb Lettuce, Romaine, Avocado, Cranshaw Melon,
Fresh Orange and Grapefruit Segments, Watercress

Lorenzo Dressing

Cheese Wafers

Almaden Special
Selection
Vintage 1972,
Magnums
Cabernet Sauvignon

Petit Filet Mignon, Mushroom Caps

Monterey Sauce

Burgandy Wine Sauce

Artichoke Bottoms with Puree of Carrots

Buttered Stringbeans

French Cut, topped with Shredded Jicamas
Parsley

Assorted Rolls with Butter Balls

Almaden Champagne
Blanc de Blanc

Cassata Camino Real

Vanilla Ice Cream, Lemon Sherbet, Candied Fruits,
Walnuts, Almonds

Raspberry Sauce

Coffee

DO YOU PANIC AT THE THOUGHT OF SERVING MORE THAN EIGHT GUESTS AT A "SIT-DOWN" DINNER?

Opening the Biltmore Hotel on October 2, 1923, Chef Matthew Gottwaldt provided a gargantuan feast for 3,000 diners. Tables were set in the main Dining Room, Palm Room, Sunken Grill, Supper Room, Ballroom and its foyer, and the Music Room.

Seven orchestras were stationed strategically and played for dancing. A fifty-piece concert orchestra was featured in the lobby under the direction of Herman Heller. Prior to dinner, guests were given a grand tour of the hotel where songbirds trilled from cages placed in secluded corners, with huge vases and baskets of flowers everywhere.

Some of the prominent citizens hosting tables were Dr. and Mrs. Frank F. Barham, Jack Dempsey, Mr. and Mrs. A. P. Giannini, Mr. and Mrs. Secundo Guasti, Capt. and Mrs. G. Allan Hancock, Mr. and Mrs. James Irvine, Jr., Dr. Peter Janss, Don Lee, Sol Lesser, Mrs. Bob Montgomery, Pola Negri, Henry Newby, and a special private trainload of 100 guests from New York City.

DINNER

Supreme of Fruits Valencia
2,000 Oranges; 1,000 Grapefruit; 1,300 Apples; 250 Casaba Melons;
75 Pineapples; 60 gals. Syrup made from Honey and "Other Things"

Essence of Tomato aux Quelles ·
2,000 lbs. tomatoes, 600 lbs. beef

Paillete au Fromage
40 lbs. Feuilletage, 15 lbs. Parmesan Cheese

Celery (3,400 stalks)   Almonds (175 lbs.)   Olives (150 gals.)

Crab Meat Epicurienne
240 qts. Crab Meat, 60 gals. Cream, 60 lbs. Sweet Butter

Noisette of Lamb Favorite
300 Saddles of Lamb, 60 gals. Madeira Sauce

Asparagus Tips Maltaise
500 Cans Asparagus Tips

Breast of Chicken Biltmore
6,000 lbs. Roasting Chickens; 1,000 lbs. Fowl; 150 lbs. Mushrooms,
60 Cans Whole Truffles; 60 gals. Veloute Sauce

New Peas a la Menthe
30 Hampers of Fresh New Peas

Potato Mireille
1,200 lbs. Potatoes

Bread
1,500 Loaves, 400 lbs. Butter

Victory Salade
1,000 Heads Lettuce, 300 lbs. Small Potatoes, 60 gals of Dressing
Composed of Mayonnaise, Rocquefort Cheese and Whipped Cream

Peach Hilda
3,000 Peaches, 500 qts. Ice Cream, 40 gals. Praline Sauce

Assorted Cakes
15,000 Assorted Macaroons, Lady-Fingers, Glace Cakes of Mint,
Chocolate, Raspberry, Raisin, etc.

Coffee
150 gals.

500 Waiters, 125 Cooks Plus Chef, 250 Attendents for Cleaning
and polishing silver, crystal and china

"GENTLEMEN ONLY, PLEASE! NO LADIES ALLOWED."

The first dinner ever served at the fabulous old Biltmore Hotel was a "stag" on September 28, 1923, given by the architects, Messrs. S. Fullerton Weaver and Leonard Schultz in honor of the owners.

A feminine spy, "Prudence Penny" from a local newspaper, described the manner of service..."the waiters were lined up in military order. At a given signal the cooks placed the food on the great tables, at a second signal (two whistles) the waiters serving the guests of honor took their service and moved away, at the third whistle the other waiters took their trays and all moved to the dining room in precision."

Earl Burnett and his orchestra played that night for some of Los Angeles' mightiest businessmen who were in attendance, including Dr. F. Barham, M. Baruch, W. G. Clark, B. V. Collins, Harry Chandler, E. A. Lundquist, J. Milner, W. Taylor and Cornelius Vanderbilt.

DINNER

Hors d'Oeuvres Parisienne

Petite Marmite Henry IV

Celery   Salted Almonds   Olives

Brook Trout Saute Fine Herbes

Saddle of Spring Lamb

Fresh String Beans Fleurette

Roman Punch

Filet of Duckling Oregon

Mousseline of French Peas

Potato Souffle

Cold Virginia Ham, Glacé Mandarin

Salade My Lady

Bombe Victoire

Mignardises

Coffee

"SO WHAT HAVE YOU BEEN DOING SINCE I LAST SAW YOU?"

The most popular and significant singing group since the Nine Muses, the Beatles' first public reunion after their disbanding was just as flamboyant as their career. The occasion was a celebration party Paul McCartney hosted for Wings, the new group which had just completed its first United States cross-country tour.

On June 24, 1976, 550 of his closest friends joined him at the Harold Lloyd Estate in Beverly Hills, every one of them dressed in apple green and/or white, as commanded in their invitations, and wearing the monogrammed white T-shirts given them as they arrived at the gate. A neon jukebox was at full volume for disco dancing around the pool.

Enhanced by strolling Mariachis, a "Mexican Plaza" was recreated along the cobblestone driveway. The Mexican delicacies displayed in stalls were especially popular with the British guests less familiar with this Southern California custom, including John Lennon, Ringo Starr and George Harrison. The historical acreage provided plenty of grounds for table groupings and sightseeing, but everyone gathered together before dinner to enjoy the New York Company of "The Wiz," currently playing at the Music Center, who presented two exciting renditions from "Ease on Down the Road." Among the guests applauding the performance of the Los Angeles Ballet Co. during dinner were Polly Bergen, the Jackson Five, Barbra Streisand, Sonny Bono, and Cher.

DINNER

COCKTAILS-MEXICAN VILLAGE
Tacos, Burritos, Taquitos, & Ceviche

COCKTAILS-DINING ROOM IN HOUSE
Jumbo Shrimp, Lobster & Crab Claws with Seafood Sauce

Smoked Salmon with Capers, Cream Cheese and Onions
Rye and Pumpernickel Bread
Raw Vegetables, Steak Tartare, Pate and Toast

SERVED SEPARATELY IN A PRIVATE ROOM
Linda McCartney's Own Split Pea Soup

DINNER AND DESSERT-TENT
Chateaubriand
Marinated Mushrooms, Poppy Seed Noodles
Russian Salad, Tomatoes Vinaigrette, Sweet & Sour Cucumbers
Assorted Cheeses and Fruit
Imported Crackers, Bagettes & Croissants
Ice Cream
Assorted Cakes and Cookies

DISCO AREA
Liqueurs, Brandies & Coffee

Catering by Milton, Inc.

"DOES ANYBODY HERE LIKE PEANUT BUTTER AND JELLY SANDWICHES?"

Members of Les Amis d'Escoffier look forward with great anticipation to their annual dinner held at a different hotel each year, if possible. Honoring the great chef, Escoffier, the Society is interested in good foods and good wines, and the proper way to enjoy them.

Before World War I, Auguste Escoffier, who presided over the Carlton Hotel in London for sixteen years, sent proteges and students all over the world, mainly to Canada and the United States. His name became synonomous with the highest standards in cooking.

The Los Angeles chapter of Les Amis d'Escoffier numbers about 160 people from all walks of life and is one of many throughout the world who bring together members of the culinary profession and their friends. They maintain strict traditions regarding the proper manner in which to appreciate fine food.

We are privileged to bring you the first public peek at the menu placed before each diner, which includes the following admonition excerpted from their Bylaws.

DINNER RULES

The napkin must be tucked under the collar. There will be no reserved seats. Person under the influence of liquor will not be permitted to sit at the table.

The wines, carefully selected to accompany and enhance the delicacy of each course, must be drunk during the course for which they are intended. To enforce this ruling, the glass — even if full — will be removed at the end of each course.

Smoking is absolutely forbidden up to the time dessert is served. A person who smokes while eating does not deserve the title of "Gourmet"

A WARNING

Since "Les Amis d'Escoffier" Society is dedicated to the art of good living only, it is forbidden under threat of expulsion to speak of personal affairs, one's own work or specialty, and more particularly to attempt to use the Society as a means of making business contacts. It is unecessary to elucidate further upon this delicate subject which everyone understands. Further, at these dinner-meetings reference will never be made to the subjects of politics, religious beliefs, or the personal opinions of either members or guests irrespective of their profession or social status.

In addition, there are never salt and pepper on the table at any meeting of a gourmet society dinner; no ashtrays on the table during dinner; and no smoking after dinner until the chairman gives his permission.

On December 4, 1961, Les Amis d'Escoffier met in the Rendezvous room of the Biltmore Hotel and were served the usual unusually excellent banquet.

AVANT DE PASSER A TABLE

Vermouth Cassis

Dubonnet

Noilly Prat Vermouth

Byrrh

Campari

Chablis Chanson

Le Saumon Fume de la Nouvelle Ecosse

Les Pinces de Crabe, Sauce Moutarde

La Quiche Lorraine

Le Caviar sur Socle de Glacé

LE DINER

La Manzanilla

Muscadet

Clos des Pierres Blanches

1959

Nuits Saint Georges

1957

Pommery Greno

1952

La Soupe de Tortue Verte au Xeres

La Pailletes Dorees

La Fruite de Riviere Marguery

Les Pommes Parisienne

Entrecote Double, Grille, Maitre d'Hotel

Les Endives de Belgique Braises

Les Fonds d'Artichaut Clamart

Le Pate de Lievre

La Salada d'Automne

Les Fromages de France

Le Gateau Glacé a la Biltmore

Sauce Cardinal

Les Friandises

Demi-Tasse

Les Liqueurs

Willium Luchman

Chef de Cuisine

"HAPPY BIRTHDAY, MR. PRESIDENT...I'LL VOTE FOR YOU!"

Back in the days when a ten-dollar dinner was considered "very expensive," the $100-a-plate supper was the backbone of every major political fund-drive. Few were done with such style as the birthday dinners given for President Dwight D. Eisenhower on January 27, 1960, to kick off his re-election campaign.

With closed-circuit television to bring his address and Irene Dunne's introduction to all those present, 84 parties were given simultaneously across the nation. The dinner Ike chose to attend was the one catered by the Hollywood Palladium at the Pan-Pacific Auditorium in West Hollywood.

Harold E. Ramser, chairman of the dinner Committee, planned the evening in the manner of an old Eisenhower family meal such as might have been served in a Kansas home around the turn of the century. Each of the 6,500 diners at the Pan-Pacific received a beautiful leatherette-bound menu containing portraits of the President, President Lincoln and the Eisenhower home in Abilene. Each course was described and accompanied by appropriate sketches.

DINNER BEGINS WITH

Eisenhower Vegetable Soup
This is the President's own recipe.
Next, because this is the big meal of the day, we have

Platters of Tender Beef
Roasted country style
Then a heaping bowl of nice, crisp

Oven Browned Potatoes
And from the farm, fresh corn made into

New England Corn Pudding
To accompany this...here are all the favorites of yesteryear

Cottage Cheese
made this morning

Applesauce
made from the apples on the winesap tree
that probably shades the kitchen window

Plum Jelly
Like the Eisenhower boys helped make
In the big pot on the stove

Sour Cream Cole Slaw
An everyday favorite

Remember the wonderful aroma that filled the kitchen just
Before the oven door opened to loaf after loaf of

Home-Made Bread
Then, the most American dessert of all

Apple Pie
Oven fresh and warm

And because we want to be sure that there is enough for everyone,
A second dessert made from the nuts the boys gathered in the grove

Old-Fashioned Hickory Nut Cake
Topping it off...

Big Steaming Cups of Coffee
and
Pitchers of Cold Milk

"YOU'D BETTER NOT SAY THE BABY LOOKS JUST LIKE HIS 'FATHER'!"

For sheer entertainment, there's no other charity ball quite like the Greater Los Angeles Zoo Association's Beastly Ball, according to Los Angeles Times reporter, Tia Gindick. On September 16, 1978, 435 of the Southland's animal lovers arrived at the Zoo "dressed as zoo will"...safari gear complete with pith helmets, missionary frocks with the motion picture "The African Queen" inspiring quite a few.

The Clark Keene orchestra was providing music for dancing but the live animals wandering among the guests took most of the attention and felt quite at home as the Zoo's theme building had been transformed into a jungle. The R'Wanda Lewis Afro-American Dance Company created more excitement with colorful native dances and pulse-pounding rhythms.

Anticipation mounted in the bidding for the opportunity to adopt a deserving resident of the Zoo. The animal stays at the Zoo but the proud "parent" names it, gets progress reports, has his/her name on a plaque and has all the fun with none of the responsibilities (except financial).

Some animals adopted that evening after dinner included a Nile hippopotamus, an orangutan, a sloth bear, a stump-tailed skunk, a lowland gorilla named Caesar and his baby brother, Brutus. Autographed items were going fast, especially the set of dinner napkins signed by several movie stars, a snake, a gorilla, a snow leopard and a cockatoo! (How...?)

Co-chairmen, Mmes. David R. Cudlip, Jeffrey M. Hobbs and James M. Stewart were busy all evening greeting the star-studded guests, among them the Gregory Peck family, Anthony Hopkins, Earl Holliman, the Gary Berghofs, Betty White and Allen Ludden, Charlton Heston, the Max Jamisons and, of course, Mrs. Stewart's husband, Jimmy.

HORS D'OEUVRES

Silver-tray passing of Hors d'Oeuvres
Stuffed Mushrooms
Cheddar Ramekin with Ortega Chilies
Artichoke Hearts Romano
Spanokopitta
Zucchini Pancakes

BUFFET DINNER

Chef-carving Chateau of Sirloin
Boneless Breast of Chicken
with
Apricot Brandy Sauce and Cashew Nuts
Wild Rice Medley with Pine Nuts
Sliced Beefsteak Tomatoes topped with Avocado and Watercress
Celery Seed Dressing
Chilled Broccoli Helene with Lemon Cream
Miniature Rolls and Croissants, Whipped Butter
Chocolate Mocha Crepes with Chocolate Mint Sauce
Coffee

Rococo, Custom Catering Service

"IT'S A BIRD! IT'S A PLANE! IT'S SUPER-DIRIGIBLE!"

Residents of Los Angeles stood excitedly in the streets and on rooftops to watch the awesome sight of the Graf Zeppelin's arrival on August 26, 1929. After a 79-hour voyage across the Pacific from Tokyo, the first time in the world such a journey had ever been accomplished, Commander Hugo Eckener of the Graf Zeppelin sat down to dinner in the Ambassador Hotel on Wilshire Boulevard.

Only two cities, Los Angeles and New York City, were to be given the opportunity to fete the Zeppelin's occupants on the North American leg of this first great round-the-world aerial trip, which had been underwritten by William Randolph Hearst. He proudly hosted about 1,500 of the most distinguished members of the community to honor the Commander, crew and passengers.

In the Hotel's Coconut Grove, a replica of the Graf Zeppelin was suspended on invisible wires overhead and circled an imaginary world with the orchestra playing appropriate national themes as it traveled, ending with the audience participating in "California Here I Come." Among those in attendance were Governor C.C. Young; Los Angeles Mayor John Porter; Sir Hubert Wilkins, Arctic explorer; and Dr. Robert Milliken, discoverer of the cosmic ray.

Other guests included Mr. and Mrs. Paul Bern, Mr. and Mrs. Harry R. Champlin, Mr. and Mrs. Lon Chaney, Charles Spencer Chaplin, Miss Marion Davies, Mr. and Mrs. Douglas Fairbanks, Sr., Sid Grauman, David Wark Griffith, Mr. and Mrs. Herbert J. Hoover, Mr. and Mrs. Harold Lloyd, Mr. and Mrs. Ernst Lubitsch, Rabbi and Mrs. Edgar F. Magnin, Mr. and Mrs. Louis B. Mayer, Mr. and Mrs. Hunt Stromberg, Mr. and Mrs. C. E. Toberman, and Dr. and Mrs. Rufus B. von KleinSmid.

DINNER

Graf Zeppelin Melon — Sir Hubert

Klare Zwiebelsuppe — Rosendahl

Kassentagen

Forellen in Butter — Hearst

Kartoffel Kugeln

Entbohntes junges Huhn — Eckener

Gebratene Kartoffeln   Grune Erbsen

Romischer Salad von Weigand

Gefrorenes Biscuit — Lady Hay

Kuchen Schiller

Mocha

Looking southeast at the intersection of Sunset Boulevard across the left and Western Avenue across the center. The Fox Western Avenue Studios in the center shows Standing Sets in the "back lot" above. The circled complex of houses is the original home and Tearoom of Assistance League of Southern California.

Circa 1923

"YOU OUGHTA BE IN PICTURES,
OH, WHAT A HIT YOU'D BE . . ."

— 1934

Photograph reproduced
through courtesy of
MARC WANAMAKER
BISON ARCHIVES

"STEWARDESS, THE GARDENIA IN MY FINGERBOWL SEEMS A LITTLE WILTED."

At the end of August, 1929, the Graf Zeppelin sedately made its way across the North American continent to Lakehurst, New Jersey.

Chef Otto Manz had a chance to relax, however, as the nine meals anticipated to be eaten during this time had been prepared in advance by the Biltmore Hotel in Los Angeles. The Biltmore engraved nine sets of menus on cards for the diners and a sample dinner menu shows that they ate in style.

DINNER

Hors d'Oeuvres   Melha Toast

Consommé Julienne

Ruck of Lamb

New Peas and Carrots, Bonne Femme

Potato Sauté

Boston Cream Pie

Assorted Cheese and Crackers

Coffee

"TO SPEAK THE PHARAOH'S NAME IS TO GIVE HIM ETERNAL LIFE."

...a quote found in the tomb.

With exotic Egyptian melodies providing an appropriate background, the Los Angeles County Museum of Art officially became the new temporary home for King Tutankhamun on February 14, 1978.

The Egyptian delegation accompanying the boy ruler and his possessions was headed by the Ambassador, Ashraf Ghorbal, and was welcomed by Museum Trustees president, Richard Sherwood, at the Preview Reception given for a select group of invited guests. The long-awaited exhibit had finally arrived midst much publicized fanfare and excitement. In a city usually blasé to Superstars, King Tut was a SUPER STAR!

Almost as dazzling as the golden artifacts, a 24-foot buffet in the atrium was decorated with four mirrored pyramids, ranging up to 48" in height, reflecting flames from the profusion of candles surrounding the bases. Six-foot grasses accented arrangements of lilies of the Nile, papyrus, Kafir lilies and bachelor buttons (a traditional Egyptian flower) set on the Nile-blue cloth.

Among those enjoying the tour of the exhibit and the authentic Egyptian delicacies were Mrs. Gerald Ford, Dr. and Mrs. Franklin D. Murphy, Betsy and Alfred Bloomingdale, the Holmes Tuttles, Mr. and Mrs. Armand Deutsch, George Sidney, Mervyn and Kitty LeRoy, Lizabeth Scott, Cary Grant and daughter Jennifer, and Mrs. Vincent Price.

BUFFET

Sfeeha
Pizza

Yogurt-Tahini Dip

Foul Madamas

Baba Channouj
Eggplant Sesame Dip

Large Loaves of Sourdough Bread

Roasted Marinated Green Peppers

Tursi
Pickled sliced Turnips and Cauliflower

Tabuoleh Salad served in Romaine Lettuce

Hummus Bi Tahini

Pita Bread
Armenian Cracker Bread

Stylized Pyramid of Crisp Raw Vegetables

Tarama and Cucumber Mint Dips

Konafa

Haresa

Kourambiedes

Baklava

Queeas

Whole Wheat Wafers

Dates, Dried Figs, Dried Apricots

Middle Eastern Coffee

The Moveable Feast

...THEREFORE "TUT LIVES TONIGHT"

Many local organizations gave their members special opportunities to view the King Tutankhamun exhibition, but by far the most exciting was the Junior League of Los Angeles benefit "Night on the Nile, Saturday, April 8, 1978 A.D."

A trained camel was stationed at the Wilshire Boulevard entrance to the 15,000 square-foot California Federal Savings & Loan parking structure to greet arriving guests. From that moment the days of Egyptian glory in the Valley of the Kings returned. Massive structural pillars were wrapped in black and appliqued with shining gold motifs representing each major local business that had "purchased" a pillar, thus helping underwrite this charity benefit. Colorful tables and gilded chairs were set on oriental rugs with giant pillows tossed about and private areas were tented with gossamer curtains.

Belly dancers wandered amongst the diners and cries of "Tut Lives Tonight," the evening's motto, were heard as toasts were drunk from the golden goblets each guest was allowed to take home as a souvenir.

Against a gleaming gold and turquoise backdrop of a symbolic Egyptian vulture 8 feet high and 28 feet across, students of the Fashion Institute of Design presented a fashion show to native melodies. Models appeared in the traditional stylized black wigs, carried sceptres, ankhs, etc. (courtesy of 20th-Century Fox Studios and Bob Mackie) and wore their own creations based on their research into classic Egyptian design.

Among guests who could be seen studying their pocket itineraries containing a split-second timing schedule were the John Argues, the Z. Wayne Griffins, Esther and Thomas Wachtell, Greta and Frederick R. Waingrow, Dr. and Mrs. Alton Ochsner, George C. Paige, Julie and David Eisenhower, Jr.

The entire assemblage of 1,500 guests were divided into three color-coordinated groups which whould have rivaled the logistics of building the Great Pyramid of Giza. The"Blue of the Nile" guests dined at turquoise tablecloths, carried turquoise itineraries to their buses upon arrival and visited the Museum on the "first shift," returning to have their buffet dinner.

The "Sands of the Desert" guests were served first from their sandy-beige covered tables, and attended the exhibition on the "second shift." The "Red Earth of Egypt" group were given a late supper at their bright terra cotta tables and enjoyed the "late shift" tour. When all had returned at Midnight "On the Oasis" they were treated to the Aman Folk Ensemble, famed belly dancer Aisha Ali, and dancing to the music of the Michael Paige orchestra. King Tut himself couldn't have done it better.

IN THE SOUK
Marketplace:

Khoudar
Vegetable Stand

Crisp Raw Vegetables
Yogurt-Cucumber Mint & Tarama Dips

Foul Madamas in Pita
Fava Beans, Olive Oil, Lemon

Hummus Bi Tahini in Pita
Chickpea Salad

Sfeeha with Yogurt Sauce
Lamb Pizza

Kasseri, Kashkavali, Feta, Kochkaese
Cheeses

Baba Ghannouj
Eggplant & Sesame Relish

Cracker Bread

Tursi
Pickled Cauliflower & Turnips

THREE PHARAOH'S BUFFETS:

Biram Ruzz
Baked Rice with Chicken

Lahma Danee
Roast Leg of Lamb with Yogurt

Laban Zabate
Mint Sauce

Mousakka's
Eggplant, Chickpeas & fresh tomatoes

Tzatziri
Cucumber & Feta Cheese Sauce

Salatat Tamatum
Sliced Beefsteak Tomatoes with Marinated Vegetables

Tabbouleh bel Khas
Bulgar Salad with Romaine

Domates

THREE DESSERT TABLES

Konafa
Shredded Wheat laced with Honey

Haresa
Sweet Farina Cakes

Menana
Shorthread Wafers in Powdered Sugar

Paklava & Baklavu
Honey Cakes

Sweet Tahini
Whole-wheat Wafers

Molabbas alla Loz
Candied Almonds

Tamr Lelhindy
Dried Apricot Cones filled with Crushed Ice

Meckasarat
Dried Fruits & Nuts

Kahwa Arabi
Middle Eastern Coffee

Shay Bel-nahnah
Spiced Mint Tea

The Moveable Feast

HANDY

KITCHEN

HINTS

To Keep yolks of eggs from drying out, place them in a cup or bowl and cover with cold water. They will stay fresh in the refrigerator for several days.

To keep egg whites for future use, store in ice trays and freeze. The white of one egg will fit into one cube space. They may be defrosted later for meringues, or (a beauty secret) facial masks!

To determine the age of an egg, place it in the bottom of a bowl of cold water. If it lays on one side it is fresh. If it stands at an angle it is a least 3 days old, and if it stands on end it is ten days or more.

To slice a hard-cooked egg, wet the knife before each slice to prevent crumbling.

To eliminate distress after eating cooked dried beans, use ¾ teaspoon of baking soda in the water when boiling the beans.

To cook vegetables of the cabbage family without the after effects of gas, use 2 pots of boiling water. Into one pot, put one level teaspoon baking soda, boil vegetables for three minutes. Remove from fire, strain water and fill from second pot or kettle of boiling water. Instead of baking soda, add one level tablespoon of salt per quart of water and allow vegetables to boil uncovered.

To hasten the cooking of cabbage, cauliflower, or brussel sprouts, cut a deep cross in the bottom of stalk base before putting each head into the boiling water.

To keep cooked cauliflower clear and white, add a little milk to the water while cooking.

To keep corn fresh for more than one day, cut a small piece off the end of the stalks, then stand ears on end in one inch of water in a bowl.

To cut or peel onions without eyes watering, hold a piece of bread between the teeth. Keep the mouth slightly open and breathe through the mouth.

To bake potatoes more rapidly, soak potatoes in salt water for 20 minutes, dry with paper towels.

To keep baked potato jackets moist and tasty for eating rub with oil, butter or bacon fat before baking.

To reheat mashed potatoes, use a double boiler, or heavy pot over low heat, add butter and melt, add cold mashed potatoes and a little salt. Slowly stir in a little milk, mixing milk, butter and cold potatoes with a fork. Whip mixture until smooth, being careful not to add too much milk to keep the proper consistency.

To reheat previously cooked food (including gravy), when adding water or milk, add salt and butter or margarine to avoid diluting the flavor.

To use a general rule in cooking vegetables properly, remember that:

If it grows beneath the ground (root vegetables) it grows covered by the cold earth; so you start it in cold water and cover the pot.

If it grows above the ground (green vegetables, squashes, corn, etc.) it grows uncovered in the hot sun; so start it in boiling water and leave the pot uncovered.

To cook vegetables lightly in the "waterless" method, use a wide-bottomed saucepan or frying pan with a tight cover. Heat and blend in the pan a mixture of half butter or margarine and half oil, lay the vegetables over this and spread wet lettuce leaves over the vegetables. Cover pan tightly, cook over low heat until just tender. Discard lettuce leaves (or chop and add to vegetables), season to serve.

To keep salad greens fresh and crisp in the refrigerator always store uncovered. Wash and separate lettuce leaves, fluff out and separate alfalfa, chop off heads of watercress etc., and store in separate open plastic bags; do not allow tops to close. Greens will stay crisp for days and not get soggy. Also radishes, celery, green onions, leeks, etc.

To keep cucumbers crisp and fresh for days, slice and place in a bowl or container of cold salted water, UNCOVERED, and refrigerate.

To keep cheese and cold cooked meats in the refrigerator, wrap in paper towels put in plastic bags and mold the bags tightly around the cheese or meat to eliminate air and tie off opening securely. From time to time check paper towels for dampness and change to fresh dry towels if necessary.

To keep raw meat for a day or two before using, store in refrigerator UNWRAPPED.

To tenderize meats naturally, use papaya juice, wine, lemon juice or lime juice. Rub into the meat and let stand at least one or two hours if a small piece, or overnight if a large piece. At room temperature meat tenderizes quicker than when refrigerated and the heat of cooking stops the process.

Fish boiled is fish spoiled. It should be poached slowly in water or wine.

To eliminate fish odor while baking or broiling salmon, rub lemon juice on both sides of salmon steak or on cut surface of salmon and let stand in the refrigerator at least one hour before cooking.

To prevent raisins from sinking to the bottom of a cake batter, dust them with flour after boiling to plump them and drying with paper towels. Then add to batter.

To keep lemons from drying out in the refrigerator, place them in a jar of water and cover securely.

To keep sliced fruit from discoloring, sprinkle lemon, lime, orange or pineapple juice over and toss gently to coat evenly.

To prevent a soggy crust on custard-type pies, bake at a high temperature for about ten minutes, then lower to finish baking.

To repair damaged crust on uncooked frozen pie, dip broken piece in milk and press firmly into place before baking.

To cut angel food cake or pound cake into layers, wrap clean white thread around, cross ends and pull slowly through cake.

To make smooth gravy, dissolve flour in hot fat or butter — never in milk or water. Remove meat and most of the drippings from the pan, leaving about 1 tablespoon. Stir in 1 tablespoon flour, mix until smooth, then add 1 cup cold water and boil for 2 or 3 minutes and season. To increase amount, use these proportions, and double, triple, etc.

To thin sauces, never use water as it weakens the flavor. Depending on the base, use wine, broth, cream or tomato juice.

To remove excess salt from soup, drop in a slice of raw potato and boil for 5 to 6 minutes.

To put out fire in grease or fat in a pan or broiler, smother with salt — NEVER use water.

To stop grease from spattering in a frying pan, sift a very slight amount of flour over the grease.

To use salt properly

soups and sauces —	add salt early
meats —	add just before removing from stove
cakes —	mix with eggs
vegetables —	add to water before cooking
fish —	add to pan while frying

To cook with wine properly:

cream soups —	sherry, Madeira
clear soups —	dry wines
fish sauces —	dry Chablis, sweet or dry sauterne
tomato or game sauces —	red Burgundy, claret, cabernet or zinfandel
red meat —	same as above
chicken —	sherry, sweet vermouth

If you must use sweet wine on a main-course dish, counteract the sweetness with a little lime or lemon juice.

SUBSTITUTIONS

FOR: SUBSTITUTE:

1 whole egg for thickening   = 2 egg yolks
or baking

1 cup butter or margarine   = 1 cup shortening plus ½ tsp. salt
for shortening
1 square (ounce) chocolate   = 3 or 4 tbsp. cocoa plus 2 tbsp. shortening

1 cup sour milk for baking   = 1 cup sweet milk mixed with either 1 tbsp.
                                vinegar, or 1 tbsp. lemon juice, or 1¾ tsp. cream
                                of tartar

1 cup whole milk   = ½ cup evaporated milk plus ½ cup water
                              = 4 tbsp. dry whole milk plus 1 cup water
                              = 4 tbsp. nonfat dry milk plus 2 tsp. table fat and 1
                                cup water

1 cup skim milk   = 4 tbsp. nonfat dry milk plus 1 cup water

1 tbsp. flour for thickening = ½ tbsp. cornstarch or arrowroot
                              = 1 tbsp. granulated tapioca

1 cup all-purpose flour   = up to ½ cup bran, whole wheat flour
for baking bread   or corn meal plus enough all-purpose flour to
                                make 1 cup

To thicken gravies and sauces with something other than "flour and water":

Egg yolks   Beat one egg yolk for every ½ cup liquid to be thickened, add a little cream and mix well. Remove sauce from fire, stir in mixture and serve. Eggs will curdle if sauce is cooked further, but it may be heated up if done quickly.

Cheese   Add 2 to 4 tbsp. grated dry cheese to sauce and stir well. Heat only long enough to soften, serve at once.

Arrowroot   Mix 1 or 2 tbsp. with a little of the basic liquid, stir slowly into the sauce and cook, stirring constantly until thickened. Especially suitable for fruit sauces and oriental sauces.

TABLE OF EQUIVALENTS OF U.S. WEIGHTS AND MEASURES

Note: All measures are level.

Pinch or dash — less than ⅛ teaspoon

3 teaspoons — 1 tablespoon

2 tablespoons — 1 fluid ounce

4 tablespoons — ¼ cup

5 tablespoons plus 1 teaspoon — ⅓ cup

8 tablespoons — ½ cup

10 tablespoons plus 2 teaspoons — ⅔ cup

12 tablespoons — ¾ cup

16 tablespoons — 1 cup

1 cup — 8 fluid ounces

2 cups — 1 pint

2 pints — 1 quart

4/5 quart — 25.6 fluid ounces

1 quart — 32 fluid ounces

4 quarts — 1 gallon

2 gallons (dry measure) — 1 peck

4 pecks — 1 bushel

4 ounces — ¼ pound

8 ounces — ½ pound

16 ounces — 1 pound

1 jigger — 1 ½ fluid ounces

VARIATIONS OF MEASUREMENTS

Cracker crumbs:	23 soda crackers	= 1 cup
	15 graham crackers	= 1 cup
Eggs:	1 egg	= 4 tbsp. liquid
	4 to 5 whole eggs	= 1 cup
	7 to 9 whites	= 1 cup
	12 to 14 yolks	= 1 cup
Flour:	1 pound all-purpose	= 4 cups
	1 pound cake	= 4½ cups
	1 pound graham	= 3½ cups
Lemons:	Juice — 1 medium	= 2 to 3 tbsp.
	5 to 8 medium	= 1 cup
	Rind — 1 lemon	= 1 tbsp. grated
Shortening or butter:	1 pound	= 2 cups
Sugar:	1 pound brown	= 2½ cups
	1 pound cube	= 96 to 160 cubes
	1 pound granulated	= 2 cups
	1 pound powdered	= 3½ cups

WHAT IT WILL MEAN TO COOK WITH METRIC MEASURES

The metric system is a way of measuring based on the decimal system with larger measures being subdivided into units of ten. Food researchers and European cooks have always used the metric system because it is more precise than American weights and measures.

In recipes, the principal difference between our present way of measuring and the metric is that dry ingredients like flour and sugar are weighed rather than measured in a cup.

Meats, fruits, and vegetables will be sold by the kilogram instead of the pound and, in recipes, will be called for by weight rather than by cup (whether sliced, diced, or whole).

Small measures — tablespoons, teaspoons, and fractions thereof — are not likely to change.

Liquids are measured in measuring cups, but the calibrations are marked in liters, ½ liters, and milliliters instead of cups. There will be no more such cumbersome measurements as ½ cup plus 1 tablespoon or 1 cup minus 3 teaspoons.

TEMPERATURE

32 degrees F.	0 degrees centigrade
68 degrees F	20 degrees centigrade
212 degrees F	100 degrees centigrade

METRIC MEASURES MADE EASY

SPOONFULS

¼ tsp .... 1.25 milliliters
½ tsp .... 2.5 milliliters
¾ tsp .... 3.75 milliliters
1 tsp .... 5 milliliters

¼ tbsp. .... 3.75 milliliters
½ tbsp .... 7.5 milliliters
¾ tbsp .... 11.25 milliliters
1 tbsp .... 15 milliliters

OUNCES

¼ ounce .... 7.5 milliliters
½ ounce .... 15 milliliters
¾ ounce .... 22.5 milliliters
1 ounce.. 30 milliliters

CUPS

½ cup ....59.0 milliliters
⅓ cup .... 78.66 milliliters
½ cup.. 118 milliliters
⅔ cup... 177 milliliters
1 cup .... 236 milliliters

PINTS-QUARTS-GALLONS

½ pint... 236 milliliters
1 pint .... 473 milliliters
1 quart .... 946.3 milliliters
1 gallon .... 3785 milliliters

WEIGHT IN OUNCES

¼ oz... 7.1 grams
½ oz .... 14.17 grams
¾ oz .... 21.27 grams
1 oz .... 28.35 grams

POUNDS-KILOGRAMS

¼ lb .... 113 kilograms
½ lb .... 227 kilograms
¾ lb .... 340 kilograms
1 lb .... 454 kilograms
1 kilogram.................................... 2,205 lbs.

RECIPES

APPETIZERS

And I, being provided thus,
Shall, with superb asparagus,
A book, a taper, and a cup
Of country wine, divinely sup.

ROBERT LOUIS STEVENSON

ABALONE COCKTAIL

1 can abalone tidbits
(rinsed in fresh water)
1 bottle clam juice (use just
enough to moisten)
Lemon juice (just a squeeze)
½ cup tomato pieces (peel
and chop 1 medium size
tomato)
Taco sauce or salsa to taste

Mix all ingredients together. Chill for 30 minutes.

Adapted from those served by the street vendors at La Bufadora below Ensenada.

Serves 4.

NANCY COCHRAN

PHILADELPHIA GOOD STUFF

2 cans flat anchovy filets
(save oil)
1 jar Progresso red roasted
peppers
1 red bermuda onion
¼ cup red wine vinegar
½ cup olive oil

Cut anchovies and peppers into bite size pieces. Quarter and slice onion. Mix all ingredients including oil from anchovies and marinate in refrigerator for 3 hours or more. Drain carefully. Serve with party rye.

Serves 4-6

ELIZABETH HABERMAN

ARTICHOKE APPETIZER

1 cup mayonnaise
1 cup Parmesan cheese
(freshly grated)
1 can (8 oz.) artichoke
hearts (chopped fine)

Mix all ingredients and place in a 6" square pyrex dish.

Bake at 350° for ½ hour or until bubbly.

Serves 4-6

MRS. WM. F. STEINER

ARTICHOKE QUICHE

3 small jars marinated
artichoke hearts (chopped)
1 onion (finely chopped)
1 clove garlic
8 eggs (beaten slightly)
½ tsp. salt
¼ tsp. pepper
Dash of Tabasco sauce
½ tsp. Worcestershire
sauce
10 unsalted crackers
(crumbed)
4 tbsp. parsley (chopped)
1 lb. yellow cheese
(shredded)

Drain the artichokes, saving the oil. Chop artichokes and put aside.

Saute the onion and garlic in 3 tbsp. of the artichoke oil until the onion is transparent. Remove the garlic clove and discard

Beat eggs with salt, pepper, Tabasco sauce and Worcestershire sauce. Add the remaining ingredients. Blend well.

Pour mixture into a well-oiled 8" x 12" pan and bake at 325° for 40 minutes until firm.

Cut into one-inch squares and serve warm. Makes 72 bite-size pieces.

This recipe may be prepared in advance and, after cooling, it can be frozen.

A food processor is a great help in preparing this appetizer.

MRS. ELNA BURNS

BOW-KNOTS

1 loaf of white sandwich
bread
1 can mushroom soup
1 pound of bacon

Cut crusts from slices of bread and flatten with rolling pin. Spread slices with undiluted mushroom soup. Roll up from two opposite corners and put one-half slice bacon around center of roll and skewer with a toothpick.

Bake thirty minutes at 350°   These can be made ahead and are popular served with a salad or at a cocktail party.

Serves 10-12.

MRS. BLAIR W. STEWART

CEVICHE

2 lbs. white fish (boned and skinned), crabmeat or scallops
1 cup lemon juice
1 tsp. salt
2 large onions
2 tomatoes
2 bay leaves
1 tsp. chili powder
¼ cup small stuffed olives
1 cup dry white wine
½ cup oil

Cut fish into small pieces. Combine with lemon juice and salt. Refrigerate 4-6 hours.

Peel and chop onions and tomatoes.

Drain fish and combine with onions, tomatoes, bay leaves, chili powder, olives, wine and oil. Stir gently to blend. Refrigerate until ready to serve.

Serve with crackers, sour dough bread, etc.

Makes 4 cups.

MRS. JAMES E. GRIFFIN

CHEESE BALL FOR SPECIAL OCCASIONS

Everyone loves this and it's a favorite of mine.

1 6-oz. Kraft Blue Cheese
2 5-oz. Kraft Old English Cheese
2 8-oz. Kraft Philadelphia Cream Cheese
1 tbsp. onions (chopped)
1 tbsp. Worcestershire sauce
½ cup pecans
½ cup parsley (chopped)

Soften to room temperature, mix cheese and add onions and Worcestershire sauce. Form into a ball, then roll it either into pecans or parsley or both.

★ JANE WITHERS
Actress, comedienne
Top child star, films include BRIGHT EYES; well known as TV commercial JOSEPHINE, THE PLUMBER.

*Part of the success in life
is to eat what you like.*

MARK TWAIN

CAVIAR MOLD

1 tbsp. gelatin (unflavored)
¼ cup boiling water
1 cup sour cream
2 tbsp. mayonnaise
2 tsp. fresh lemon juice
3 tsp. onion (grated)
¼ tsp. sugar
2 eggs (hard-boiled and grated)
Dash of Tabasco sauce
4 oz. caviar or lumpfish caviar
Salt, pepper and white pepper to taste
Crackers or pumpernickle bread slices

Dissolve the gelatin in boiling water. In a saucepan heat the sour cream slowly over low heat. Add the softened gelatin to the sour cream. Stir until the gelatin is completely melted. Remove from heat and add mayonnaise, lemon juice, onion, sugar, grated egg and Tabasco sauce. Mix well.

Wash caviar carefully under cold water and drain very thoroughly. (This is very important in order to rinse out the juice.) Add caviar to the sour cream mixture and pour into an oiled 2-cup mold. Chill until firm.

Unmold when ready to serve and decorate with dollops of sour cream and a little caviar in each dollop. Serve with your favorite crackers or thin slices of pumpernickle bread.

Serves 6.

MRS. CHARLES J. BROSKA

CAVIAR PIE

1 8-oz. pkg. cream cheese
½ cup sour cream
¼ cup onion (grated)
1 jar black caviar
1 hard-boiled egg (chopped)

Soften cream cheese. Mix with sour cream and grated onion. Spread evenly in 4" x 8" shallow dish. Use spatula and spread caviar evenly over top of mixture. Sprinkle hard-cooked egg on top. Serve with mild or French-onion crackers.

Serves 8.

MRS. ROBERT E. MITCHELL (SUE)

CREAM CHEESE AND LOX MOUSSE

½ lb. lox
½ lb. whipped cream cheese
3 8-oz. pkgs. cream cheese
4 hard boiled eggs
4 green onions (sliced paper thin)
2 tbsp. white onion (grated)
4 tbsp. cucumber (grated)
1 tbsp. horseradish
1 tsp. dillweed
1 cup fresh snippets of parsley

GLAZE:
1 tbsp. Knox gelatin (dissolved)
4 tbsp. lemon juice
1 cup boiling water

Beat together cream cheese, whipped cream cheese and horseradish. Fold in eggs, onions, cucumber and dill. Butter a 6-cup round mold. Dip each piece of lox into ungelled glaze and line mold. Partially set glaze and add to cheese mixture. Pour into lox-lined mold and chill overnight. Unmold on platter. Garnish with parsley and serve with flat English biscuits, crackers, or bagels. (Left over great for stuffing omelets or baked potatoes).

GLAZE:
Dissolve gelatin in lemon juice and add water.

Serves 12.

MRS. WILLIAM J. REA

ONION CHEESE PUFFS

⅓ cup Parmesan or Romano cheese (grated)
¾ cup mayonnaise
½ cup onions (finely minced)
½ tsp. Worcestershire sauce
½ tsp. white pepper
Pepperidge Farm bread or cocktail rye

Combine and mix all ingredients well. Spread on rounds of whole wheat Pepperidge Farm bread or cocktail rye.

Bake on upper third of 400° preheated oven for 5 minutes or until golden brown and puffy.

Serve immediately.

Makes 3½ dozen appetizers on 1¾" bread rounds.

These puffs can be frozen before baking. When baking frozen puffs, allow a few more minutes for cooking. This is a quick and simple recipe to make, but delicious.

MRS. FRED C. KEMMERLING, JR. (CARLEEN)

CHEDDAR CHEESE CARROT BALL

8 oz. cheddar cheese
(shredded),
room temperature
3 oz. cream cheese
½ cup salted peanuts
(finely chopped)
¼ cup carrot (shredded)
2 tbsp. red onion (finely chopped)
⅛ tsp. dillweed

Beat together cheeses at room temperature. Stir in rest. Chill. Form into a ball or can be formed in shape of carrot with parsley at large end so it looks like a carrot. Serve at room temperature with crackers.

MRS. ROBERT STEINER

CHEESE-EGG SPREAD

1 small green pepper
1 cup stuffed green olives
2 hard boiled eggs
½ lb. sharp cheddar
cheese (grated)
2 tbsp. onion (grated)
Garlic juice
Salt and pepper to taste.

Chop pepper, olives and eggs fine or put through grinder. Add grated cheese and onion, garlic juice and seasonings. Mix well and serve as spread for crackers. Also good on crackers or toasted bread under broiler.

Makes 1 cup of spread.

MRS. ROBERT E. JOHNSTON

CREAM CHEESE NUT DIP

1 8-oz. pkg. cream cheese
2 tbsp. milk
½ cup sour cream
1 3-oz. jar chipped beef
(chopped fine)
¼ cup green pepper
(chopped fine)
2 tbsp. onion flakes (dried)
½ tsp. garlic salt
½ cup pecans (chopped)
2 tbsp. butter(melted)

Blend cream cheese, milk and sour cream. Add chipped beef, green pepper, onion flakes and garlic salt. Blend together until smooth. Pour into 7" or 8" glass pie dish (or square pyrex glass baking dish) evenly. In a bowl stir pecans into melted butter and spread over top of other mixture evenly. Bake 20 minutes at 350° in glass dish. Serve hot with chips.

Serves 6-8.

★ MRS. JOHNNY MANN (LYNN)
JOHNNY MANN: Author, Choral director, composer, conductor, pianist, producer, recording artist. Founder and leader of JOHNNY MANN SINGERS.

SPICY CHEESE SPREAD OR DIP

1 crock 10-oz sharp cheddar cold pack cheese
2-oz. jigger bourbon or brandy
Cayenne pepper to taste

Soften cheese. Beat in bourbon or brandy. Add Cayenne pepper to taste.

Makes about 1 cup.

★ MARION LEDERER
FRANCIS LEDERER: Actor, educator.
Many films include BRIDGE OF SAN LUIS REY, DIARY OF A CHAMBERMAID and STOLEN IDENTITY; instructor of drama class.

CHEESE SOUP IN BREAD

1 loaf of squaw or rye bread (unsliced)
1 can of cheese soup
1 8-oz. jar of Cheez Whiz with Jalapeno pepper
1 7-oz. can of green chili salsa

Remove top and part of insides of bread and tear into bite-size pieces leaving sides and bottom of loaf intact. Place bite-size pieces on a serving tray with loaf in center.

Heat cheese soup, Cheez Whiz and green chile salsa together and pour into hollowed-out loaf of bread. Sides and bottom of loaf should be torn off by guests as soup level lowers.

This is a delicious and fun first course for an informal dinner.

NOTE: Plain Cheez Whiz can be used if a less spicy soup is desired.

Serves 12.

MRS. C. S. KLOEPPEL

CHEESE SPANISH SPREAD

1 lb. sharp Tillamook cheese (grated)
2 large onions (chopped)
1 large clove garlic (minced)
1 4-oz. can Ortega peppers (diced & drained)
2 tbsp. vinegar
1 8-oz. can tomato sauce
½ cup salad oil
1 can olives (chopped)
French bread

Mix all ingredients together. Slice French bread thin and toast it. Spread with Spanish spread and broil well-done.

This spread keeps well in the refrigerator and is nice to have on hand.

Makes 4 dozen or more

ALPHA MacCORMACK

CHICKEN WINGS PACIFICA

3 or more lbs. chicken wings
1 stick butter or margarine
1 cup soy sauce
1 cup brown sugar
¾ cup water
½ tsp. dry mustard

Arrange wings in shallow baking pan. Heat butter or margarine, soy sauce, sugar, water and mustard until butter and sugar melt. Cool. Pour over wings and marinate at least two hours turning once or twice. Bake in same pan in 375° oven for 1¼ to 1½ hours turning occasionally. Drain on paper towels.

Makes about 24 wings.

★ BETTY WHITE AND ALAN LUDDEN

Actress, comedienne, singer
Actor, TV host
Her many TV appearances include MARY TYLER MOORE SHOW, co-star LIFE WITH ELIZABETH, and star BETTY WHITE SHOW. — He is host of PASSWORD and PASSWORD PLUS TV series.

BAKED CHICKEN WINGS

2 lbs. chicken wings
½ cup sherry
¼ cup butter
4 tbsp. catsup

Cut tips off chicken wings then cut in half. Place in shallow pan and sprinkle generously with garlic salt. Pour sauce over and bake 1 hour at 400° turning once or twice. Good hot or cold.

Makes about 16 wings.

★ DOROTHY MALONE
Actress
Many films include THE BIG SLEEP, WRITTEN ON THE WIND (Academy Award Best Actress 1956); co-star PEYTON PLACE TV series.

CHILI CHEESE APPETIZER

½ cup butter
10 eggs
½ cup flour
1 tsp. baking powder
1 8-oz. can green chilies
 (chopped)
1 pint cottage cheese
1 lb. Jack cheese
 (shredded)
Dash salt

Melt butter in 9" x 13" pan. Beat eggs lightly in large bowl. Add flour, salt and baking powder and blend. Add melted butter, chilies, cottage cheese and Jack cheese and mix until blended. Turn batter into pan and bake at 400° for 15 minutes. Reduce heat to 350° and bake 35-40 minutes longer. Cut into squares and serve hot.

Makes about 24 one-inch squares.

May be made in advance and may be cut in half using a 9" square pan and baking for 50 minutes.

GLENDA GRIBBEN

CHILI DIP

1 1-lb. pkg. Velveeta cheese
 (grated)
1 1-lb. can chili (with or
 without beans)
6-8 green onions including
 tops (fine chopped)
1 7-oz. can green chilies
 (chopped)
Crackers

Chill cheese in the freezer for ½ hour to make grating easier.

Mix all ingredients well and bake one hour at 300°. Cool and then refrigerate for 24 hours.

Serve at room temperature with crackers.

Variation: If served hot, it can be served like a fondue with French bread instead of crackers.

This recipe may be frozen.

MRS. FRANK E. PICKETT

GREEN CHILI DIP

1 8-oz. pkg. cream cheese
1 cup sour cream (or Imo)
1 can (small) diced green
 chilies
1 tsp. garlic salt
Bacon bits

Mix ingredients together. Put in bowl and serve with Fritos or tortilla chips. Prepare 24 hours in advance.

Serves 12.

MRS. ROBERT L. HEMMINGS

BROILED DEVILED CLAMS

24 hard-shelled clams (small)
¾ cup butter, (softened)
3 tbsp. Dijon-style mustard
¼ cup shallots (minced)
1 tbsp. lemon juice
Salt and pepper to taste
Stale bread crumbs
Rock salt

Clean and shuck clams, discarding the top shell, and release them from the bottom shells. In a bowl combine the butter, mustard, shallots, lemon juice, salt and pepper. Divide the butter mixture among the clams, spreading it evenly over each clam, so clam is completely covered. Cover clams with plastic wrap and chill 30 minutes. Sprinkle 2 tsp. of bread crumbs over each clam and arrange the clams on a bed of rock salt in a shallow baking pan. Broil clams 2 inches from flame for 3 to 4 minutes until the crumbs are golden.

Serves 4.

★ CAROL BURNETT
Actress, comedienne, dancer, singer
Many TV appearances include GARRY MOORE SHOW and star CAROL BURNETT SHOW (countless Emmy Awards); theatre roles include ONCE UPON A MATTRESS on broadway.

CLAM DIP IN A LOAF

1 large round loaf sourdough bread
1 8-oz. cream cheese (softened)
2 cans minced clams (drained, save juice)
2 tbsp. lemon juice
½ cup clam juice
1 tsp. salt
1 green onion (chopped)
Parsley (chopped)

Cut off top and hollow out 1 large round loaf of sourdough bread. Mix rest of ingredients. Place mixture inside hollowed-out bread. Wrap in foil. Bake 3 hours at 250°. Break unused bread into cubes to use as dipper.

GLENDA GRIBBEN

CRAB OR LOBSTER DIP

1 7-oz. can crab or lobster
   meat or 8-oz. fresh
   meat (flaked)
½ cup celery (chopped)
¼ cup scallions (chopped)
1 clove garlic (mashed)
3 tsp. olive oil
1 tsp. salt
¼ tsp. black pepper
⅓ tsp. oregano
¼ tsp. coriander
½ tsp. sugar
½ tsp. curry powder
1½ tbsp. lemon juice

Combine all ingredients and marinate in refrigerator serveral hours or overnight. Serve with crackers.

MRS. ROBERT K. OSTENGAARD

GINNY'S CRABMEAT MOLD

2 tbsp. gelatin
¼ cup water
1 can mushroom soup
6 oz. cream cheese (soft)
1 small onion (grated)
7 oz. can crabmeat
1 cup celery (chopped)
1 cup mayonnaise

Dissolve gelatin in water for about 5 minutes. Add to heated soup and stir until the gelatin is thoroughly dissolved. Let stand until cold. Mix with other ingredients.

Turn into mold (or dish) and chill. Unmold on bed of lettuce. Serve with crackers or toasty rolls.

HINT: This can be frozen if you wish to keep it up to three months.

Serves 8-12.

MRS. ROBERT W. YATES (FIJI)

MADAME WU'S CRAB PUFFS

1 cup fresh crab meat
(cooked)
⅓ cup cream cheese
1 egg white
¼ tsp. salt
1 pinch white pepper
20 square wonton wrappers
1 qt. vegetable oil

First, make a paste of the crab meat, salt and pepper, then add the cream cheese and mix it until it is smooth.

With a pastry brush wet the four edges of the wonton wrappers with egg white. Put 1 tbsp. of the crab mixture in the center of the square and bring the edges together to form a triangle, carefully sealing the edges. Then take two angles of the triangle, carefully bring them to the third angle, after brushing the edges with egg white for a sealer. Appetizers are now ready to be deep-fried or stored in the regrigerator for future use.

Heat one quart vegetable oil in a deep kettle until it is very hot (375°). Submerge the puffs and turn them over until they are uniformly browned (about 2 minutes). Remove and drain on paper towelling.

Makes 20 puffs, and I guarantee that they will be the first eaten on your hors d'oeuvres tray.

★ MADAME WU
Author, Lecturer, Restaurateur
Book - MADAME WU'S ART OF CHINESE COOKING

CURRIED COCONUT BALLS

2 3-oz. pkgs. cream cheese
(softened)
2 tbsp. pickle relish
(well drained)
¾ tsp. curry powder
Salt to taste
Flaked coconut

Blend cream cheese, relish, curry and salt to taste. Chill well. Drop by teaspoonfuls into coconut and roll into balls. Chill and spear on picks to serve.

Makes 30-35.

MRS. ARNOLD BERG

GREEN GODDESS DIP

1 tbsp. anchovy paste
1 green onion (chopped) or
    preferably about ⅓ cup
    green onion stems
⅓ cup parsley (chopped)
1 tsp. dry tarragon
½ cup mayonnaise
½ cup sour cream
4 tsp. tarragon vinegar
Tiny pinch of garlic powder
        or
    rub mixing bowl with cut
    clove of garlic

Mix all together and chill several hours. Serve with all sorts of raw vegetables or thin with a few tablespoons of buttermilk and use as salad dressing.

Yields about 1 ⅓ cups.

SUE HIRSCH

ITALIAN EGGPLANT HORS-D'OEUVRE

2 medium eggplants (peeled
    & diced)
½ cup olive oil
2 onions (sliced)
2½ cups canned Italian
    plum tomatoes
1 cup celery (diced)
½ cup green pepper (diced)
4 tbsp. capers
2 tbsp. pine nuts
2 tbsp. wine vinegar
2 tbsp. sugar
Salt and pepper
4 tbsp. Florio Dry Marsala

In large frying pan saute eggplant in olive oil for about 8 minutes until soft and lightly browned. Remove eggplant to a bowl and set aside. To oil remaining in skillet add onions and saute until golden, adding more oil if needed. Add tomatoes, celery and green peppers. Simmer for 15 minutes. Add capers, pine nuts and eggplant. Mix thoroughly.

In small saucepan heat wine vinegar and sugar stirring until sugar is dissolved. Stir mixture into the eggplant. Add salt and pepper to taste. Bring eggplant mixture to boil, cover, simmer over very low heat for 20 minutes, stirring occasionally. Remove from heat. Stir in 4 tbsp. Marsala, or to taste. Turn into serving bowl and chill before serving.

Serves 12.

NEOMA AMENT

". . . THE DAYS OF WINE AND ROSES,
AND YOU."

— 1962

Lyric by JOHNNY MERCER
Music by HENRY MANCINI
© 1962 Warner Bros. Inc.
All Rights Reserved
Used by Permission

Photography by
MICHAEL JARRETT
OCB Reprographics, Inc.
Irvine, Ca.

DUNKER'S DELIGHT

1 cup mayonnaise
2 tsp. tarragon vinegar
Salt, pepper and curry to taste
2 tsp. chili sauce
Pinch thyme
Dried chives or chopped onions

Chill throughly. Excellent for crab, shrimp or raw cauliflower buds or slender sticks of yellow squash.

★ MARTHA SLEEPER STELLING
Actress, designer.
Films include DINNER AT EIGHT and BELLS OF ST. MARY; featured in many early silent Hal Roach Comedies.

QUICKIE LO-CAL PROTEIN FIX

1 pint low-fat cottage cheese
1 med. size egg (well beaten)
1 tbsp. green onions or chives (finely chopped)
1 tbsp. celery (finely chopped)
1 tbsp. green peppers (chopped fine)
2 tbsp. pimiento (finely chopped)
1 tbsp. parsley (finely chopped) or 1 tsp. dried parsley
Garlic salt
Lawry's salt
Pepper
Paprika
Crisp greens
Lettuce leaves

Mix beaten egg with cottage cheese gently but well. Fold in other ingredients after draining thoroughly. Season to taste with garlic salt, Lawry's salt and pepper. Dust with paprika and serve on greens with tomato wedges, or use as dip for fresh vegetables, potato chips, tortilla chips, or triscuits. (Cut down on any salt if using any of the last three).

Serves 2.

★ LOLA ALBRIGHT
Actress, singer.
Many TV roles include co-star PETER GUNN TV Series; films include A COLD WIND IN AUGUST and co-star LORD LOVE A DUCK (Berlin Film Festival Best Actress Award)

SWISS FONDUE

½ lb. imported Swiss cheese
1½ tbsp. flour
1 cut clove of garlic
1 cup white wine
Salt and pepper to taste
Dash of nutmeg
2 tbsp. light rum
   or brandy

Cook at the table (or on range and transfer). Shred Swiss cheese and dredge with flour. Rub cooking utensil well with clove of garlic.

Pour in wine. Place over low fire. When wine is heated to point where air bubbles rise to surface (never boiling), stir with a fork and add cheese by handfuls, stirring thoroughly before adding each handful. (Be sure it is thoroughly dissolved.) Keep stirring mixture until it starts bubbling lightly. Add salt and pepper and a dash of nutmeg, light rum or brandy.

Place all in warmed casserole or in chafing dish. Keep it bubbling while serving.

Serves 4 or more.

DOYNE WOOD

GUACAMOLE

2 avocadoes (ripe)
½ cup each mayonnaise,
   sour cream
2 tbsp. green taco sauce
1 large or 2 small cloves of
   garlic or ¼ tsp. garlic
   powder
½ onion (finely chopped) or 2
   tsp. onion powder
½ tsp. cilantro (optional)

Mash avocados coarsely, then mix in all other ingredients, adding tomatoes at the last. According to taste you can add more of any of these ingredients. More might be needed according to the size of avocados.

PAULA TREHARNE

CHINESE PINEAPPLE MEATBALLS

MEATBALLS
2 lbs. ground round
½ cup celery (minced)
½ cup almonds or pecans
  (chopped)
2 tsp. salt
½ cup cornflakes
4 eggs
2 tbsp. soy sauce
Dash garlic powder
Dash Accent
Flour
Oil

SAUCE:
2 cups chicken bouillon
1 cup sugar
6 tbsp. corn starch
1 cup pineapple juice
½ cup vinegar (try
  ¼ cup first)
2 tbsp. soy sauce
1 cup pineapple (crushed)
1 green pepper (chopped)

Mix first nine meatball ingredients and form into small cocktail size balls. Roll in flour and fry in very hot oil.

Drain pineapple. Mix all sauce ingredients together except the crushed pineapple and green pepper. Cook until thickened, stirring constantly. Then add the chopped green pepper and the crushed pineapple. Pour over the meatballs and heat slowly. When bubbly, pour into serving dish with warmer. Serve with toothpick.

Serves 10.

SUSAN HARDESTY

ELEGANT MEATBALLS

1 lb. pork sausage
1 lb. ground beef
2 cups fresh bread crumbs
2 eggs
½ cup chopped onion
2 tbsp. parsley
2 tsp. salt
2 tbsp. butter or margarine
½ cup smoky barbecue sauce
1 10-oz. jar apricot jam.

Shape first 7 ingredients into meatballs. Brown in butter. Place in casserole and pour mixture of jam and barbecue sauce over all. Bake at 350° for ½ hour.

ILAMAY TALLAKSON

CHESTNUT MEAT BALLS

1 cup soft bread crumbs
   (1½ slices)
½ cup milk
1 tbsp. soy sauce
½ tsp. garlic salt
¼ tsp. onion powder
½ lb. beef (ground)
½ lb. bulk-pork sausage
1 can water chestnuts
   (drained and fine
   chopped)

Combine bread crumbs, milk, soy sauce, garlic salt and onion powder. Add beef, pork and chestnuts. Mix well. Form into 1" balls. Place on baking sheets and freeze or bake in 350° oven 25-30 minutes. Serve with sweet and sour duck sauce by Chetten House, or add Chinese duck sauce.

Makes 20

JEANNE HAYES

TINY MEAT BALLS

1 lb. ground beef
1 tsp. salt
¼ tsp. pepper
¼ tsp. nutmeg
1 4-oz. can mushroom (stems
   and pieces) or 4-oz. fresh
   mushrooms (minced
   or ground)
1 egg (well beaten)
½ cup fine bread crumbs
1 clove garlic (pressed)
1 onion (minced or ground)
1 tbsp. parsley (minced)
Olive oil or butter
½ cup Burgundy wine

Mix the beef, salt, pepper, nutmeg, mushrooms, beaten egg and bread crumbs. Heat oil (or butter) in pan and saute garlic, onion and parsley until soft. Add wine and pour over meat mixture and mix well. Dip hands in cold water, form meat into tiny balls and roll in flour, lightly. Place meat balls in refrigerator until chilled. Fry gently in olive oil or butter until brown on all sides; shake pan. At this point these freeze beautifully in plastic countainer. Place in chafing dish to serve, adding a bit more wine to prevent sticking. (Leftovers are great in spaghetti).

Makes about 20.

MRS. WILLIAM J. REA

LAMB SATES

3 tbsp. olive oil
1 cup onion (finely chopped)
2 cloves of garlic (finely chopped)
1 tbsp. curry powder
1 tbsp. chili powder
1 tsp. pepper (fresh)
⅔ cup soy sauce
2 tbsp. honey
⅓ cup olive oil
⅓ cup lime juice
2-3 lbs. lamb, cut in small pieces

Saute onion, garlic in 3 tbsp. oil until tender. Add curry, chili and pepper and turn burner to low. Combine remaining incredients and add to saute mixture. Remove and chill. Marinate lamb for serveral hours. Thread on skewers. Broil in oven or on barbeque and turn occasionally.

Serves 4-6.

DICK MILL

LATIN LUSH

1 6-oz. can tomato paste
1 tbsp. salad oil
4 cans (5 oz. each) green chili salsa (LaVictoria brand is best)
1 2-oz. can ripe olives (sliced and drained)
1 clove garlic (pressed)
2 slices onion (finely minced)
1½ cups cheddar cheese (shredded)
Corn chips

Combine all ingredients, except corn chips, thoroughly. May be served immediately but tastes better if it has marinated 2-3 hours. The amount of green chili salsa may be varied according to how hot spicy one desired the dip.

Serve with corn chips.

Serves 8.

MRS. WELLS WOHLWEND

MARINATED COCKTAIL MUSHROOMS

½ cup white wine vinegar
1 tbsp. parsley (chopped)
½ tsp. salt
½ tsp. pepper
½ tsp. sugar
1 tbsp. lemon juice
½ tsp. oregano
⅔ cup oil (not olive oil
   as it does not refrigerate
   well)
1 lb. fresh mushrooms
1 clove garlic (chopped fine)

Combine all ingredients except mushrooms and garlic in a large jar. Shake well.

Wash mushrooms well being careful not to break them into pieces. Cut the stems from the mushrooms and discard them or save for soup. Add mushrooms to the other ingredients in the jar along with the garlic. Marinate covered at least 24 hours in the refrigerator. Stir occasionally.

To serve, remove the mushrooms from the marinade and place on hors d'oeuvre tray with toothpicks. (Keeps several weeks in the refrigerator).

Serves 8.

SUSAN HARDESTY

SUPREME STUFFED MUSHROOMS

12 large mushrooms
Lemon juice
STUFFING:
2 tbsp. butter
2 cups swiss cheese
   (grated)
½ cup bread crumbs
2 tbsp. parsley
   (minced)
½ clove garlic
   (minced)
1 tbsp. onion (minced)
Salt and pepper to taste
2-4 tbsp. California
   Sherry
Parmesan cheese (grated)

Wash mushrooms. Remove stems leaving caps intact. Set stems aside. Sprinkle few drops lemon juice on each cap. Set aside.

For stuffing, mince stems very fine and saute in butter. Meanwhile, combine cheese, bread crumbs, parsley, garlic, onion, and salt and pepper in a bowl. Add stems and enough sherry to moisten mixture. Pile stuffing into mushroom caps. Sprinkle with additional bread crumbs and dot with butter. Sprinkle with Parmesan cheese.

Bake at 350° for 15 minutes.

Makes 12.

MRS. JOHN ALCANTARA

MUSHROOM PIROSHKI

PASTRY:

1 cup butter
1 8-oz. pkg. cream cheese
(softened)
½ tsp. salt
2 cups flour
1 egg yolk
2 tsp. milk

FILLING:

½ lb. mushrooms
(finely chopped)
2 tbsp. butter
½ cup onions (chopped)
½ tsp. salt
Pinch of pepper
1 tsp. lemon juice
2 tsp. flour
½ cup sour cream
1 tsp. dried dill
Pinch of nutmeg

PASTRY:

Beat together butter, softened cheese and salt in mixer. Work in flour by hand. Form into 8" x 16" rectangle. Wrap in foil and chill overnight. Remove 10 minutes before using. Divide pastry in half, roll into rectangle ⅛" thick. Fold into thirds and roll again. Fold into thirds and roll again. Fold into thirds and roll into 10" square. Cut into 2½" rounds. Stack trimmings, re-roll and cut. Put level tsp. of filling in center. Moisten edges and fold over filling. Lay on side and press edges together with a fork. Set pastries seam side up on ungreased cookie sheet. Brush with mixture of egg yolk and milk. Flatten slightly and pinch ends up. Bake 25-30 minutes at 350°. May be frozen before baking.

Makes 4 dozen.

FILLING:

Wipe mushrooms with damp cloth and chop fine. Heat butter; add mushrooms and onions; cook briskly, stirring for 4 minutes. Sprinkle with salt, pepper, nutmeg, lemon juice and flour. Cook and stir 2 minutes longer. Remove from heat. Blend in sour cream. A little work, but worth it.

NADINE JOHNSON

SPINACH STUFFED MUSHROOMS

1 pkg. frozen chopped spinach
(defrosted and water
removed)
¼ lb. butter
2 oz. curry powder
Salt and pepper to taste
12-18 mushroom caps
3 oz. cheddar cheese

Mix all ingredients well (except mushrooms and cheese). Stuff mushroom caps with mixture and top with cheese.

Bake at 350° for 8-10 minutes. Delicious as an appetizer or served with dinner.

Serves 6.

NINA BOYER CARMER

CALIFORNIA COUNTRY PATÉ

1 lb. sweet Italian sausage
1 lb. chicken livers
½ lb. very fresh
  San Francisco sour
  dough bread
2 tbsp. parsley (minced)
¼ tsp. pepper
¼ tsp. nutmeg
3 large shallots (chopped)
¾ cup dry sherry
2 tbsp. brandy
2 eggs (extra large, beaten)

Lightly freeze sausage and livers to make handling easier. Break up bread and soak in wines. Remove casings from sausage and grind with livers. Add all ingredients to bread and mix. (Very tasty if some wine-soaked bread lumps remain.) Turn into lightly greased 9" x 5" glass loaf pan. Cover with foil and lid. Bake at 350° 1½ hours. Pour off excess liquid and cool with a heavy casserole on top of pate to weight it down. Allow to cool before chilling overnight. Unmold.
  Serve with small sweet gherkins.

Makes 20 slices.

MRS. KELLY STUMPUS

JOHN'S SPECIAL PATÉ

1 lb. chicken livers
2 onions (chopped)
¾ cup butter
1 lg. clove garlic (pressed)
1 tbsp. flour
¼ tsp. sugar
1 tsp. salt
½ tsp. pepper
3 tbsp. cognac

Saute onions and garlic in ½ cup butter. Remove and add balance of butter. Saute livers until they lose their color. Sprinkle with flour, salt and pepper. Cool, add onions and put in a food processor, adding cognac slowly. Refrigerate.
  Serve with French Onion Crackers or Rye Rounds.
  Recipe may be cut in half but cannot be frozen.

Makes 2 cups.

JOHN ALCANTARA

STEAMED PORK DUMPLINGS SHAO-MAI

1 pkg. wonton wrappers
1½ lbs. lean pork (finely
  ground)
2 tbsp. scallions (finely
  chopped)
2½ stalks Chinese
  celery cabbage
1½ tbsp. soy sauce
1 tsp. fresh ginger
  (minced)
1 tsp. cornstarch
1 tbsp. Chinese rice wine
  or white wine
1½ tsp. sesame seed oil
⅓ cup canned bamboo
  shoots (finely chopped)
SAUCE:
4 tsp. smooth peanut butter
2 tbsp. peanut oil
3 tsp. sugar
¾ tsp. cayenne pepper
¼ cup soy sauce
1½ tsp. garlic (minced)

Remove cabbage root stems, chop finely and squeeze out water. Combine pork, scallions, cabbage, soy sauce, ginger, cornstarch, wine, sesame seed oil, bamboo shoots. Place wrapper in hand. Use one tsp. filling, place in center. Gather sides of wrapper, pleating and gently squeeze center. Flatten bottom. Place dumplings on greased plate. Refrigerate 3 hours. Place in covered steamer for 30 minutes.

SAUCE: Combine ingredients. Chill. Warm to room temperature. Try without sauce. Sauce is strong so use sparingly.

Makes 40-50 pieces.

THOMAS E. KING, JR.

SAUSAGE PUFFS

1 pkg. skinless sausages
4 Pepperidge Farm patty
  shells
1 cube butter or margarine
Garlic or garlic salt
¼ cup Parmesan cheese
2 tsp. oregano
1 cup sherry
2 tbsp. Worcestershire sauce
2 tbsp. onion (grated)
2 tbsp. dry mustard
4 tbsp. brown sugar

Fry sausages and cut each into 4 pieces and marinate in mixture of sherry, Worcestershire sauce, onion, mustard and brown sugar (best to marinate for 24 hours). Thaw patty shells. Roll each one into 8" x 4" rectangle. Cut into 2" squares. Brush with garlic butter and sprinkle with Parmesan cheese mixed with oregano. Place a sausage on top. Fold to form triangle. Press edges together and dip edges in garlic butter. Sprinkle remainder of Parmesan cheese on top. Place on ungreased cookie sheet and bake at 425° for 15-20 minutes.

GERI BUTTKE

SCAMPI

2 lb. large shrimp
2 tbsp. olive oil
2 tbsp. butter
½ tsp. each salt and pepper
2 tbsp. lemon juice
¼ cup vermouth
2 green onions (minced)
Garlic
1 tbsp. parsley (chopped)
¼ tsp. Tabasco Sauce
1 tsp. Worcestershire Sauce
1 tbsp. A-1 Sauce

Peel shrimp and devein. Combine oil and butter in skillet. Add shrimp and saute until golden brown. Remove. Add onions and saute lightly. Add other ingredients and simmer 2 minutes. Pour over shrimp and serve.

Serves 8.

KEN DAVIDSON

MARINATED SHRIMP

3 tbsp. lemon juice
2 lbs. cooked shrimp
MARINADE:
3 red onions (sliced very
   thinly)
1 2-oz. jar of capers and juice
1 tbsp. parsley (chopped)
2 bay leaves
1 cup olive or vegetable oil
¾ cup white champagne
   vinegar
2 tsp. Worcestershire sauce
Salt to taste
¼ cup sugar
1 tsp. garlic powder
1 tsp. dry mustard
GARNISH:
Black olives
Lemon slices

Pour lemon juice over shrimp and set aside. Mix marinade ingredients together, pour over shrimp. Toss and seal with plastic wrap. Store in refrigerator one day. Drain before serving. Garnish with black olives and paper thin lemon slices.

Serves 12.

MRS. J. O. YUNGFLEISCH

SCALLOP TART

1 recipe whole wheat
  pastry
2 cups fresh scallops
½ cup small seedless
  grapes
⅓ cup walnuts (chopped)
⅓ cup red onions
  (chopped)
1 cup each grated Swiss
  cheese and mild Cheddar
⅓ cup half & half
Salt and pepper
Butter

WHOLE WHEAT PASTRY:

1 stick of butter
1 cup bleached all-
  purpose flour
½ cup whole wheat flour

Prepare and bake one 9" tart shell. Meanwhile, saute in butter until soft the red onion and then add the scallops. Stir over medium fire for 2-3 minutes. While stirring, add half & half, salt and pepper, grapes and walnuts. Be very careful not to overcook the scallops as they will become tough. Pour into tart shell. Add cheeses and sprinkle with paprika. Place in preheated 400° oven until cheese bubbles.

WHOLE WHEAT PASTRY:

Prepare in Cuisinart with steel blade as follows: Lodge butter (cut in 6 parts) closely to blade and add flour and whole wheat flour. Turn machine on and off and mix until coarse. Add a little water at a time to mixture until dough forms into a ball. Roll dough to fit in a tart shell. Butter underside of foil and place on top of dough. Cover foil with bakers pellet or rice and bake at 420° for 15 minutes (be sure butter and water are very cold). Excellent hors d'oeuvres made in the Cuisinart.

MRS. FRED C. KEMMERLING, JR. (CARLEEN)

MYSTERY SPREAD

10 oz. Gruyere cheese
10 oz. Emmenthal cheese
1 lb. baby shrimps (cooked)
⅔ cup scallions
1 tbsp. dillseed
1 ½ cups mayonnaise

Chop very fine by hand or with a food processor each of the first four ingredients. Combine together in a bowl and add the dillseed and mayonnaise. Mix thoroughly. Refrigerate before serving.

  The spread is best served on stone ground wafers.

Serves 12.

MRS. J. O. YUNGFLEISCH (MARY)

SHRIMP DIP

⅓ cup cream
2 tsp. lemon juice
¼ tsp. onion juice
Dash of Worcestershire
   sauce
8-oz. pkg. cream cheese
¾ cup shrimp (chopped,
   cooked or canned)

Gradually add cream, lemon juice, onion juice, and dash of Worcestershire sauce to the cream cheese. Mix well. Add the drained and chopped shrimp and mix again.

Serve with lightly salted crackers or ruffled potato chips.

Makes 1 cup

MRS. CHARLES K. MAIR

ROSY SHRIMP MOLD

1 envelope unflavored gelatin
¼ cup water (warm)
½ cup onion (finely chopped)
¾ cup celery (finely
   chopped)
1 cup mayonnaise
3 cans small shrimp (drained)
1 8-oz. pkg. cream cheese
1 can tomato soup
Parsley or watercress

Soften gelatin in warm water for 5 minutes. Mix onion, celery and mayonnaise with shrimp. Heat cheese and soup together. Combine all ingredients and pour into a lightly-oiled fish mold. Refrigerate until firm.

Unmold on a bed of parsley or watercress and serve with crisp crackers.

Hint: 1 pound of fresh small bay shrimp may be substituted for canned shrimp.

Serves 12.

ARLEEN KLOEPPEL

SHRIMP AND WATER CHESTNUTS

3 cans shrimp
   (finely chopped)
2 cans water chestnuts
   (chopped)
juice of ½ lemon
3 to 4 small green onions
   (chopped)
½ tsp. curry powder
Lots of mayonnaise

Mix well. Will be thin consistency.

Can be used as cocktail spread or dip.

Makes 1½ cups.

FLORENCE LEIGH

SHRIMP ROLL VERONICA

3 8-oz. pkg. cream cheese
1 8-oz. carton whipped sweet butter
4 green onions (chopped very fine)
4 French or sourdough loaves (flutes)about 12" long each
1 3-oz. jar capers (chopped)
1 lb. cooked medium size shrimp (chopped)
3 tbsp. horseradish (or more to taste)
Pistachio nuts (shelled and diced)

At room temperature, cream together the butter and cream cheese until well blended. Add onions, shrimp and horseradish and blend. Add capers last and mix in lightly. Warm French loaves slightly. Slice them in half long-wise and scoop out bread inside, leaving two shells. Press shrimp mixture firmly into bottom half and mound. Replace top half and press so that sides meet. Wipe away excess. Chill several hours or overnight.

Slice thinly, dicarding end slices. Arrange on serving platter and sprinkle garnish of diced pistachio nuts liberally over the dish. Great for a picnic without the garnish. Recipe may be cut in half.

Serves 12.

KATHY PARKER

SOUR CREAM SPINACH DIP

2 cups sour cream
1 cup mayonnaise
¾ pkg. dry leek soup mix
1 10-oz. pkg. frozen, chopped spinach (well drained and rechopped)
½ cup parsley (finely chopped)
½ cup green onions (finely chopped)
1 tsp. dill seed
1 tsp. salad seasoning mix
Pinch garlic salt

Combine sour cream and mayonnaise. Add and combine well: soup mix, spinach, parsley, green onions, dill, seasoning mix and garlic salt.

Makes 3½-4 cups dip.

MRS. CHARLES E. HORNING, JR.

TERRINE DE LANGOUSTINES (SHRIMP PATE)

¾ lb. langoustines or Spanish red shrimp (shelled and cleaned)
2 tbsp. butter
½ tsp. salt
⅛ tsp. white pepper
2 tbsp. cognac
1-¼ lbs. shrimp (shelled and cleaned)
2 tbsp. salt
4 tsp. nutmeg
¾ tsp. white pepper
3 cups whipping cream

Heat butter in a 10" skillet, add langoustines, salt and pepper. Gently toss until just cooked. Turn off heat, add cognac. Toss to coat langoustines. Set aside. Puree remaining ingredients in food processor. Remove 1 tbsp. of pureed mixture, cook in small skillet, and taste. If necessary to adjust seasonings, it should be a bit on salty side. (Over-season all recipes to be served cold, chilling deadens flavors.) Gently combine sauteed langoustines and pan juices with pureed mixture. Place in well-buttered 2 qt. pyrex loaf pan. Smooth top, pressing mixture to avoid air bubbles after it has been baked. Cut rectangle of wax paper to exactly fit top of pan. Butter one side, place buttered side down on mixture. Cover tightly with foil. Place in water bath whose depth reaches half-way up pan. Bake at 300° for 75 minutes. Remove terrine from water bath, allow to cool in pan. Refrigerate. When thoroughly chilled cut into ½" slices.

Serves 8-10.

★ L'ERMITAGE
Jean Bertranou
West Hollywood

TUNA SPOONLETS

2 tbsp. each of lemon juice parsley and minced onion
2 6½-oz. cans tuna (or salmon)
⅛ tsp. pepper
2 eggs (beaten)
½ cup flour
Oil for frying

Mix ingredients except oil. Drop by spoonfuls in hot salad oil and fry at 375° until brown. Serve with lemon juice.

Serves 10.

LIZ CONGDON
RITA LIVINGSTON

BEVERAGES

There was a young lady of Lynn
Who was uncommonly thin
  That when she essayed
  To drink lemonade
She slipped through the straw and fell in.

LANGFORD REED

FROZEN OLD FASHIONEDS

Ice
1 small can lemonade
  concentrate
1 tbsp. orange juice
  concentrate
1 can water
1 can bourbon

Fill blender with ice. Add all ingredients and blend. Serve immediately. May be topped with slice of orange and maraschino cherry.

GLORIA ARNETT

ORANGE JULEP

1 qt. orange juice
6 limes (juice or
  finely sliced)
1 cup powdered sugar
½ cup chopped mint leaves
Carbonated or alcoholic
  beverage

Chill all ingredients 1 hour. Pour over crushed ice in tall glasses. Then fill with carbonated water or a mild alcoholic beverage. Stir gently. Garnish with mint leaves or an orange slice.

Serves 4 people.

MRS. ROY ALLISON RICHARDSON

PINK MAGNOLIA

1 qt. vodka
1 qt. skim milk
1 qt. pink lemonade
Pernod to taste

Mix vodka, skim milk and pink lemonade. Add Pernod carefully to taste. (The Pernod has a licorice flavor and not much is needed.)

Makes 30 3-oz. cups.

MRS. BERNARD MELONE

RAMOS FIZZ

1 can frozen lemonade
  concentrate
1 equal can gin
1 equal can half
  & half
1 tbsp. frozen orange
  concentrate
1 egg

Fill blender with crushed ice. Add lemonade, gin, half & half and orange juice. Blend one minute. Add whole egg. Blend one more minute.

Serves 4 people

STEVEN E. SMITH

CHAMPAGNE PUNCH
(A La Harry Mynatt)

1 qt. good champagne
1 qt. soda water
1 qt. ginger ale
6 oz. brandy
6 oz. rum
3 oz. orange curacao
3 oz. triple sec
4-5 dashes bitters (angostura)
3 oz. lemon juice or
  Rose's lime juice
6 oz. orange juice
½ cup sugar (optional)

Pour all ingredients into a large punch bowl over a medium cake of ice. The following may be added for color:
  Lemon slices
  Orange slices
  Strawberries
  Pineapple slices
  Banana slices
  Fresh mint leaves dipped
    in powdered sugar

Makes 30 4-oz. drinks.

MRS. HARRY MYNATT

CRANBERRY-BOURBON PUNCH

1 qt. cranberry juice
1 46-oz. can pineapple juice
1 cup orange juice
½ cup lemon juice
1-2 cups bourbon
2 bottles ginger ale (28 oz.)
  (chilled)

In punch bowl combine juices and bourbon. Refrigerate. Just before serving add ginger ale.

Serves 20-25.

JEANENE COOK

FROZEN FRUIT NOG

1 quart prepared eggnog
2 pkgs. (10-oz. each) frozen
  raspberries or strawberries
  with syrup
1 6-oz. can frozen
  concentrated orange
  juice (thawed)
Cinnamon sticks
Ground nutmeg

Chill eggnog. Thaw fruit according to package directions. Combine eggnog and undiluted orange juice concentrate. Beat until thick and foamy. Place thawed fruit with syrup into bottom of punch bowl or pitcher. Add eggnog mix. Stir gently to swirl fruit through nog. Serve in punch cups or small mugs. Garnish each with cinnamon stick and sprinkling of nutmeg.

SOPHIE GLANZMAN

THE DRINKING MAN'S PUNCH

1 large can grapefruit
  juice (unsweetened)
1 large can pineapple juice
  (unsweetened)
1 fifth vodka
1 fifth sauterne
1 large bottle ginger ale
1 fifth Champagne (or more)

Mix all ingredients. Pour over cake of ice. For stronger punch substitute 1 fifth light Bacardi Rum for sauterne.

Serves 20 people

JOHN ALCANTARA

DOROTHY'S CYCLONE PUNCH

5 6-oz. cans frozen lemonade
  (undiluted)
2 6-oz. cans frozen orange
  juice (undiluted)
1 jigger lime juice
  concentrate
1 quart vodka
2 quarts 7-Up
Fresh fruit to float
Large chunk of ice
Red food coloring

Mix all ingredients together in large punch bowl.

MRS. BERNARD G. RAMOS

PUNCH IN THE PINK

3 tbsp. red hot cinnamon
  candies
¼ cup sugar
½ cup warm water
1 46-oz. can pineapple-
  grapefruit juice (chilled)
1 qt. ginger ale (chilled)
1 qt. California Light
  Muscat (chilled)

Cook candies, sugar and water over low heat until candies are dissolved. Cool. Mix with all except ginger ale. Chill. Just before serving add chilled ginger ale.
Variation: For a less sweet punch substitute soda water for ginger ale.

Makes 27 4-oz. cups.

MRS. JAMES R. SOULÉ

CHAMPLIN CHAMPAGNE PUNCH

Commencing in 1860, my family was in the wine business in upstate New York for nearly a century. One of my great-great grandfathers was the first professional champagne-maker in the United States, so I thought the traditional family formula for our champagne punch might be a suitable contribution.

¼ lb. powdered sugar
2 quarts champagne
1 quart Perrier or
 sparkling mineral water
2 oz. brandy
2 oz. Maraschino liqueur
2 oz. Curacoa liqueur

Mix well in a punch bowl that has been surrounded with cracked ice (never put ice in the bowl).

★ CHARLES CHAMPLIN
Author, critic, editor
Entertainment Editor of Los Angeles Times; many books include FLICKS.

CHAMPION SANGRIA

1 gal. burgundy
¼ bottle gin
⅓ bottle Cointreau
3 qts. orange juice
2 qts. apple juice
2 tsp. lemon juice
5 tbsp. granulated sugar
2 bottles CHEAP champagne
Sliced fresh peaches
Sliced raw apples
Sliced oranges and lemons
Whole strawberries

Mix ingredients in large container. The champagne must be added last before the fresh fruit and must be inexpensive so it will integrate properly. Good Champagne is too dry and will overpower the delicate blend. Serve in a punch bowl over ice.

Serves 70.

★ JOHN CHAMPION
Author, Director, Producer.
Creator McHALE'S NAVY and Producer LARAMIE TV series; Many films include SHOTGUN and MUSTANG COUNTRY; Books include HAWKS OF NOON and MUSTANG COUNTRY.

SWEDISH APRICOT NECTAR

1 lb. dried apricots
1/5 May wine
1 quart brandy
1 quart water
1 small cinnamon
   stick

Combine all ingredients in a gallon container or divide equally in 16 8-oz. jars. Age at room temperature one month. Will keep at room temperature after aging for 6 months. After 6 months will keep indefinitely in refrigerator. Nice to give as a gift! Serve plain in liquer glasses or over ice cream.

Makes 4 qts. or 16 8-oz. bottles

MRS. ROBERT L. HICKS

PINEBERRY JUICE
(non-alcoholic)

1 cup pineapple
   juice (strained)
1 cup cranberry
   juice cocktail
2 tsp. lemon juice

Combine juices and chill.

Makes four 4-oz. cups.

MRS. ROY ALLISON RICHARDSON

TOM AND JERRY

2 eggs beaten
   until yellow
½ box powdered sugar
1 jigger Rum or
   Brandy mix
Rum flavoring (optional)
Milk

Add sugar to eggs gradually. Beat until thick. (Can add rum flavoring) Put one large spoonful of mixture in cup. Add one jigger rum or brandy mix, stir. Fill cup with hot milk. Sprinkle nutmeg on top.

KAREN MARSHALL

SOUPS

This Bouillabaise a noble dish is
  A sort of soup, or broth, or stew
Or hotchpotch of all sorts of fishes,
  That Greenwich never could outdo.

WILLIAM THACKERAY

CREAM OF BROCCOLI SOUP

2½ lbs. fresh broccoli
1 cup chicken broth
½ tsp. salt
1 cup Swiss cheese (grated)
2 tbsp. flour
1 cup chicken broth
1 pkg. instant chicken broth (Lipton Cup-O-Soup)
1 cup whipping or light cream

Cut the broccoli into flowerets (the tender part of the stem can also be used) and place in a saucepan with 1 cup of chicken broth and salt. Cover and simmer 20 minutes until tender. Grate the Swiss cheese in a food processor. Add the hot broccoli with its broth and flour. Process until smooth. Return the puree to the saucepan and stir in the remaining ingredients. Simmer for a few minutes to blend flavors, stirring often.

Serves 8.

★ CESARE DANOVA

Actor

Many films include TENDER IS THE NIGHT, MAIN STREET, and ANIMAL HOUSE; TV roles include star GARRISON'S GORILLAS TV series; theatre roles include co-star TIME OF THE CUCKOO at Music Center.

CHICKEN CORN SOUP

1 3-to 4-lb. chicken
6 cups water
3 tsp. chicken seasoned stock base
1 tsp. salt
10 pieces saffron
2 cups noodles
Dash of M.S.G.
2 cups whole kernel corn
½ tsp. parsley flakes
1 tsp. green onions (shredded)
¼ tsp. black pepper
⅛ tsp. celery salt
2 hard cooked eggs

Cut chicken into pieces. Cook in water with chicken stock base, salt and saffron about 1½ hours. Remove chicken from stock, take meat off bones and cut into bite-size pieces. Put pieces back in stock and bring to a boil. Add other ingredients except eggs. Simmer 15 minutes. Chop eggs and add to soup.

Makes 2½ quarts.

MRS. WILLIAM STEINER

CHILI BEEF SOUP

1 lb. pinto beans
2 quarts water
1 lb. lean ground beef
1 onion (chopped)
1 green pepper (chopped)
2 tbsp. chili powder
1 tsp. each cumin, oregano,
   seasoned salt
2 beef bouillon cubes
1 26-oz. can tomatoes
1½ tsp. paprika
½ tsp. garlic powder

Soak pinto beans in 2 quarts of water overnight. Bring to a boil. Add other ingredients and simmer for several hours, or until beans are very soft.

Serves 6.

SUE HIRSCH

QUICK BOUILLABAISE

1 can onion soup
1 can tomato soup
⅓ cup red burgundy wine
1 tbsp. Worcestershire sauce
⅛ tsp. A-1 sauce
⅛ tsp. Lawry's Seasoning Salt
¼ tsp. dill
⅛ tsp. sugar
¼ lb. cooked shrimp
¼ lb. cooked crabmeat

Pour the two soups into a cooking pot. Do not add water. Blend with a wire whisk until smooth; add wine, sauces and seasonings. Bring to a boil but do not allow it to boil. Lower heat and add seafood. Any combination of cooked seafood may be used. Heat for about 5 minutes and serve with ½ slice lemon in each bowl as garnish.

Serves 2.

LORRAINE WOOD

VEGETABLE CLAM CHOWDER

6 scallions (sliced)
2 tbsp. butter or margarine
3 medium potatoes (peeled
   and sliced thin)
2 medium carrots (diced)
¾ cup dry white wine
1 7-oz. can minced clams
1 7-oz. can green peas
½ tsp. dill
1 ½ cups light cream
Salt

Saute the sliced scallions in butter 5 minutes. Add sliced potatoes, carrots, wine, liquid from clams and peas and dill. Salt to taste. If liquid does not cover potatoes add enough water to make sure it does. Cover and simmer for 25 minutes. Add peas and clams together with cream. Heat to just before boiling stirring in clams during last couple of minutes.

Serves 6.

FRAN ARMSTRONG

CIOPPINO
(An Italian Fish Soup)

SOUP BASE:

2 tbsp. olive oil
2 medium onions (chopped)
4 cloves garlic (chopped
  finely)
1 green pepper (chopped)
2 28-oz. cans pear
  tomatoes
2 6-oz. cans tomato paste
2 8-oz. bottles clam juice
Salt and pepper to taste
1½ tbsp. thyme
1 tbsp. oregano
1 large or 2 small bay leaves
1 tbsp. fennel seeds
1 tbsp. sugar
2 cups dry white wine

FISH STEW:

24 raw clams in shells
  (scrubbed)
2 lbs. raw fish in chunks (red
  snapper, halibut, sea bass)
8 large shrimp in shells
1 lb. scallops
6 to 8 sprigs of parsley
  (snipped)

Saute onions lightly in oil in a large kettle. Add garlic, then green pepper and saute lightly.

Drain and chop Italian pear tomatoes, reserving juice. Add to kettle along with tomato paste, juice from pear tomatoes, clam juice, seasonings and wine, and simmer for about 20 minutes. Soup base may be held at this point until needed.

About 20 minutes before serving, add raw clams and fish in chunks. After 10 minutes, add scallops and shrimp. Stir carefully so that fish chunks are not broken up. Add parsley and serve in large soup plates with hot Fench bread for dunking.

Serves 8.

VERONICA PLESTED
KATHY PARKER

Two things are essential in life:
to give good dinners and
to keep on fair terms with women.
          CHARLES MAURICE DE TALLEYRAND

CRAB BISQUE

1 cup crab meat
½ cup sherry
1 11-oz. can tomato
   bisque soup
1 10 ½-oz. can green
   pea soup
¼ tsp. curry powder
1 soup can half and half
½ tsp. paprika

Put crab meat in a bowl, pour over sherry and let stand 1 hour. Blend soups, cream, curry and paprika. Heat slowly, but do not boil. Add the crab meat. Reheat to boiling point and serve immediately.

Serves 6.

ARLEN O'HARA

LENTIL LAMB SOUP

Leftover roast leg of
   lamb bones (or 2 or 3 pkgs.
   lamb neck will do)
2 ½ quarts cold water
2 tbsp. salt
1 small clove garlic
½ tsp. peppercorns
   (8 or 10)
1 medium onion (sliced)
1 cup celery tops
1 bay leaf
4 sprigs parsley
1 12-oz. pkg. quick
   cooking lentils
2 cups carrots (sliced)
⅛ tsp. pepper

Place lamb bones or necks in large kettle. Cover with cold water and add salt. Tie garlic, peppercorn, onion, celery tops, bay leaf, parsley in cheesecloth; add to water and bones. Cover and simmer 4 hours. Remove bones and bag, leaving meat. At this point can be chilled in order to remove fat easily.

Add lentils and cook 30 minutes. Add sliced carrots and pepper and continue cooking until carrots and lentils are tender - about 20-30 minutes.

Makes 6 1½-cup servings.

FRAN ARMSTRONG

LAMB SHANK BORSCHT

6 lamb shanks
1 can chicken broth (47 oz.)
1½ cups water
6 whole black peppers
1 tsp. salt
1 bay leaf
1 small green pepper (diced)
3 medium carrots (diced)
1 medium onion (chopped)
4 small beets (diced)
4 cups cabbage (shredded)
1 small potato (diced)
2 tbsp. lemon juice

Cover the lamb shanks, bay leaf, salt and pepper with broth and water. Simmer 2 hours. Take out shanks and remove meat from bone. Return meat to broth. Put in refrigerator overnight. Skim grease. Put in all vegetables and simmer 15-20 minutes. Remove from heat and add lemon juice.

Serves 6.

MRS. W. BERNARD MELONE

PERFECT CREAM OF LETTUCE SOUP

2 medium onions
  (thinly sliced)
½ lb. butter
1 cup chicken broth
1 head Boston lettuce
  (shredded)
2 cups milk
2 cups heavy cream
Salt and pepper

Cook onions in ¼ lb. butter over low heat 1 hour. Heat together chicken broth and remaining butter until butter is melted. Add lettuce; bring to a boil; reduce heat and simmer 15 minutes. In a blender or food processor, puree onions with lettuce mixture. Add milk and cream and reheat carefully. Add salt and pepper to taste.

Serves 6-8.

MRS. BRIAN L. COCHRAN

MINESTRONE

1 quart or 14-oz. can
  tomato juice
4 cups water
2 tsp. sugar
2 tsp. salt
1 tsp. sweet basil
⅛ tsp. pepper
½ clove garlic (minced)
2 large carrots (thinly
  sliced)
3 large stalks celery
  (diced)
2 medium sized potatoes
  (diced)
2 leeks (sliced)
2 medium size unpeeled
  zucchini (sliced)
½ small, unpeeled eggplant
  (diced)
¼ cup parsley (chopped)
1 lb. fresh lima beans
  (shelled)
1 lb. fresh or frozen peas
  (shelled)
¼ lb. fresh or frozen
  green beans (tipped and
  cut)
2 tbsp. olive or salad oil
1 cup fine egg noodles
½ cup grated Parmesan
  cheese

Simmer tomato juice, water, sugar, salt, basil, pepper, garlic, carrots, celery, potatoes, leeks, zucchini, eggplant, parsley, for one hour in large pot. Then add and simmer lima beans, peas, green beans and oil for 30 minutes more. Then add and simmer for 10 minutes more, or until the vegetables are tender: noodles and cheese. Stir in cheese well; soup will be thick. Soup should be served piping hot with additional Parmesan cheese sprinkled over top.

Serves 8.

GRACE SEMER

So munch on, crunch on, take your muncheon,
Breakfast, supper, dinner, luncheon.
THE PIED PIPER OF HAMELIN

FRENCH ONION SOUP

3 large onions
(finely chopped)
4 tbsp. sweet butter
6 cups beef bouillon
1 tbsp. Worcestershire
sauce
1 tsp. pepper (no salt,
the bouillon is salty
enough)
Sour dough bread (toasted)
Swiss cheese
Parmesan

Brown onions in butter; add bouillon. Add Worcestershire sauce and pepper. Simmer until onions are tender.

Suggestion: If you have oven-proof bowls, serve soup in bowls with a slice of French or sourdough bread dusted with cheese and placed in soup. Put under broiler until cheese is melted.

Serves 6.

MRS. HARRY MYNATT

SUPER CREAM OF PEA SOUP

2 pkgs. frozen peas
1 cup chicken broth
1 med. size onion
(sliced)
1½ pints light cream
Salt and pepper

Cook peas and onions together in chicken broth until tender. Puree first in blender then put through fine sieve. Add half and half. Salt and pepper, keep hot in double boiler. Serve with chopped chives sprinkled on top of 1 tbsp. whipped cream.

Serves 4 to 6 people.

★ BEULAH BONDI
Actress.
(Still going strong, her motto is "Live In The Now"!)
Many films include OF HUMAN BONDAGE, OUR TOWN, SISTER KENNY and SNAKE PIT; TV series include THE WALTONS--for episode THE PONY CART (Emmy Award Best Actress 1977); National Honorary member Phi Beta.

FRESH PEA SOUP

Although Tony's favorite dish is Beef Stroganof, this is one he really enjoys.

4 cups fresh peas
½ cup water
1½ quarts milk
¼ tsp. marjoram (4 sprigs)
Pinch thyme (1 sprig)
2 mint leaves
1 tbsp. herb salt
1 tbsp. sugar

Heat but do not boil fresh peas in water. Liquefy in blender with milk (brought to room temperature), add marjoram, thyme, mint leaves, herb salt and sugar. Put through a sieve then heat over water (double boiler) to serving temperature. DO NOT BOIL.

Serves 8.

★ MRS. TONY TRABERT (EMERYL)
TONY TRABERT: Sportsman.
U.S. Tennis Open Champion at Wimbledon; U.S. Davis Cup Captain 1976, 1977, 1978, 1979.

PEANUT SOUP

2 cups chicken stock
4 medium onions (chopped)
1 cup cream
1 cup coconut milk
4 tbsp. peanut butter
Dash cayenne
Dash lime juice
Fresh mint leaf (chopped)

In saucepan combine 2 cups of chicken stock with 4 medium onions (chopped). Bring liquid to a boil, and simmer the mixture for 30 minutes. Strain the liquid into a bowl and stir in one cup each of cream and coconut milk. Add 4 tbsp. of peanut butter and a dash of cayenne. Transfer mixture and blend for a minute. Chill the soup.

Add a dash of lime juice, and garnish each cup with chopped fresh mint leaf prior to serving.

Makes 4 cups.

★ RANGOON RACQUET CLUB
Beverly Hills

MY FAVORITE THICK VEGETABLE SOUP

½ cup dry white beans
4 cups vegetable (use
  at least 4 different
  kinds). Choose from okra,
  turnips, carrots, peas,
  zucchini, cauliflower
  (or what have you). Cut
  in small pieces.
4 tbsp. butter
¼ lb. salt pork (diced)
⅓ cup celery
  (thinly sliced)
4 tbsp. onions (finely
  chopped)
1 cup canned sliced
  baby tomatoes
2 quarts chicken stock
1 bay leaf
Salt and pepper
¾ cup of following:
  rice, barley or macaroni
  (wagon wheels are fun)
Sweet basil
1 tbsp. parsley flakes
Minced garlic
Parmesan cheese
  (freshly grated)

Cook beans according to direction. Drain and set aside. Saute vegetables in butter until lightly coated. Set aside. Fry salt pork in 6-8 quart stock pot until crisp and brown; lift out pork with slotted spoon; set aside. Saute celery and onions in remaining fat until lightly browned. Stir in tomatoes, vegetables, chicken stock, bay leaf, salt and pepper. Bring to boil; reduce heat and simmer for 30 minutes. Add the grain or macaroni, beans and salt pork. Cook another 20 minutes or until grain is tender. Season with sweet basil, chopped parsley and minced garlic. Serve with lots of freshly grated Parmesan cheese and hunks of French bread. This freezes beautifully.

Serves 10.

MRS. BRIAN L. COCHRAN

There were three sailors of Bristol City
Who took a boat and went to sea.
But first with beef and captain's biscuits
And pickled pork they loaded she.
                    WILLIAM MAKEPEACE THACKERAY

SOUR AND HOT SOUP   SAUN-LA-T-AUG

5 cups chicken broth
  (not canned)
6 dried Chinese mushrooms
  (2-3 inches in diameter)
3 squares Chinese bean
  curd (Tofu)
¾ cup (canned) bamboo
  shoots
½ lb. boneless, lean pork
½ tsp. ground white pepper
1½ tbsp. soy sauce
4 tbsp. white vinegar
1 egg (beaten)
2 scallions (whole)
  (finely chopped)
3 tsp. sesame seed oil
2½ tbsp. cornstarch mixed
  with 4 tbsp. water

Slice pork ⅛ inch thick and cut ¼ inch wide, 2 inches long. Cut bamboo shoots and bean curd into similar sizes. Soak mushrooms (30 minutes in warm water) and cut into same shape. Combine stock, pork, bamboo shoots, mushrooms, salt and soy sauce in 3-quart or larger cooking pot. Bring quickly to boil. Reduce heat; simmer 4 minutes. Drop in bean curd (try not to break), pepper and vinegar and bring to boil again. Stir in cornstarch mixture. Stir until soup thickens. Then, while stirring, pour in beaten egg. Remove to serving bowl. Stir in sesame seed oil. Sprinkle scallions on top. Soup can be varied by including 10-12 tiger lily buds and ⅓ cup Chinese fungi (cloud's ears.)

Serves 4-6.

THOMAS E. KING, JR.

FRESH TOMATO SOUP

2 cups water
3 large onions (chopped)
5 lbs. fresh tomatoes
1 bunch parsley
  (chopped)
6 strips bacon
1 cup sugar
2 tbsp. salt
2 stalks celery
  (minced)
1 tbsp. mixed spices
2 tbsp. flour

Cut tomatoes in quarters. Add sugar, water, salt, spices, onions, celery and parsley. Bring to a boil. Simmer 1½ to 2 hours. Cut bacon into small pieces. Add flour and brown lightly. Put tomatoes, vegetables, spices through a food mill. Then add bacon with the flour and bring all to a boil.

Serves 10-12

GLENDA GRIBBEN

CREAM OF CUCUMBER SOUP

2 cups cucumber
  (peeled and coarsely
  chopped)
1 cup chicken broth
1 cup light cream
¼ cup celery leaves
  (chopped)
3 sprigs parsley
¼ cup chopped chives
2 tbsp. flour
3 tbsp. soft butter
Lemon rind
Salt and pepper
Dill weed

Put all ingredients in blender and mix until smooth. Season with salt and pepper. Serve hot or cold. If cold, garnish with some grated lemon rind and finely chopped cucumber. If hot, garnish with a small amount of dill weed.

Serves 3-4.

MRS. SPENCER LAWSON

EMERALD SOUP

1 pkg. frozen chopped
  spinach
2 cans cream of
  chicken soup
3 dashes of Tabasco sauce
1 soup can of milk
1 garlic clove

Defrost but do not cook spinach. Place in blender with 2 cans of soup and one can of milk. Add one large or 2 small cloves of garlic and Tabasco. Blend well and chill. Serve in chilled bowls. For color sprinkle with paprika. Can also be served hot.

Serves 4.

★ MRS. PAUL FRANCIS WEBSTER (GLORIA)
*PAUL FRANCIS WEBSTER: Author, lyricist
Film scores include ROSE MARIE, APRIL LOVE,
SECRET LOVE (Academy Award 1953), LOVE IS
A MANY-SPLENDORED THING (Academy Award
1955), and SHADOW OF YOUR SMILE (Academy
Award and Grammy Award 1965); Awarded
Diploma Di Benemeranza Hall of Artists, Nice,
France and Auguste Messinese Gold Award, Italy.*

CHILLED AVOCADO SOUP

3 large ripe
   avocados (1⅔ cups)
1 14-oz. can chicken broth
1 tbsp. lemon juice
½ tsp. salt
½ tsp. pepper
1½ cans water
½ cup light cream
3 slices bacon
   (cooked and chopped)

Mash avocados and combine with broth, lemon juice, salt, pepper and 1½ cups water. Press through sieve. Refrigerate two hours. Stir in cream and top with bacon.

Serves 4.

MRS. JAMES E. GRIFFIN

CHILLED AVOCADO CURRY SOUP

My mother, who gave me this recipe, is a real gourmet! It is one of our favorite summer luncheon soups.

1 tbsp. butter
½ tsp. curry powder
1 pkg. chicken
   noodle soup
2 cups water
1 cup light cream
1 medium size avocado

Melt butter. Stir in curry powder. Add water. Bring to boil and add soup mix. Cover and simmer 7 minutes. Stir in cream and re-heat but do not boil. Put in blender with half of the avocado. Blend until smooth. Add remaining half avocado cut in small pieces. (Do not blend the second half avocado but leave it there so there are bits of it in the soup when it is served.) Chill thoroughly and serve sprinkled with a bit of fresh ground nutmeg.

Serves 6.

★ MRS. LUIS W. ALVAREZ (JAN)
DR. LUIS W. ALVAREZ: Physicist, scientist Expert in research of sub-atomic particles (Nobel Laureate 1968) Einstein Medal and California Scientist of the Year 1960 .

CONSOMME SUPREME

This recipe is from a farming community near Capetown, South Africa.

1 tin Campbell's consomme
1 small package Philadelphia
   cream cheese
1 clove garlic

In blender mix the cheese with half the consomme and the garlic very finely chopped. Divide equally into four ramekins or small sherbet glasses. Place in refrigerator until quite set. Top with the remaining half tin consomme spooned gently over cheese mixture. Allow to set in refrigerator.

Serves 2.

BETTY BERRINGTON

GAZPACHO

2 stalks celery
1½ cucumbers
1½ large tomatoes
1½ medium green
   peppers
1 tsp. diced chili
   pepper (canned)
3 tbsp. lemon juice
¼ cup olive oil
½ tsp. freshly
   ground pepper
2 tsp. garlic salt
1 cup chicken broth
2 cups tomato juice
3 tsp. Worcestershire
   sauce
1½ tsp. salt
2-3 drops Tabasco sauce

Dice finely celery, cucumbers, tomatoes and peppers. Combine all ingredients. Chill. Serve with croutons or top each serving with a drop of sour cream and diced avocado.

Makes 3 quarts.

MRS. MICHAEL LIVINGSTON

NO-CAL GAZPACHO

6 large tomatoes
  (peeled and seeded)
1 cucumber (peeled
  and seeded)
1 clove garlic
1 large onion
1 green pepper
  (diced fine)
Salt to taste
Tomato juice (as
  needed to thin soup)

Place tomatoes, cucumber, onion and garlic in blender. Add ¼ cup tomato juice to facilitate blending. This is a thick soup — add more tomato juice if desired. Add salt to taste. Chill. Serve in bowls and top with diced green peppers. Unlike other gazpacho recipes no oil is used.

Serves 6.

★ MRS. ROBERT BARKER (DOROTHY)
BOB BARKER: actor, announcer, TV host.
Host PRICE IS RIGHT TV series; MISS U.S.A.,
MISS UNIVERSE and ROSE BOWL PARADE TV
Specials.

COLD RASPBERRY SOUP

3 cups fresh or frozen
  raspberries
½ cup sour cream
½ cup sugar
1 cup cold water
1 cup red wine
  (Italian Swiss)
1 tsp. lemon juice
Rind of ½ lime
  (finely grated)

Work the raspberries through a fine sieve. Combine the juice with the sour cream and sugar. Add remaining ingredients and serve chilled.

Serves 4.

MRS. GRAHAM POLK

Jack Sprat could eat no fat,
His wife could eat no lean;
And so between them both, you see,
They licked the platter clean.
(NURSERY RHYMES 1639)

WADE'S VICHYSSOISE SUPREME

Wade created this recipe for the Foreign Correspondents Club in Tokyo, a favorite to this day.

4 large onions
(sliced thin)
4 large potatoes
(cut in pieces)
4/5 quart chicken
stock (extra rich)
3 cups heavy cream
1½ cups milk (or
all cream may be used)
3 tbsp. butter
Salt and pepper
to taste
Chives (chopped)
Paprika

Brown onions in butter. Add potatoes and cook, stirring constantly until coated. Add stock and simmer until potatoes are tender. Remove from stove, cool and refrigerate. When mixture is chilled, blend until pureed. Add salt, pepper, milk and/or cream and mix well. Return to refrigerator until well chilled. Just before serving sprinkle chives and paprika over the top.

Serves 6-8.

★ MRS. WADE L. BINGHAM (VIRGINIA)
WADE L. BINGHAM: Director, cinematographer, producer.
TV credits include 60 MINUTES, CBS REPORTS, SEE IT NOW, and TWENTIETH CENTURY with Walter Cronkite; Far East Bureau Chief, CBS TV News; War Correspondent in Korea and Viet Nam.

FROSTY ZUCCHINI SOUP

2 large zucchini (sliced)
1 medium green
pepper (sliced)
½ cup onion (chopped)
3 cups chicken stock
1 cup yogurt or sour cream
1 tsp. parsley (finely
chopped)
½ tsp. fresh dill
(finely chopped)
or ¼ tsp. dried dill
Salt and pepper
4 slices raw zucchini garnish

Place zucchini, green pepper and onion and chicken stock in saucepan. Save some raw zucchini for later. Simmer for 20 minutes.

Strain and reserve the stock.

Place sour cream or yogurt, parsley and dill in food processor or blender. Add the vegetables and process. With the machine running slowly add the stock. Add some raw zucchini at the end for extra crunch.

Season to taste and chill. Place a slice of raw zucchini on the side of bowl or goblet.

Serves 4.

MRS. PAUL W. MIKOS

SALADS

Cool in the summer is salad,
And warm in the winter is love;
And a poet shall sing you a ballad
Delicious thereon and thereof.

MORTIMER CALLINS

AVOCADO
AND FRESH MUSHROOM SALAD

DRESSING:
⅓ cup olive oil
1 tbsp. dry white wine
1 tbsp. fresh parsley
  (chopped)
1 clove garlic (pressed)
1 tsp. salt
Fresh pepper (coarsely
  ground)
Juice of 1 lemon
½ lb. fresh mushrooms
  (sliced)
3 avocados (peeled and
  sliced in rings)

Layer mushrooms and avodaco slices in shallow crystal serving bowl. Pour dressing over, cover tightly with Saran wrap and chill for one hour before serving. Garnish with sprigs of parsley and more cracked pepper, if desired.

Serves 6.

MRS. WILLIAM J. REA

BROCCOLI SALAD

2 pkg. frozen broccoli
  (chopped)
1 small jar stuffed or
  plain olives (chopped)
3 hard-boiled eggs
  (chopped)
1 bunch fresh green
  onions (chopped,
  include some tender
  green tips)
½ cup celery (chopped)
Salt
¾ cup mayonnaise

Barely cook broccoli (about half the time directions call for). Drain broccoli well and chill until very cold. Add olives, eggs, onions and celery. Season with salt. Combine with mayonnaise.

Serves 12.

CORENE ELLIOTT

CAESAR SALAD

¼ cup olive oil
¼ cup vegetable oil
¼ cup lemon juice
1 egg (room temperature)
4 anchovy filets or
  1 tsp. anchovy paste
¾ tsp. salt
1-2 garlic cloves
¼ cup Bleu cheese (minced)
½ tsp. dry mustard
⅓ tsp. hot pepper sauce
¾ cups Parmesan (grated)
2 heads romaine lettuce

Put all ingredients (except last two) into blender and blend until smooth. Chill. Serve over greens (Remainder will keep.)

Serves 12.

JEANNE HAYES

CHINESE CHICKEN SALAD WITH JAPANESE SALAD DRESSING

3 chicken breasts
Sliced ginger
1 head lettuce (shredded bite size)
½ pkg. rice sticks or 2 oz. bean thread (deep fried) (may be fried day or two ahead and held in plastic bag)
3-6 green onions (vertically slivered)
1 small pkg. toasted almonds
¼ cup toasted sesame seeds

MIYAKO SALAD DRESSING:
1 cup Japanese rice vinegar
1 tsp. salt
¾ cup sugar
1 tbsp. mirin (sweet sake)

Cook chicken breasts in water with sliced ginger 20 minutes or until done. Drain and cool. Shred. Assemble all ingredients, adding rice sticks and salad dressing and serve immediately.

Combine vinegar, salt and sugar and heat stirring until sugar is dissolved. Remove from heat and stir in mirin. Chill.

Serves 6-8.

BETTY KEMP

CHUTNEY CHICKEN SALAD

1 cup raisins (white
  wine to cover)
2 lbs. chicken breasts
1 ½ cups mayonnaise
1 cup peanuts
1 cup mango chutney
2 cups bananas (sliced
  diagonally)
Salt and pepper to taste
1 cup coconut (flaked)
2 avocados

Plump raisins in white wine overnight. Use 2 full chicken breasts baked at 350° for 1 hour. Cool, skin, bone and tear into bite-size pieces. Mix all ingredients except avocado. Serve on lettuce leaves and garnish with avocado slices.

Serves 8.

MRS. KENNETH WILLIAMS

OVEN CHICKEN SALAD

1 cup mayonnaise
1 tsp. capers (crushed
  or sliced)
2 cups chicken (cubed)
2 tbsp. onion (grated)
2 cups celery (chopped
  fine)
1 can water chestnuts
  (sliced)
½ cup toasted almonds
  (slivered)
1 cup herbed croutons
2 tsp. lemon juice
½ tsp. salt
½ cup Parmesan cheese
  (grated)

Mix all ingredients together into a 9" x 9" dish. Bake 10 minutes in 450° oven. May be prepared the night before and kept in refrigerator but let stand until at room temperature before baking.

Serves 4-6.

DR. SHERRIE ATKINSON

CHICKEN WITH A DATE

¾ cup sour cream
1 tbsp. onion (minced)
2 tbsp. orange juice
1 tbsp. lemon juice
1 tsp. salt
Pepper to taste
1 cup celery (chopped)
3 cups chicken (cubed)
2 tbsp. toasted almonds
1 cup dates (cut up)
1 tbsp. pimiento (chopped)

Combine and mix ingredients. Garnish with mandarin oranges and serve on lettuce.

Serves 8.

INGRID HEDBERG

COBB SALAD

½ head of lettuce
½ bunch watercress
1 small bunch chicory
½ head romaine
2 medium tomatoes (peeled)
2 breasts of boiled roasting chicken
6 strips crisp bacon
1 avocado
3 eggs (hard-cooked)
2 tbsp. chives (chopped)
½ cup imported Roquefort cheese (finely grated)
1 cup Brown Derby Old-Fashioned French Dressing

Finely cut lettuce, watercress, chicory and romaine and arrange in salad bowl. Cut tomatoes in half; remove seeds; finely dice and arrange in a strip across the salad. Dice breasts of chicken and arrange over top of chopped greens. Chop bacon finely and sprinkle over the salad. Cut avocado in small pieces and arrange around the edge of the salad. Decorate the salad by sprinkling over the top the chopped eggs, chopped chives and grated cheese. Just before serving mix the salad thoroughly with French dressing.

MRS. ROBERT COBB

COLE SLAW SUPREME

DRESSING:
1 onion (chopped)
1½ cups salad oil
1 cup sugar
½ cup rice vinegar
½ tsp. poppy seed
½ tsp. celery seed
½ tsp. salt
1 head cabbage
White raisins
Almonds (slivered)

Place dressing ingredients in blender and mix. Grate a head of cabbage. Add raisins and slivered almonds. Add dressing and toss well.
    Makes 2 cups of dressing.

Serves 8.

ALPHA MacCORMACK

MEREDITH WILLSON'S MOTHER'S COLE SLAW

This was Meredith's mother's recipe.

1 cup apple cider vinegar
1 cup granulated sugar
Salt and pepper to taste
½ cup unpeeled red apple (crisp) (finely chopped)
Cabbage (chopped)
6 ice cubes or large piece of ice
1 cup heavy cream
1 tsp. prepared mustard
1 tsp. salad dressing

Mix vinegar with sugar. Add salt and pepper. Finely chop ½ cup crisp unpeeled red apple, combine with chopped cabbage and cover with vinegar mixture, adding ice cubes. Let stand in the refrigerator for about 6 hours. Meanwhile, whip salt and cream, adding mustard and salad dressing.

When ready to serve, squeeze the cabbage mixture, one handful at a time, until it is entirely free of the vinegar juice. Just before serving combine cabbage with the whipped cream mixture, one tbsp. at a time, until it is a nice slaw or salad consistency.

Serves 6 to 8.

MRS. MEREDITH WILLSON (ROSEMARY)

★ *MEREDITH WILLSON: Author, composer, conductor, flutist.*
Flute soloist with John Philip Sousa Band; theatre scores and librettos include THE MUSIC MAN (New York Drama Critics, Tony and Grammy Awards 1965) and THE UNSINKABLE MOLLY BROWN; songs include 76 TROMBONES, MAY THE GOOD LORD BLESS AND KEEP YOU, TILL THERE WAS YOU and IOWA FIGHT SONG.

COPPER MEDALLIONS

¾ cup white vinegar
1 cup sugar
2 lbs. carrots (sliced and cooked)
1 green pepper (chopped fine)
1 medium onion (chopped fine)
1 can tomato soup
½ cup salad oil
1 tsp. prepared mustard
1 tsp. Worcestershire sauce

Cook carrots only until just crisp-tender (about 10 minutes).

In separate pan boil vinegar with sugar until sugar dissolves. Add remaining ingredients and refrigerate at least 8 hours. Serve cold. Keeps in refrigerator for several weeks.

Serves 8.

MRS. RICHARD A. WEAVER

CRABREAD SALAD

1 standard loaf white sandwich bread (decrusted, buttered and cubed finely)
1 onion (chopped fine)
2 cans crab
2 cans shrimp
8 hard boiled eggs (chopped)
2 cups mayonnaise
Salt and pepper
2 cup celery (finely chopped)
½ cup green pepper (chopped fine)

Mix lightly bread and onion; cover tightly; refrigerate. Next day add crab, shrimp and hard boiled eggs. When ready to serve add mayonnaise salt and pepper, celery and green pepper. Mix well. Serve on lettuce leaf garnished with cherry tomatoes.

Serves 12 amply.

PAT ALCANTARA

CUCUMBER SESAME

3 medium cucumbers
   (sliced fine)
2 tsp. salt
½ cup vinegar
5 tbsp. sugar
2 tbsp. ginger root
   (chopped finely)
1 tsp. sesame seeds

Pare cucumbers. Leave part green. Cut in halves, remove seeds and slice fine. Place in bowl, add salt and allow to stand 10 minutes. Squeeze off excess water. (Use cheese cloth.) Mix vinegar, sugar, ginger root and sesame seeds in a pot and allow to boil. Pour over cucumbers. Serve cold as pickles or a garnish.

(The cucumbers have a tangy, ginger taste.)

Makes 1½ to 2 cups.

MRS. JOHN T. MASTERS (TIMMI)

TUNISIAN EGGPLANT SALAD

1 12½-oz. can chunk-
   style tuna
1 lb. eggplant
½ cup boiling water
1 large green pepper
   (chopped)
1 clove garlic (crushed)
½ cup olive oil
⅓ cup red wine vinegar
1 tsp. oregano
1 tsp. salt
1 large tomato (seeded and
   chopped)
Crisp salad greens
¼ cup crumbled feta cheese

Drain tuna. Cut eggplant into 1" cubes. Steam over boiling water 2 to 5 minutes until eggplant is tender. Drain. Arrange with green pepper in a 2-quart shallow casserole. Combine garlic, oil, vinegar, oregano and salt in a screw-top jar. Shake well. Pour over eggplant mixture. Cover and refrigerate 1 hour. Drain marinade and reserve for other use. Toss marinated vegetables with tomato and tuna. Spoon into salad bowl lined with crisp greens. Top with crumbled feta cheese.

Serves 4.

MRS. BAXTER HALLAIAN

MACARONI SALAD ITALIAN STYLE

1 lb. elbow macaroni
1½ cups mayonnaise
1 cup cooked ham (diced)
1 cup scallions (sliced)
1 tbsp. Dijon mustard
Salt and pepper to taste
1 tbsp. tarragon vinegar
1 tbsp. red wine vinegar
¼ tsp. rosemary
¼ tsp. garlic (minced)
¼ cup vegetable oil
1½ tbsp. olive oil
1 tbsp. hot water
Hard boiled eggs (sliced)
Ripe olives (pitted)

In a bowl of an electric mixer combine the tarragon vinegar, red wine vinegar, rosemary, garlic and salt and pepper to taste. With the motor at high speed add the vegetable oil combined with olive oil in a stream. Beat in the hot water and continue to beat for 5 min. In a larger bowl combine the cooked macaroni while still warm with above mixture. Add the mayonnaise, ham, scallions and mustard. Add salt and pepper to taste. Garnish the salad with sliced hard boiled eggs and ripe olives.

Serves 10 people.

INGRID POLLAKOFF

MEXICAN SALAD BOWL

1 box cherry tomatoes
1½ lbs. lean beef
1 head lettuce
2 ripe avocados
1 medium onion
1 pkg. Fritos, partly
    crunched
1 pkg. Tillamook cheese
    (grated)
1 pkg. Monterey Jack cheese
    (grated)
1 can ripe olives
1 can Ranch Beans (partially
    drained)
1 pkg. Ranch salad dressing

Cut tomatoes in half and brown meat. Shred lettuce, slice avocados, chop onions, crunch Fritos and grate cheeses.

Mix all ingredients and serve.

Great for a luncheon or a family summer dinner.

Serves 6.

TRACY E. GRIFFIN

MUSHROOM SALAD

1 lb. fresh mushrooms
4 ½ tbsp. Poupon mustard
4 ½ tbsp. red wine vinegar
   with tarragon
¾ cup olive oil
½ tsp. salt
¼ tsp. freshly ground pepper
½ tsp. oregano
Freshly chopped parsley

Slice mushrooms. Prepare salad dressing. Toss salad and sprinkle with parsley.

Serves 6.

MRS. ARVID S. PETERSON

MUSHROOMS — LEEK SALAD

16 fresh mushrooms
Vinaigrette dressing
2 fresh leeks
1 head lettuce
1 bunch watercress
1 can mandarin oranges
Ground black peppercorns

Marinate sliced fresh mushrooms in vinaigrette dressing the day before. Slice white ends of leeks very fine and separate the rings. Place lettuce leaves on salad plates; sprinkle generously with chopped watercress; add marinated sliced mushrooms; top with leek rings and mandarin oranges. Serve with vinaigrette dressing. Sprinkle ground black peppercorns over salad.

Serves 8.

★   PEGGY GOLDWATER
BARRY GOLDWATER, SR: Civic leader, pilot, statesman
Member United States Senate from Arizona, former Republican Nominee for President, United States.

SALAD NIÇOISE

DRESSING:

1 heaping tbsp. Dijon
   mustard
¼ cup wine vinegar
1 cup olive oil
2 tbsp. salt
1 tbsp. fresh black pepper
½ cup fresh basil

1 handful of green beans
   (cooked)
2 large tomatoes
   (cut in wedges)
2 medium potatoes (cooked,
   peeled and cubed)
1 large head of lettuce
   (iceberg, romaine or Bibb)
2 peppers, red, yellow or
   green (sliced)
3 stalks of celery
   (quartered long-ways
   and sliced thin)
1 large cucumber (seeds
   removed and sliced thin)
3 scallions (sliced)
1 small can tuna (drained)
6-12 anchovy fillets
¼ cup Italian black olives
3 hard cooked eggs
   (quartered)
Fresh basil leaves
   (chopped)

Prepare the dressing several hours before serving and marinate the green beans and potatoes in about ½ of it while they are still warm. You can also stick a toothpick in a garlic clove and drop it into the salad dressing. Be sure to remove it before you dress your salad. Rub a bowl with a cut garlic clove. Then arrange the lettuce leaves around the outside of the bowl. Place the tomatoes on the lettuce.

Prepare the remaining vegetables. Arrange them attractively on the lettuce. Add the tuna in fairly large chunks. Sprinkle on some of the chopped basil. Remember to add the marinated potatoes and green beans. Decorate the top with the anchovy fillets wrapped around the black olives as well as the hard-boiled eggs. Sprinkle with more chopped basil and a few scallions, if desired. Add dressing and mix well.

Serves 8-10.

KATHRYN B. MURPHY

SALAD A LA ROSE

6 oz. uncooked linguini
Pinch saffron
1 tsp. chicken base
½ tsp. powdered garlic
½ tsp. olive oil
2 tbsp. lemon juice
18 oz. San Francisco Bay
    shrimp
1 large cantaloupe
½ cup Thousand Island
    dressing
½ cup oil and vinegar
    dressing
3 whole tomatoes
3 whole eggs (hard boiled)
12 black olives (pitted)
1 lemon (sliced into wedges)

Boil linguini with saffron (saffron optional if unavailable, but saffron will "add a jewel to the crown"), chicken base, garlic, olive oil and lemon. Cook until tender but not soft. Strain under cold water and dry on towel.

Marinate linguini in oil and vinegar dressing for ½ hour.

Mix Bay shrimp with slivers of cantaloupe. Add Thousand Island dressing. Drain off excess liquid before placing in center of a large plate. Surround shrimp with marinated linguini. Surround outside of plate with ½ slices of tomatoes and sliced boiled eggs. Top egg slices with ½ black olive.

Place one lemon wedge on each serving.

Serves 6.

★ THE MUSIC CENTER PAVILION
Los Angeles
Lothar Kuehndahl, Executive Chef

We may live without poetry,
music and art;
We may live without conscience,
and live without heart;
We may live without friends;
we may live without books;
But civilized man
cannot live without cooks.
                    EDWARD ROBERT BULWER

YANKEE POTATO SALAD

2 lbs. potatoes
(boiled, cooled
and peeled)
1 cup green pepper
(finely chopped)
½ cup celery (finely
chopped)
½ cup onion (finely
chopped)
2 tbsp. parsley
(chopped)
2 tbsp. white wine
vinegar
Salt and pepper to taste
1 cup mayonnaise
2 or 3 eggs (hard boiled)

In a bowl combine the potatoes, cut into ½ inch squares, green pepper, celery, onions, parsley, vinegar and salt and pepper. Fold in mayonnaise. Chill. Garnish the salad with slices of hard-boiled egg. Sprinkle with chopped parsley.

Serves 10.

INGRID POLLAKOFF

RICE SALAD

1 pkg. Uncle Ben's white and
wild rice (cooked)
1 box cherry tomatoes
(halved)
½ bunch green onions
(chopped)
1 jar artichoke hearts
(drained)
1 jar button mushrooms
(drained)
1 bottle Wishbone Italian
dressing

Toss above ingredients with 1 bottle Wishbone Italian dressing & refrigerate overnight. Add 1 pkg. (10 oz.) frozen baby peas before serving.

★ ART LINKLETTER
Author, producer, TV host.
Radio and TV series include HOUSE PARTY and SECRET WORLD OF KIDS. Book titled KIDS SAY THE DARNDEST THINGS.

SHRIMP SALAD ELEGANTE

Green mayonnaise
  2 cups mayonnaise
  2 tbsp. parsley
  1 tbsp. chives
  1 tbsp. tarragon
  1 tsp. dill
  1 tsp. chervil
  Cream
Shredded lettuce
Shrimp
Pimiento strips
Hard-boiled egg
Drained capers
Sprigs of watercress or dill
  and lemon slices

Mix together mayonnaise, parsley, chives, tarragon, dill and chervil to make a green mayonnaise. Makes 2 cups.

In large wine goblets, line bottom with shredded lettuce and fill glasses with alternating layers of shrimp, green mayonnaise (thinned with cream) pimiento strips, sieved hard-boiled egg, shredded lettuce and drained capers.

Top each goblet with 1 or 2 shrimp and garnish with sprigs of watercress or dill and lemon slices.

MRS. FRED C. KEMMERLING, JR. (CARLEEN)

SHRIMP AND VERMICELLI SALAD

1 pkg. (16 oz) vermicelli
3 lbs. fresh shrimp (deveined)
3 cups celery (finely diced)
2 4½-oz. cans black olives
  (sliced)
2 4-oz. cans pimientos
½ cup parsley (minced)
6 tbsp. mayonnaise (Best
  Foods)
Salad dressing (16 oz.
  Bernsteins Italian)
Salt and pepper

Cook vermicelli according to package directions (al dente). Cool, chop to 1" pieces. Add remaining ingredients. Toss with approximately ¾ bottle of salad dressing, add mayonnaise and mix. Add salt and pepper to taste. Marinate overnight; then the next day, add remaining salad dressing, according to taste.

Serves 20 at a buffet.

GLORIA DAHL

SALLY'S SAUERKRAUT SALAD

2 ½ green peppers
  (sliced thin)
2 ¼ cups celery
  (cut medium)
2 medium onions
  (sliced round)
1 can sliced pimiento
1 large can sauerkraut
  (washed and drained)
3 cups sugar
1 ¼ cups cider vinegar
⅔ cup salad oil
½ tsp. garlic powder
⅔ cup water
½ tsp. salt

Mix together first 5 ingredients. Cover with sugar, vinegar, salad oil, garlic powder, water and salt. Cover tightly and marinate in refrigerator for 24 hours, stirring occasionally. Drain well.

Keeps in refrigerator for at least a week.

Serves 20 or more.

DOYNE WOOD

DELICIOUS HOT SEAFOOD SALAD

1 cup celery (chopped)
1 green pepper (chopped)
1 cup crab meat (shredded)
1 cup medium-size shrimp
  (cleaned)
¼ cup onion (grated)
3 hard boiled eggs
  (chopped)
¼ cup mayonnaise
Buttered crumbs.

Toss all ingredients together. Place in baking pan and toss buttered crumbs on top. Bake about 30 minutes in 350° oven.

Hint: To serve 12, increase shrimp and crab each to 1½ lbs. and triple all other ingredients.

Serves 4

MRS. BRUCE APP LOWMAN

JOHN'S SPINACH SALAD

Soy oil
Red wine vinegar
Salt
Pepper
Salad herbs
Extra dry and crisp
  crumbled bacon (fresh)
Chopped white Bermuda
  onion
Coarsely chopped crisp red
  apples
Spinach leaves

Mix oil, vinegar, salt, pepper, and salad herbs in quantities to make a good oil and vinegar french dressing (in proportion to overall amount of fresh spinach.) Marinate in quantity a generous amount of extra dry and crisp crumbled bacon (not bottled). Generous amount of coarsely chopped white Bermuda onion. Generous amount of coarsely chopped crisp red apples with skin left on. Put all in a large jar and shake thoroughly and let marinate at room temperature for a couple of hours. Then chill well before tossing with crisp spinach leaves.

★ MRS. JOHN GREEN (BONNIE)
JOHN GREEN: arranger, composer, conductor, pianist, producer, recording artist.
Many hit songs include BODY AND SOUL,. COQUETTE, I WANNA BE LOVED and SOME-THING IN THE WIND; films scored and con-ducted include EASTER PARADE (Academy Award 1951), AN AMERICAN IN PARIS (Acad-emy Award 1953) and WESTSIDE STORY (Academy Award 1961).

PERKY PEA SALAD

2 10-oz. pkgs. tiny frozen
  peas, thawed
1 cup onion, diced
1 cup celery, diced
½ cup water chestnuts,
  sliced
1¼ cups sour cream
3 tbsp. mayonnaise
Juice of ½ large lemon
Salt and pepper to taste
1 cup crisp bacon, crumbled
1 cup salted cashews

Combine all ingredients except bacon and cashews early in day. Cover and refrigerate. When ready to serve, add bacon and nuts. Mix well. Note: Can add diced, cooked chicken breast, tuna, etc.; increase sour cream and mayonnaise to moisten.

MRS. RICHARD C. NELSON

SPINACH SALAD

1 bunch spinach
4 slices bacon
1 hard boiled egg
Vinegar and oil
   salad dressing

Select tender spinach greens from the produce market. Wash thoroughly and cut off stems. Refrigerate in plastic bag for freshness. Cook bacon until very crisp. No fat should remain. Crumble bacon slices. Break chilled spinach greens into bite-sized pieces in salad bowl. Add salad dressing to taste and mix. Sprinkle top with grated hard boiled egg. Serve immediately while crisp and cold.

Serves 4.

★ ETHEL BRADLEY (MRS. TOM BRADLEY)
TOM BRADLEY: Civic leader, politician.
Mayor, City of Los Angeles

APRICOT SALAD MOLD

2 pkgs. orange Jello
3 cups boiling water, to
   dissolve Jello
1 cup small marshmallows
1 cup crushed pineapple
1 cup apricots
½ cup pineapple juice
½ cup apricot juice
1 egg
1 tbsp. butter
2 tbsp. flour
1 pkg. Dream Whip
Grated cheese

Dissolve Jello with hot water. Add marshmallows. Drain pineapple and apricots and add to Jello.

Refrigerate until firm, then add the following after cooking: pineapple juice, apricot juice, egg, butter, flour. Cool. Add Dream Whip and spread over Jello. Top with grated cheese.

Serves 8-10.

★ FRANCES RUSSELL KAY and
ELLINGWOOD KAY
Columnist, editor, writer--editor, story editor, writer.
She is former Women's Editor for North China Daily News; Society Editor for Valley News--He is former Managing Editor of Cosmopolitan Magazine, story editor Warner Bros. Films and C.B.S., Screen Gems and Four Star Television.

PICKLED BEET ASPIC

1 1-lb. can whole beets
4 tbsp. vinegar
¼ cup granulated sugar
1½ tbsp. pickling spices
  (in cheesecloth bag)
Water (as needed)
1 envelope Knox unflavored
  gelatin

Put liquid from drained beets into a one quart measuring pitcher. Add vinegar, sugar and enough water to make 1½ cups of liquid.

Transfer to saucepan (not aluminum), bring to a boil. Add spice bag and simmer 15 minutes.

Grate beets coarsely. Dissolve gelatin in ½ cup water. Add a small amount of simmered liquid, mix, combine with rest of liquid till dissolved. Add beets.

Pour into one quart mold or 8" x 8" glass pan. Allow beets to absorb flavor of pickling juices till tepid. Refrigerate.

Serve on lettuce with dressing (½ mayonnaise, ½ sour cream plus horseradish to taste). The aspic served plain is excellent as a condiment for meats.

Serves 6.

ALICE A. ANDRE

CIDER MOLD SALAD

1½ tbsp. unflavored gelatin
½ cup water
2 cups cider
⅓ cup lemon juice
½ cup sugar
½ tsp. salt
½ tsp. cinnamon
⅛ tsp. cloves
2½ cup mixture of celery,
  apples, nuts

Soak gelatin in water. Heat mixture of cider, lemon juice, sugar and salt. Add spices. Dissolve soaked gelatin in hot liquid. Chill until beginning to thicken. Add apple mix, pour into oiled, 2-quart mold. Chill until firm.

Serves 6-8.

GLENDA GRIBBEN

CRAB SALAD MOLD

2 envelopes Knox gelatin
½ cup cold water
1 can tomato soup
1½ cups celery (diced)
1 medium onion (chopped
    fine)
1 green pepper(chopped
    fine)
1 cup mayonnaise
Diced sweet pickle to taste
1 cup crabmeat (or lobster)
2 3-oz. pkgs. cream cheese

Dissolve gelatin in cold water. Heat soup and add gelatin and water to the soup, then add rest of ingredients, with cream cheese last.

Chill in mold overnight before serving.

Serves 8.

DOYNE WOOD

CUCUMBER DELIGHT

1 cup hot water
1 large pkg. lemon Jello
1 cup mayonnaise
1 pt. farmers' cottage cheese
1 cucumber, medium size
1 onion, small
½ cup celery
1 tbsp. vinegar
½ tsp. salt
Sour cream
Slivered almonds

Dissolve Jello in hot water and add mayonnaise and cottage cheese. Grate cucumber and onion. Cut celery finely. Add vegetables, vinegar and salt to gelatin mixture and blend. Pour into a 6-cup mold or several smaller molds.

Serve with sour cream topped with almonds.

Serves 8.

MRS. FRANK E. PICKETT

HOLIDAY CRANBERRY CANDLES

1 1-lb. can whole cranberry
  sauce
1 3-oz. pkg. red Jello
1 cup boiling water
¼ tsp. salt
1 tbsp. lemon juice
½ cup mayonnaise
1 apple (peeled and diced)
¼ cup walnuts or
  pecans (chopped)

Heat cranberry sauce; strain; set aside. Dissolve Jello in hot cranberry juice and water. Add salt and lemon juice. Chill until thickened. Beat in mayonnaise until light and fluffy. Fold in berries, fruit and nuts.

Divide mixture evenly into eight 6-oz. fruit juice cans. Chill four hours or longer. Unmold; garnish with mint, parsley or watercress. Inset birthday candles in the top. Light to flame.

Serves 6.

MRS. ROBERT L. HICKS

EGG SALAD MOLD

1 dozen hard boiled eggs
  (put in cold water,
  bring to boil and set
  aside for 15 minutes)
1 tsp. salt
½ tsp. + dash
  Worcestershire Sauce
¼ tsp. garlic salt
1 envelope Knox Gelatin
½ cup cold water
1 cup mayonnaise

Cook eggs (as directions state) and chop. Add mayonnaise and eggs. Add the remaining ingredients. Pour into medium mold. Chill until firm.

Serves 12.

BARBARA HARRIS
President
Assistance League of Southern California

Little Jack Horner sat in the corner,
Eating a Christmas pie:
He put in his thumb and pulled out a plum,
And said, "What a good boy am I!"
                    (NURSERY THYMES 1720)

CHEESE FLUFF

1 pkg. lemon Jello
1 cup crushed pineapple
Juice of ½ lemon
½ pint whipping cream
  (whipped)
1 cup Tillamook cheese
  (grated)
¾ cup sugar

Combine 1 pkg. lemon Jello, 1 cup boiling water and ½ cup cold water. Let set until cool. Separately, combine a cup of crushed pineapple and its juice, ¾ cup sugar and juice of ½ lemon. Boil this for 10 minutes and cool. Mix ½ pint of whipping cream, add this and 1 cup of grated cheese. Stir well together.

Serves 6.

★ MARIE WINDSOR HUPP

Actress.

65 films include THE KILLING (Look Magazine Best Supporting Actress 1956); over 100 TV roles include CHARLIE'S ANGELS, MARCUS WELBY and FANTASY ISLAND.

CHERRY PECAN MOLD

1 large (17 oz.) can pitted
  sweet black cherries
1 3-oz. pkg. lemon Jello
1 3-oz. pkg. cherry Jello
2 cups boiling water
1 cup fresh squeezed
  orange juice
1 cup juice from cherries
2 cups pecan halves
Sour cream
1 or 2 tbsp. mayonnaise
Watercress
Fresh mint

Drain cherries, reserve liquid. Dissolve Jello in boiling water. Add cold orange juice and cherry juice. Add cherries and pecans. Pour into large round mold.

Put in refrigerator until ready to serve and unmold on large round serving plate. Fill center with sour cream mixed with 1 or 2 tbsp. mayonnaise. Garnish with watercress and fresh mint.

Serves 8.

MRS. JOHN GORDON McEDWARD

SPECIAL CORNED-BEEF SALAD

2 6-oz. pkgs. lemon Jello
2¾ cups boiling water
2¾ cups very cold water
4 tbsp. fresh horseradish (or' to taste)
About 10 dashes of Tabasco
8 tbsp. cider vinegar
1½ to 2 cups mayonnaise
4 tsp. Grey Poupon french mustard
4 12-oz. cans corned beef (broken into pieces, can use food processor)
4 cups celery (finely chopped)
3 small green peppers (finely chopped)
3 small onions (finely chopped)

Dressing Ingredients
Mayonnaise
Horseradish
Mustard
Jalapeno sauce
Lemon juice
Lawry's salt

Dissolve Jello with hot water. Add cold water, horseradish, Tabasco, vinegar, mayonnaise, mustard, corned beef, celery, green peppers and onion.

Spray large mold with Pam before filling. Chill overnight or until firm.

Combine dressing ingredients to taste and in amount needed.

This is great served with sliced melon and various fresh fruit.

Serves 20-24 (can be reduced)

DOYNE WOOD

The cosy fire is bright and gay,
The merry kettle boils away
And hums a cheerful song.
I sing the sauces and the cup;
Pray, Mary, fill the teapot up,
And do not make it strong.

BARRY PAIN

JOAN'S GAZPACHO SALAD RING
a la BRUGES

3½ cups tomato juice
2 envelopes unflavored
   gelatin
1 cup chicken broth
¼ cup red wine vinegar
1 tsp. garlic (minced)
2 tsp. salt
¼ tsp. pepper (coarse)
Cayenne pepper or Tabasco
   Sauce
2 large tomatoes,
   (peeled, drained, and
   chopped about 1¾ cups)
½ cup onion
   (finely chopped)
¾ cup cucumber (finely
   chopped, peeled and
   drained)
¾ cup green pepper, (finely
   chopped, seeded)
¼ cup pimiento (finely
   chopped)
Garnish with parsley or
   watercress
Guacamole

Pour 1 cup tomato juice into a small saucepan and sprinkle with gelatin. Let stand 5 minutes. Oil a 6-cup ring mold. Heat tomato juice/gelatin mixture over moderate heat, stirring constantly until it comes to a simmer and the gelatin is dissolved. Pour into a medium mixing bowl; stir in the remaining tomato juice and chicken broth, vinegar, garlic, salt, pepper and generous dash of cayenne or Tabasco sauce. Chill until mixture begins to set. Stir in remaining ingredients.

Spoon into prepared mold and chill 2 to 3 hours. Unmold and garnish with parsley or water cress. Fill ring with prepared Guacamole to which you may add chopped pimiento.

Serves 16 to 20.

MRS. FRANK TWOHY

There was an old person of Dean,
Who dined on one pea and one bean;
For he said, "More than that,
Would make me too fat,"
That cautious old person of Dean.
                    EDWARD LEAR

SHRIMP MOLD

1½ pkg. plain gelatin
½ cup cold water
1 can tomato soup
1 large pkg. cream cheese
1 cup mayonnaise
2 cans small shrimp (flaked)
¾ cup celery (chopped)
⅔ cup onion (chopped)
⅔ cup green pepper
   (chopped)

Dissolve gelatin in cold water and set aside. Melt cheese and soup in double boiler. Add gelatin and mayonnaise. Beat together. Add the rest of ingredients and pour into mold. Set in cooler overnight.

This can be served with crackers as an appetizer or on lettuce as a salad.

SALLY GULICK

SHRIMP REMOULADE

4 tbsp. horseradish mustard
½ cup tarragon vinegar
1 cup oil (½ cup olive; ½ cup vegetable)
2 tbsp. tomato catsup
1 tbsp. paprika
1 tsp. salt
1 clove garlic (crushed or minced)
½ cup green onion with tops (finely minced)
½ cup celery hearts (finely minced)
1 tbsp. parsley (finely chopped)
1 tbsp. grated horseradish (optional)
½ tsp. cayenne pepper

Mix vinegar, mustard, salt, pepper, paprika, tomato catsup and garlic. Then add oil and beat thoroughly. Lastly add onions, celery and parsley then horseradish, if desired.

This dressing should be poured over cooked shrimp, refrigerated, and allowed to marinate for at least 4 or 5 hours (but can marinate for as long as 2 days). It should be served cold on a bed of shredded lettuce.

Recipe sufficient for 3 lbs. of shrimp.

Serving Suggestion: Very hot French bread and very cold Chablis.

★ MRS. WADE L. BINGHAM (VIRGINIA)
WADE L. BINGHAM: director, cinematographer, producer.
TV credits include 60 MINUTES, CBS REPORTS, SEE IT NOW, and TWENTIETH CENTURY with Walter Cronkite; Far East Bureau Chief, CBS TV News; War Correspondent in Korea and Viet Nam.

SALMON MOUSSE

2 envelopes unflavored
  gelatin
1½ cup cold water
1 cup dairy sour cream
1 lb. can salmon
  (drain and flake)
1 cup cucumbers (finely
  chopped and peeled)

Soften gelatin in water and dissolve. Combine mayonnaise, sour cream and stir in gelatin. Chill until slightly thickened. Fold in salmon and chopped, peeled drained cucumber. Pour into fish mold and chill.

MRS. CHARLES F. S. RYAN

TONGUE MOLD

This is our preference for a tennis brunch.

1 pkg. lemon Jello
1 pint warm water
3½ cups boiled tongue
  (finely chopped)
½ cup dill pickles
  (finely chopped)
½ cup mayonnaise
2½ tbsp. sugar
1 tsp. onion (scraped)
⅛ tsp. salt

Dissolve Jello in warm water, then add vinegar and salt. Chill until cold and a syrupy thickness. Place in a bowl of cracked ice and whip with a rotary eggbeater until fluffy and thick like whipped cream. Fold in the onion, tongue, pickles and mayonnaise, and turn into a loaf pan.
  Chill until firm.
  Unmold when ready to serve and garnish with crisp radishes and lettuce.

Serves 8.

★ LAWRENCE CASEY
Actor
Many TV roles include co-star PEYTON PLACE and guest star ONE STEP BEYOND TV series; films include GOOD GUYS WEAR BLACK.

FROZEN WALDORF SALAD

½ envelope Knox unflavored
  gelatin
¼ cup cold water
1 pkg. lemon Jello
1 cup hot water
⅛ tsp. salt
1 cup celery (chopped)
1½ cups apples (chopped)
1½ cups walnuts (chopped)
½ cup mayonnaise
1 cup cream, whipped
GARNISH:
Mayonnaise
Sour cream
Maraschino cherries

Dissolve gelatin in cold water. Dissolve Jello in hot water. Mix these two together; add salt and let cool. When cool, add celery, apples, nuts and mayonnaise and mix well. Fold in the whipped cream.

Pour into lightly greased mold or 8½"x12" pan. Place in refrigerator. Do not freeze.

This is an excellent salad with holiday dinners and can be made a day ahead.

Garnish with half mayonnaise and half sour cream and top with cherry.

Serves 10.

MRS. THOMAS O. BROWN

FROSTED LIME WALNUT SALAD

1 cup hot water
1 pkg. lime flavored
  gelatin
1 can crushed pineapple
  (drained)
1 cup cottage cheese
½ cup celery (finely
  diced)
1 tbsp. pimiento (chopped)
½ cup walnuts (chopped)
  (save 4 halves for
  garnish)
2 3-oz. pkgs. cream cheese
2 tbsp. sour cream
2 tsp. lemon juice

Pour hot water over gelatin, stir until dissolved; chill, stirring occasionally until consistency of unbeaten egg white. Mix other ingredients, and stir into chilled gelatin. Pour into 8"x8"x2" cake pan; chill until firm.

Frost with combined cream cheese, sour cream and lemon juice. Chill again. Cut into squares, place on greens, garnish with walnut halves.

Serves 6-8.

ALMA ENGER

NED'S BLEU CHEESE SALAD DRESSING

1 8-oz. pkg. cream cheese
1 4-oz. pkg. Bleu cheese
2 cups salad oil
Juice of three lemons
¾ cup sugar
1 medium to large garlic
   clove (minced)
3 tsp. salt

Bring cream cheese and Bleu cheese to room temperature. Place them in the bowl of an electric mixer and start to mix at slow speed. Add the oil slowly.

Continue to add the oil at a medium rate until all is used. Increase the speed of the mixer moderately. Beat until the mixture is smooth. Add the lemon juice, sugar, garlic and salt and mix thoroughly. Pour into a jar or jars for storage in the refrigerator. Use as needed.

This recipe will make about one quart. It will keep indefinitely in the refrigerator. When it is cold it may thicken to some degree. This does not matter. Spoon some of the dressing over cold broken lettuce and toss thoroughly.

Makes 1 quart.

MRS. EDWARD G. THOMPSON

BROWN DERBY OLD-FASHIONED FRENCH DRESSING

1 cup water
1 cup red wine vinegar
1 tsp. sugar
Juice of ½ lemon
2½ tbsp. salt
1 tbsp. ground black pepper
1 tbsp. Worcestershire sauce
1 tsp. English mustard
1 clove garlic (chopped)
1 cup olive oil
3 cups salad oil

Blend together all ingredients except oils. Add olive and salad oil and mix again. Chill. Shake before serving.

Makes 1½ quarts.

Water is optional, depending upon what degree of oiliness you desire.

Serves 6 to 8.

MRS. ROBERT COBB

MARCELLA'S DILL DRESSING

2 cups mayonnaise
4 tsp. dill weed (dried
    or frozen), or ¼ cup
    chopped fresh dill (better)
¼ cup white vinegar
2½ tbsp. prepared mustard
2½ tbsp. sugar

Place mayonnaise in bowl and beat dill, vinegar, mustard and sugar in that order into it. Beat until fluffy. Let stand 12 hours to chill. Serve at room temperature. Good for fish and salads.

Makes about 2½ cups.

★ ASSISTANCE LEAGUE OF SOUTHERN CALIFORNIA TEAROOM

PAPAYA SEED DRESSING

½ cup sugar
1 tsp. seasoned salt
1 tsp. dry mustard
1 cup white vinegar
2 cups oil
1 small onion (minced)
2 tbsp. fresh papaya seeds

Use a food processor or blender and mix the sugar, salt, mustard and vinegar. Gradually add the oil and onion. Add the papaya seeds and blend BRIEFLY — until the seeds look like coarse black pepper. Note, no pepper is used in this dressing.

Lovely with both green and fruit salads. Can store a week or so in refrigerator, stir and bring to room temperature before using.

Makes about 3½ cups.

NANCY COCHRAN

LO-CAL TOMATO VINAIGRETTE DRESSING

1 46-oz. can tomato juice
½ cup oil
½ cup vinegar
1 tbsp. thyme
1 tbsp. garlic (minced)
2 tbsp. ground pepper
1½ tbsp. fresh lemon juice
2 tbsp. salt
1 bunch parsley
1 bunch onion
½ bell pepper
Dash of vinegar

Puree in food processor parsley, onion, bell pepper and dash of vinegar. May add more vinegar to taste. Mix all ingredients together.

Makes 1 gallon

★ RUFFAGE RESTAURANT
Beverly Hills
Richard Simmons

*"IT MUST BE JELLY 'CAUSE
JAM DON'T SHAKE LIKE THAT . . ."*

— 1942

Lyrics by SUNNY SKYLAR
Music by GEORGE WILLIAMS, J. CHALMERS,
"CHUMMY" MACGREGOR
Copyright © Renewed 1971
by Dorsey Brothers Music, Inc.
Used by Permission
All Rights Reserved

Photography by
MICHAEL JARRETT
OCB Reprographics, Inc.
Irvine, Ca.

BREADS

*'A loaf of bread,' the Walrus said, 'Is what we chiefly need.
Pepper and vinegar besides are very good indeed —
Now, if you're ready, Oyster dear, We can begin to feed.'*

LEWIS CARROLL

LEA'S APPLESAUCE NUT BREAD WITH A TWIST

1 cup applesauce
½ cup brown sugar
4 egg whites
2 cups flour (sifted)
½ tsp. salt
½ tsp. ginger
¾ cup sugar
¼ cup vegetable oil
3 tbsp. milk
1 tsp. baking powder and soda
1 tsp. cinnamon and nutmeg
½ cup nuts (chopped)
1 tbsp. lemon rind

Mix applesauce, sugar, oil, egg whites, and mix thoroughly in a large bowl. Add flour, baking powder and soda, salt, cinnamon, nutmeg, ginger and lemon rind. Stir in chopped nuts. Pour batter into loaf pan 9"x5"x3", spreading evenly. Bake for 1 hour or 1 hour 15 minutes, or until slightly pulling away from the sides of the loaf pan. Bake in a pre-heated 350° oven. This is very good. Can be served warm or cool. Do hope you enjoy!!

Serves 6.

★ MRS. GREG MORRIS (LEA)
GREG MORRIS: Actor.
TV roles include co-star MISSION IMPOSSIBLE and VEGA$ TV Series.

APRICOT NUT BREAD

2 cups flour (sifted)
4 tsp. baking powder
1 tsp. salt
⅔ cup sugar
1 egg
1 cup milk
3 tbsp. shortening (melted)
1 cup pecans (grated)
1 cup dried apricots (diced)

Mix together in a bowl sifted flour, baking powder, salt and sugar. Add egg, milk and melted shortening and beat at lowest speed until blended.

Add chopped apricots and pecans and mix thoroughly with a spoon.

Place dough in a greased 5"x9" pyrex loaf pan and let it rest in the pan for 20 minutes.

Bake one hour at 350° degrees. Cool in the pan for 10 minutes; remove to wire rack to finish cooling before slicing. (If metal pan is used, raise baking temperature to 375°.)

Makes 1 loaf.

MRS. ARTHUR ARMSTRONG

CARIBBEAN BANANA BREAD

2 cups flour
¾ cups pecans (chopped)
⅓ cup granulated sugar
⅓ cup brown sugar
1 tbsp. baking powder
1 tsp. salt
¼ tsp. nutmeg
2 eggs (beaten)
1 cup ripe bananas (mashed)
½ cup milk
3 tbsp. butter (melted)
1 tsp. rum extract

Combine first 7 ingredients. Blend together eggs, bananas, milk, butter and rum extract. Add all at once to flour mixture, stirring only until flour is moistened. Turn into well-greased loaf pan and bake at 350°, 65-70 minutes, or until toothpick comes out clean. Cool 15 minutes before removing from pan.

Makes 1 loaf.

LINDA SMALDINO

CELERY BREAD

1 loaf of sandwich bread
   (unsliced)
1 cup butter (softened)
¼ tsp. salt
Dash cayenne pepper
½ tsp. paprika
1 heaping tsp. celery seed

Cut off all crusts except bottom crust. Cut vertically in half lengthwise down to but not through crust. Cut in 1" blocks across lengthwise cut (not through crust).

Mix all ingredients. With a small spatula cover every side of every block of bread with butter mix. Then frost top and side. (Don't use too much inside.) This covers everything.

Place on cookie sheet with sides.

Bake at 375° for 20 minutes or until brown and crusty. The cut bread should look like half a railroad track.

This is better when made ahead and frozen. If frozen, bring to room temperature before baking.

Serves 8-10.

MRS. W. BERNARD MELONE

CORN BREAD

My Aunt Nettie's Recipe

1 cup white corn meal
½ tsp. soda
½ tsp. salt
1 cup buttermilk
1 egg
1 tbsp. grease (bacon
  drippings are best)

Mix all ingredients while heating bacon drippings in small size cast iron skillet. When grease begins to smoke just a little, pour it into corn bread mixture and stir; it should sizzle. Pour this back into the same cast iron skillet, making sure there is enough grease coating so the blend won't stick. Delicious!!

Serves 6.

★   SUSAN HOWARD
Actress.
Many films and TV roles including PAPER CHASE TV series.

JALAPEÑO CORN BREAD

3 cups (1 pkg.) corn bread
  mix
2½ cups milk
½ cup oil
3 eggs (beaten)
1 large onion (grated)
2 tbsp. sugar
1 cup cream-style corn
¾ cup fresh or canned
  jalapeno peppers
  (chopped)
1½ cups sharp cheese
  (shredded)
¼ lb. bacon (cooked and
  crumbled)
¼ cup pimientos (chopped)

Put corn bread mix in large bowl, add milk and stir. Add all other ingredients in order listed. Bake in 3 greased 8"x8"x2" pans in a hot oven at 400° for about 35 minutes or until done. This bread freezes well.

Makes 3 loaves.

MRS. ALVIN J. LIVINGSTON (RITA)

GRANDMA DURST'S CRANBERRY BREAD

1 orange (juice and grated rind)
2 tbsp. shortening put in cup with enough warm water to make ¾ cup
1 cup sugar
½ tsp. salt
½ tsp. soda
1 egg (beaten)
2 cups flour
1½ tsp. baking powder
1 cup raw, cut cranberries
½ cup nuts (chopped)

Mix all ingredients together well. Bake 1 hour at 350°. Remove pan and wrap at once in wax paper. Let cool and keep in refrigerator.

Makes 1 loaf.

CAROL A. DURST

DILLY CASSEROLE BREAD

1 cup cottage cheese (small curd)
1 pkg. dry yeast
¼ cup warm water
2 tbsp. sugar
1 tbsp. instant onions
1 tbsp. butter
2 tbsp. dill seed
1 tsp. salt
¼ tsp. soda
1 egg (unbeaten)
2¼ to 2½ cups flour

Heat cheese until lukewarm. Dissolve yeast in warm water. Add all ingredients. Knead a bit on floured board.

Put in greased 2-quart casserole and let rise to double in bulk. Press down and let rise again to double in bulk.

Bake at 350° for 30 minutes. Put butter and garlic salt on top. Heat and serve. Good toasted.

Serves 12 generously.

EMMA L. KELLOGG

SUPER NUTRITIOUS HONEY/WHEAT GERM BREAD
(The Easy Way)

3 cakes or packets dry yeast
3 cups warm water
⅓ cup honey (or brown sugar)
1 cup wheat germ, raw
4 tsp. salt
4 cups white unbleached
   flour (sifted)
5 cups whole wheat flour
   (unsifted)
5 tbsp. salad oil

In large bowl, combine yeast and water (cake yeast 95° water; dry yeast 105-115° water). Stir to dissolve yeast. Add honey and stir. Let sit in warm place until yeast just begins to work (3-5 minutes). Stir in wheat germ and salt. Add 2 cups white flour. Add 3 cups whole wheat flour, a cup at a time. Mix thoroughly with spoon. Slowly add rest of flour, alternating whole wheat and white. Blend until batter will accept no more.

Pour oil over the dough and hand knead in the bowl for just 3 minutes. Cover, place bowl in warm (about 85°) draft-free place and let rise until bread doubles in volume (40-45 minutes).

Punch down, turn out onto lightly floured board and knead gently for about 2 minutes. Shape into loaves and place in greased loaf pans. Cover and let rise at 85° until double (about 30-35 minutes). Bake at 400° for metal pans, 375° for glass. To test for doneness, tip out loaf and tap bottom, hollow sound indicates it is done. Cool on rack. Serve warm with butter to bring out nutty, slightly sweet flavor.

Makes 2 loaves.

LYNNE MORGAN TERZIAN

*The best doctors in the world
are Doctor Diet, Doctor Quiet,
and Doctor Merryman.*

JONATHAN SWIFT

LEMON BREAD

½ cup margarine
1 cup sugar
2 eggs
1½ cups flour
1 tsp. baking powder
½ tsp. salt
½ cup milk
Grated rind of one lemon
½ cup walnuts (chopped)
GLAZE:
Juice of 1 lemon
¼ cup sugar

Cream margarine and sugar. Add eggs one at a time and beat well after each addition. Add sifted dry ingredients alternately with milk. Add grated lemon rind and walnuts. Place in a loaf pan. Bake one hour at 325°. Remove from oven.

GLAZE:
Heat lemon juice and sugar until the sugar melts. Spoon glaze over bread. Let stand one hour before serving.

Makes 1 loaf.

MRS. C. PAUL VOGEL

ORANGE NUT BREAD

2¼ cups all-purpose flour (sifted)
2½ tsp. baking powder
½ tsp. salt
1 cup sugar
1 egg (beaten)
2 tbsp. vegetable oil
1 cup orange juice
1 tbsp. orange rind (grated)
½ cup nuts (chopped, walnuts preferred but can use pecans)

Heat oven to 350°. Sift together dry ingredients. Combine egg, oil, orange juice and orange rind. Pour liquid ingredients into the flour mixture and add nuts. Stir until smooth. Bake in greased loaf pan (9"x5"x3") for 1 hour. If loaf is covered with aluminum foil for the first half hour of baking, it is less likely to crack on top.

Serves 12.

BARBARA SELDA BRASNICK

ORANGE PEEL BREAD

1 cup orange peel
Water
1¾ cups sugar
1 tbsp. butter
1 egg
2 cups milk
4 cups flour
4 tsp. baking powder
⅛ tsp. salt

Cut orange peel into small pieces. Cover with water and cook until tender. Add 1 cup sugar and boil to syrup.

Cream butter. Add remaining sugar, egg, milk and flour mixed with baking powder and salt. Beat well and add orange peel. Pour into two buttered 5"x9" loaf pans. Let stand 20 minutes.

Bake 40 to 50 minutes in 325° oven.

This is an excellent tea bread.

Makes 30 thin slices per loaf.

MRS. ARTHUR ARMSTRONG

PUMPKIN BREAD 'SOPHIE'

1⅔ cup flour (sifted)
1½ cups sugar
¼ tsp. baking powder
¾ tsp. salt
1 tsp. soda
½ tsp. cinnamon
½ tsp. nutmeg
½ cup salad oil
½ cup water
1 cup pumpkin
2 eggs
1 cup nuts (chopped)
1 cup dates (chopped)

Sift dry ingredients together. Mix together salad oil, water, pumpkin and eggs. Blend in dry ingredients. Fold in dates and nuts.

Bake in greased and floured loaf pan in 325° oven for 1½ hours. Turn out on rack to cool. Will keep well if refrigerated.

If using three 7"x3" pans, cook 45 to 55 minutes. Test for doneness at 45 minutes.

In 8½"x4½" pan, cook 1 hour, 10 to 15 minutes. Test after 1 hour, depending on how full pan is.

CHRISTINA EMERSON

ANGIE'S YUMMY BREAD

¼ lb. soft butter or
   margarine
½ cup mayonnaise
1 4-oz. Ortega chile peppers
   (diced)
1 clove garlic (crushed)
½ lb. Jack cheese or
   cheddar cheese (grated)
1 loaf French bread

Combine all ingredients except bread and chill to blend flavors. About 1 hour before serving remove from refrigerator. Split French bread lengthwise. Spread mixture on both sides; then cut sides into serving-size pieces. Broil until cheese is melted and bubbly.

May also be cut into bite-size pieces and used as an appetizer.

Serves 8.

SALLY BERGSTROM

ZUCCHINI-PINEAPPLE BREAD

3 eggs
1 cup salad oil
1½ cup sugar
½ cup brown sugar
1 tsp. vanilla
2 cups zucchini (peeled and
   shredded)
1 8¼-oz. can well drained
   crushed pineapple
3 cups all-purpose flour
2 tsp. soda
1 tsp. salt
½ tsp. baking powder
1½ tsp. ground cinnamon
¾ tsp. ground nutmeg
1 cup walnuts (chopped)

With mixer beat eggs. Add salad oil, sugar and vanilla; continue beating mixture until thick and foamy. Stir in shredded zucchini and pineapple.

Combine flour, soda, salt, baking powder, cinnamon, nutmeg and walnuts; stir gently into zucchini mixture just until blended. Divide equally between two greased and flour dusted 5"x 9" loaf pans. Bake in 350° oven for 1 hour. Cool in pans 10 minutes. Turn onto rack and cool.

Makes 2 loaves.

JEWELL WATERS

MUFFIN BLINTZES

½ cup Bisquick
3 eggs
1 pint cottage cheese
½ cube soft margarine
1 tsp. vanilla
2 tbsp. sour cream

Blend all ingredients in blender. Fill greased muffin tins ¾ full and bake at 350° for 45 minutes. When removing from tin, turn upside down and cool on rack.

Serve with sour cream.

Variation: In miniature tins, bake 20 minutes - use for appetizers - makes 4 dozen.

Makes 1 dozen.

SHARON SIMON

NEIGHBOR MAY'S HEALTHY BRAN MUFFINS

2½ cups unprocessed El Molino bran flakes
2 cups wheat germ
1 cup sesame seeds (toasted)
2 cups brown sugar
5 cups whole wheat flour
5 tsp. soda
1 tsp. salt
1 cup honey
½ cup molasses
1 cup oil
4 eggs (slightly beaten)
1 quart buttermilk
2 cups boiling water

Optional additions:
Raisins
Dates
Nuts
Grated orange peel

Mix first 7 ingredients with next 6 ingredients. Mix well. You may add the optional ingredients. Bake at 375° for 15-20 minutes. The muffins may be frosted. The batter may be stored in the refrigerator for 30 days, and no sifting is necessary for the dry ingredients in the recipe above. Be sure to start with a large bowl!

Makes 6 dozen.

HOPE S. KELLY

TUPPERWARE MUFFINS
(For Camping)

1 cup shortening
2½ cups sugar
4 eggs
1 quart buttermilk
4 cups Kellogg's All-Bran
2 cups boiling water
5 cups flour
5 tsp. soda
1 tsp. salt
2 cups Nabisco 100% Bran

Mix shortening, sugar, eggs and buttermilk. Soak All-Bran in cooled boiling water. Add soaked All-Bran to shortening mix. Add rest of ingredients. Stir just until mixed. Refrigerate in Tupperware. Use as needed.

Spoon into muffin cups. Do not stir ever. Fruit may be added to muffins before baking. Bake at 350° for 20-25 minutes. Keeps many weeks in refrigerator.

Makes 1 dozen.

MRS. J. L. VAN BUREN

RON FAIRLY'S FAVORITE 'ANGEL'
APPLE PANCAKE

A nutritious energy booster, pre-day game as part of breakfast, or post-nightgame as a snack with milk.

2 apples
Butter
3 eggs
½ cup milk
½ cup flour
½ tsp. salt
1 tbsp. sugar

Peel, core and slice apples into ⅛" wedges and slice across. Saute in butter in Corning Ware casserole.

Mix together in small bowl eggs, milk, flour, salt and sugar and beat with rotary beater. Add mixture to apples and butter in casserole and put uncovered into a preheated 450° oven for 10 minutes. Remove and dust with granulated sugar and cinnamon, if desired. Dot with butter and return to oven for a minute or two.

★ MARY FAIRLY
RON FAIRLY:Sportsman.
Baseball outfielder and first baseman for Clubs including Los Angeles Dodgers and California Angels.

BUTTERHORNS

4 cup flour (sifted)
1 cup butter (softened)
2 tbsp. sugar
1 tsp. salt
1 cake yeast
1 cup warm milk
3 egg yolks (beaten)

Mix flour, butter, sugar and salt into a crumbly mixture (like a pie dough).

Dissolve yeast in warm milk and mix with beaten egg yolks.

Add yeast mixture to the flour mixture and blend. Place in a greased bowl and cover tightly. Refrigerate overnight or for several hours.

Roll out three circles of dough and cut each into 12 wedges. Stretch the base of each triangle to widen. Roll toward the tip to form crescent shaped rolls.

Cover with a towel and let rise for 2 to 3 hours in a warm place (80° to 85° F.)

Bake 10 minutes at 425°

Hint: When letting rolls rise in a warm place, you may place the bowl in an open oven with pilot light on.

Makes 36 rolls.

GINNY DEWEY

HERB ROLLS

¼ cup butter
1½ tsp. parsley flakes
¼ tsp. onion flakes
1 tbsp. Parmesan cheese
½ tsp. dill seed
1 pkg. refrigerated
  buttermilk biscuits

Place butter, parsley, dill, onion flakes and cheese in a pie plate, heat to melt butter and stir to blend ingredients.

Cut biscuits into halves or quarters and swish around in herbed butter. Arrange in pie plate so pieces touch. Bake at 425° for 12-15 minutes.

HINT: This can be made ahead of time and kept covered in the refrigerator.

Serves approximately 8

MRS. D. KEITH COLWELL (DONNA)

POPOVERS

4 eggs
2 cups milk
2 tbsp. melted butter
2 cups flour (sifted)
½ tsp. salt

Preheat oven to 375°.

Beat together eggs, milk and butter. Blend in flour and salt.

Butter 8 to 10 custard cups and fill half full. Bake at 375° for 60 minutes.

Make small slit in top of each popover 10 minutes before done.

Makes 8-10.

JANIE WILEY

SOUFFLE CRACKERS

Soda crackers
Ice water
Melted butter
Sesame seeds or seasoned salt

Soak white soda crackers in ice water for 10 minutes. Lift with slotted spatula (draining as much as possible) to heavy cookie sheet. Brush with melted butter. Sprinkle with sesame seeds or seasoned salt. Place in pre-heated 400° oven until crisp.

JANIE WILEY

SOUR DOUGH SLICES

6 sourdough French rolls
1¼ lb. butter
1 tsp. beef extract (Bovril)
Parmesan cheese

Slice rolls into rounds as thin as possible. Combine butter and beef extract and spread on slices. Sprinkle lightly with Parmesan cheese. Place on a cookie sheet and bake at 325° for 8 minutes. Reverse pan and bake 8 minutes longer. Should be lightly brown and crisp. Excellent served with soup.

Serves 20.

FRAN ARMSTRONG

BEIGNETS SOUFFLES

According to Alan Fisher, her famed British butler, 'This recipe is used frequently in the Crosby home and never has been given out before.'

1 cup water
½ cup butter
½ tsp. salt
1 tsp. sugar
1 cup flour (sifted)
4 eggs
1 tsp. orange flavored liqueur
   or rum
Powdered sugar
OPTIONAL: Raspberry
   sauce

Combine water, butter, salt and sugar in a saucepan and bring to a boil. When butter is melted, add all at once sifted flour and cook, stirring vigorously until the mixture leaves the sides of the pan. The stirring vigorously is extremely important.

Remove from the fire and add eggs one at a time, beating well after each addition. Add orange flavored liqueur or rum, according to taste.

Drop the dough by teaspoons into hot deep fat (370°) raising the temperature a little when the beignets begin to color. The beignets turn over of their own accord when one side is browned. Drain well on absorbent paper. Sprinkle with powdered sugar. Serve hot.

Traditionally these do not need an accompaniment, but I like sometimes a hot or cold raspberry sauce with them.

★ KATHRYN CROSBY
BING CROSBY: Actor, raconteur, recording artist, singer, sportsman.
Countless films include ROAD TO...Series and GOING MY WAY (Academy Award Best Actor 1944); awarded at least 26 Gold Records; founder Bing Crosby National Pro-Am Golf Championship.

VEGETABLES

This is every cook's opinion:
No savoury dish without an onion.
But lest your kissing should be spoiled
Your onions must be thoroughly boiled.

DEAN SWIFT

ARTICHOKE CASSEROLE

2 pkgs. frozen artichoke
  hearts
2 cups fresh mushrooms
  (sliced)
½ cup butter
1 tsp. salt
1 tsp. basil
½ tsp. oregano
¼ tsp. garlic powder
1 tbsp. dry bread crumbs
1 tbsp. lemon juice
½ cup Parmesan cheese

Arrange defrosted and drained artichokes in bottom of a 1½ qt. casserole. Saute mushrooms in butter, adding spices. When mushrooms are soft, add bread crumbs and lemon juice. Spoon mushroom mixture over artichokes. Dot with butter and top with cheese. Bake at 350° for 30 minutes.

Serves 6.

MRS. DONALD BOWERS

ASPARAGUS SUPREME

2 tbsp. butter
2 tbsp. flour
1½ cups cheddar cheese
  (grated)
1½ cups asparagus pieces
  (cooked)
¾ cup milk
1 tsp. white onion (chopped)
3 eggs
1 tbsp. green pepper (cut)
Salt and pepper to taste

Melt butter in double boiler top; add flour, seasonings, onion and milk to make a smooth sauce. Add eggs, well beaten, then cheese and asparagus. Blend well. Place in buttered casserole and bake at 325° for about 45 minutes.

Serves 4.

VALLIE BOWMAN

The proof of the pudding is in the eating.

HENRY GLAPTHORNE

WESTMORE'S GLORIFIED BAKED BEANS

2 cans medium baked beans
2-3 onions (chopped)
12-14 pitted prunes (cooked)
2 cloves garlic (pressed)
4 tbsp. sugar
2 tbsp. chili powder
2 cups cheddar cheese
(grated)

Chop prunes and onions. Mix all ingredients (except cheese) in a casserole. Bake at 325° for 1 hour. Refrigerate overnight. Next day cover with grated cheese and reheat at 325° for ½ to ¾ of an hour.

Serves 10-12

★ MRS. MICHAEL G. WESTMORE (MARION)
MICHAEL G. WESTMORE: Makeup artist, business executive, author, educator. Makeup credits include ROCKY film and ELEANOR AND FRANKLIN TV series (Emmy Award 1976): developed special medical makeup for accident and burn victims, Rancho Los Amigos, U.C.L.A.; book, ART OF THEATRICAL MAKEUP FOR STAGE AND SCREEN.

MISS KITTY'S GREEN BEAN CASSEROLE

2 pkgs. French-style green
beans
1 can cream of mushroom
soup
1 can french fried
onions
¼ lb. fresh mushrooms

Cook beans in boiling salted water until barely tender. Drain and while hot add mushrooms which have been sliced and sauted in butter and the mushroom soup. Pour into ungreased casserole, put onions on top and bake at 350° for 25 to 30 min. While this is sort of an old stand by-the mushrooms add a great punch.

★ MERVYN LEROY
Business executive, director, producer.
75 films include THE WIZARD OF OZ, LITTLE WOMEN, GYPSY, MADAME CURIE, THE HOUSE I LIVE IN (Academy Award 1945), and QUO VADIS (French Victoire Award and Star of Italy 1952) the only director ever to win all 3 awards; Hollywood Park Racetrack executive.

PARTY GREEN BEAN CASSEROLE

3 lbs. green beans (wash, Frenchcut, cook, covered, over low heat in ½" boiling water with a beef or chicken boullion cube ten minutes)
6 eggs
1½ tsp. seasoned salt
½ tsp. coarse pepper
½ tsp. paprika
2 tsp. prepared mustard with horseradish
1 tsp. savory
⅓ cup parsley (chopped)
¼ cup toasted almonds (chopped)
½ cup minced onion, slightly cooked in skillet with ½ lb. sliced mushrooms
2 cups cottage cheese
3 cups Swiss cheese (shredded)
¼ lb. butter (melted)
1 small can water chestnuts (sliced)

Spread half of cooked beans in greased 3-quart casserole.

Beat together eggs, salt, pepper, paprika, mustard, savory, parsley, almonds, mushrooms, onion and cheeses, one half the butter and the water chestnuts. Pour half over beans. Layer remaining beans and top with remaining cheese mix and butter.

Bake at 350° for 30 minutes or until set. May be topped with chopped cooked bacon, Parmesan or canned fried onions.

Serves 10-12.

BARBARA CRITTENDEN SCHOTT

PIQUANT GREEN BEANS

1½ lbs. string beans
4 strips bacon
2 tbsp. red wine vinegar
¼ tsp. sugar
1 tbsp. Worcestershire sauce
¼ tsp. dry mustard
2 drops Tabasco sauce

Steam beans until tender.

Cut bacon into ½ inch strips, saute and remove from fat. Add remaining ingredients to fat and bring to boil, stirring constantly. Pour over beans, add bacon and mix well.

Serves 4.

LINDA SMALDINO

BEETS WITH PINEAPPLE

2 cans diced beets and juice
1 can (small) pineapple
  chunks
3 tbsp. cornstarch
3 tbsp. melted butter
6 tbsp. sugar
½ cup vinegar

Heat beets. Combine sugar, corn starch, butter and vinegar. Add to hot beets and stir until smooth. Add pineapple that has been drained and heat.

Serves 8-10.

NOLA ROBERTS

BROCCOLI CASSEROLE SUPREME

2 10-oz. pkgs. broccoli
  spears
1 jar Cheez Whiz (8-oz.)
1 can cream of mushroom
  soup
1 cube butter (melted)
1 small loaf white bread
  (unsliced)

Cook two packages of frozen broccoli spears. Drain. Melt Cheez Whiz and mushroom soup together. Grease casserole, 9"x9", and place cooked vegetables in it. Pour Cheez Whiz and soup over the vegetables.

Take chunks out of bread (no crust). Put on top of casserole. Push in half way and pour melted butter on top of bread. Bake 30 minutes at 350°.

Serves 6.

MRS. GILBERT NUÑEZ (BETTY)

RED CABBAGE

1 head red cabbage
2 tbsp. bacon drippings
1 onion (finely chopped)
2 carrots (finely chopped)
1 cup beef consomme
1 cup red wine
1 bay leaf
2 apples (peeled and finely chopped)
2 tbsp. wine vinegar
Salt and freshly ground pepper.

Remove the cabbage core. Cut the cabbage into quarters and then into medium fine slices as you would for cole slaw. In a large saucepan heat the bacon drippings and add the onions and carrots. Saute for approximately 3 minutes. Add the cabbage and toss well so that it is lightly coated with the bacon fat. Mix in consomme, wine, bay leaf, apples, vinegar and salt and pepper to taste. Stir well and bring to a boil. Reduce heat, cover, and simmer for 1 hour.

Serves 6-8.

GLORIA DAHL

GATEAU DE CARROTES

2 lbs. carrots (sliced)
4 oz. butter
¼ lb. mushrooms (sliced)
1 lb. spinach
4 eggs
4 oz. Swiss cheese (grated)
1 tsp. salt
½ tsp. pepper

Saute carrots slowly in 2 oz. butter until tender. Chop coarsely and reserve in large mixing bowl. Saute mushrooms in 1 oz. butter quickly until tender, chop coarsely and add to carrots. Saute spinach in remaining butter. Reserve. Beat together the eggs and cheese. Combine thoroughly with carrots and mushrooms. Add salt and pepper to taste and correct seasonings. Line a 9"x 4"x3" baking pan with aluminum foil. Butter foil generously and fill with half the carrot mixture. Spread spinach over this and fill with remaining mixture. Place baking pan in large pan filled with hot water and bake in preheated 400° (hot) oven 45 minutes or until knife plunged into center comes out clean. Invert onto warm serving platter and remove foil. Slice and serve immediately.

Serves 6-8.

★ MA MAISON
West Hollywood

CARROT RING

1½ cups shortening
1 cup brown sugar
4 eggs
2½ cups flour
2 tsp. baking soda
2 tsp. baking powder
1 tsp. salt
4 tbsp. cold water
2 tbsp. lemon juice
3 cups shredded raw carrots
Peas, cooked

Cream shortening and sugar. Add eggs. Mix dry ingredients and add to mixture. Add water, lemon juice and carrots. Mix well.

Grease large ring mold. Fill with mixture and bake 1 hour at 350°. Unmold and fill center with cooked peas when ready to serve.

Serves 8.

ANNE SHUMSKY

COINTREAU CARROTS

6 carrots (shredded coarsely)
2 tbsp. butter
2 tbsp. Cointreau

Cook carrots 2-3 minutes in 1-2 tbsp. butter. Add Cointreau.

Serves 4.

GLENDA GRIBBEN

CELERY CASSEROLE

4 cups celery (chopped)
Boiling water to cover
1 can cream of chicken soup
½ cup grated sharp cheese
1 tbsp onion (grated)
½ cup sliced almonds

Cook the celery for 10 minutes in boiling water. Drain into colander and let sit for at least one hour. In small casserole, put celery, soup, cheese and onion. Mix and cover with sliced almonds. Bake 1 hour at 375°.

Serves 4.

MRS. W. BERNARD MELONE

CALIFORNIA CAULIFLOWER CASSEROLE

1 medium head cauliflower,
   broken into flowerettes
   (about 2 lbs.)
1 cup dairy sour cream
1 cup cheddar cheese
   (shredded)
1 tsp. flour
2 tsp. chicken seasoned
   stock base
1 tsp. dry mustard
⅓ cup walnuts
   (coarsely chopped)
¼ cup fine bread crumbs
1 tsp. butter (melted)
1 tsp. dried marjoram leaves
   (crumbled)
½ tsp. onion salt

Heat 1" salted water (½ tsp. salt to 1 cup water) in Dutch oven to boiling point; add cauliflower. Heat to boiling, reduce heat and cover. Simmer until tender, about 15 minutes, drain. Heat oven to 400°. Mix sour cream, cheese, flour, stock base and mustard. Place cauliflower in baking dish 10" x 6" x 2". Spoon cheese mixture over cauliflower. Mix walnuts, bread crumbs, butter, marjoram and onion salt; sprinkle over cheese and cauliflower. Bake until hot and bubbly, about 15-20 minutes.

Serves 4.

MRS. KAYE VAHAN (ROXANNA)

CORN AU GRATIN

1 lb. whole kernel corn
12 oz. whipping cream
1½ tbsp. clear butter
1½ tbsp. flour
½ tsp. salt
2 tbsp. sugar
½ tsp. Accent
3 tbsp. Parmesan cheese

Put corn in cream on the fire and bring to one boil. Separate corn from cream and return to fire.

Make roux (paste) from clear butter and flour, adding paste to cream to thicken. Simmer 5 minutes and season.

Return corn to cream and bring back to a boil over low heat.

Transfer creamed corn to casserole. Sprinkle evenly with Parmesan cheese, dot the top with melted butter and brown under broiler.

Serves 8.

MRS. RON SMITH

CARNABE

1 cauliflower,
  including leaves
1 egg
¼ cup flour
½ cup tomato paste
Juice of 1 lemon
Salt and pepper to taste
3 tbsp. of oil or as needed.

Trim leaves from cauliflower, cut off the flowerettes, and trim off end of the core. Wash well, cut leaves into thirds and dice the core. Cook all in salted water about 15 to 20 minutes, or until slightly cooked but still firm. Drain and allow to cool. Beat egg in one dish and place flour, salt and pepper in another dish. Place oil in frying pan, heat to medium. Dip flowerettes, separately, into flour, beaten egg, then flour again. Place flower side down in frying pan and fry to golden brown. Turn right side up, add leaves, tomato paste, cubed core, water and lemon juice. Cover and cook 350° for 30 minutes.

★ BILLIE GRANT (MRS. HANK GRANT)
HANK GRANT: Author, columnist, commentator, singer.
Columnist for the Hollywood Reporter; KNX radio news commentator.

ESCALLOPED EGGPLANT

1 medium-sized eggplant
Salt and pepper to taste
1 egg, beaten
2 tbsp. melted butter
1 small onion (chopped)
1 cup dry bread crumbs
½ cup buttered bread crumbs

Pare and cut eggplant in one-inch cubes. Cook in small amount of water until tender. Drain well. Add salt and pepper to taste. Add egg, butter, onion and dry bread crumbs. Mix thoroughly.

Place in greased 1 qt. baking dish. Cover with buttered crumbs. Bake in 375° oven about 30 minutes.

Serves 6.

CHARLOTTE MEIER

ITALIAN FRIED EGGPLANT

1 large eggplant, cut in
  slices ½ inch thick
1 egg (beaten)
Flour
Oil
2 cans tomato sauce
Garlic
Salt
Pepper
Sweet Basil
Grated Italian cheese

Dip eggplant into egg and flour batter. Fry in oil until golden brown and set aside. Prepare sauce of tomato sauce, garlic, salt, pepper, sweet basil. Cook sauce slowly for 10 to 15 minutes.

In casserole place layer of eggplant slices; layer of sauce. Sprinkle with grated Italian cheese. Repeat layers until all ingredients used. Bake in 325° oven about 10 minutes. Leftovers can be made into sandwiches.

Serves 4.

LEONORA CICERO

EGGPLANT STEW

1 eggplant
1 cup onion (chopped)
½ cup mushrooms (sliced)
1 red pepper (diced)
1 green pepper (diced)
Dash salt, pepper &
  season salt
1 lg. can seasoned stewed
  tomatoes
Olive oil

Peel, slice and dice one eggplant. Soak in salt water for ½ hour. Drain. Rinse and drain again. Saute 1 cup chopped onion and ½ cup sliced mushrooms in olive oil (enough to cover bottom of pan). Add diced red and green pepper, 1 can seasoned stewed tomatoes, dash salt, pepper and season salt. Add eggplant and simmer until vegetables are done. Serve hot. As left over serve cold. Do not reheat.

Serves 4.

★ ROBERT F. (BOBBY) KNOOP
Sportsman
Infielder for California Angels baseball club. Coach with California Angels. Led American League at second base in fielding average 1966. Set many records for double plays.

STUFFED EGGPLANT

3 medium eggplants
2 tbsp. butter
1 large onion (minced)
1 can mushrooms (chopped)
1 tsp. parsley (minced)
¼ lb. butter
½ lb. sausage meat
1 cup cream of tomato
  soup
¼ cup bread crumbs
Cheese

Cut in two and scrape out part of eggplant, leaving thin shell. Salt and fry carefully. Make stuffing by browning the onion in 4 oz. of butter, add 1 cup mushrooms, ¼ cup crumbs, parsley and browned sausage. Moisten with tomato soup. Mix well. Fill eggplant sections with stuffing, sprinkle with bread crumbs, dot with butter and cheese. Bake at 350° for 20 minutes until tender.

Serves 8-10.

GRACE H. McKNIGHT

HOMINY CASSEROLE

4 cans hominy (14-16 oz.,
  drained)
1 medium onion
  (chopped)
½ lb. fresh mushrooms
  (sliced and sauteed with
  onion)
3 tbsp. butter
2 cups sharp cheese (grated)
1 can mushroom soup
1 can milk
½ cup sherry
1 tsp. seasoned salt
½ tsp. seasoned pepper
1 tsp. Worcestershire sauce
1 small bunch parsley
  (chopped)
2 eggs (beaten)
1½ cups breadcrumbs
½ cup butter
Paprika

Put hominy in a 9" x 13" x 2" buttered pyrex casserole.

Saute onion and mushrooms in butter in a heavy pan.

Add 1 cup grated cheese, soup, milk, sherry, salt, pepper, Worcestershire sauce, parsley and eggs to the onion mixture. Pour over hominy. Sprinkle remaining cheese over the top. Spread bread crumbs evenly over the casserole and dot with butter. Dust with a little paprika.

Cook at 350° for 30 minutes or until brown on top.

Two or three small cans of Vienna sausage may be added for a main dish or this may be used as a brunch dish with bacon, ham, sausage, etc.

Serves 8-10.

BARBARA CRITTENDEN SCHOTT

MUSHROOMS IN SOUR CREAM

1 lb. fresh mushrooms
(whole)
2 tbsp. butter
1 clove garlic (crushed)
1 tsp. dill weed
1 tsp. salt
½ tsp. pepper
1 tbsp. lemon juice
¼ cup sherry
1 cup sour cream

Wash and drain mushrooms; trim ends. Melt butter in 2-quart pan. Add mushrooms, garlic, dill weed, salt, pepper, lemon juice and sherry. Cook 20 minutes over low heat.

Blend a few mushrooms with some sauce into the sour cream. Then add all of the mushrooms and sauce to the sour cream. When cool, cover and refrigerate at least 8 hours or overnight. Heat and serve in chafing dish.

Serves 6 generously.

MRS. TERENCE C. McGAUGHEY

GEPPETTO'S "THAT'SA MUSHROOMS"

1 lb. fresh mushrooms
Butter
½ cup celery (chopped)
½ cup green onions
½ cup green pepper
1 cup mayonnaise
¾ tsp. salt
¼ tsp. pepper
8 slices white bread
2 eggs
1 can cream of mushroom
soup (undiluted)
1 cup cheddar cheese
(grated)
2 slices bread (buttered
up and cubed)

Coarsely slice mushrooms, saute in butter. Mix mushrooms with celery, green onions and green peppers. Blend in mayonnaise, salt and pepper.

Trim crusts and butter bread; cut into 1" cubes. Place half the cubes on bottom of a buttered 3-qt. pyrex baking pan. Top with vegetable mixture. Layer remaining cubes over vegetables.

Beat eggs slightly with milk. Pour over casserole and refrigerate at least 1 hour. (May be made a day ahead) Spoon mushroom soup over top. Sprinkle 2 more slices of buttered cubed bread over soup.

Bake uncovered 1 hour and 15 minutes at 300°. Top with grated cheese. Bake 10 minutes more.

Serves 8.

MRS. LYNN P. REITNOUER

RED PEPPERS, ONIONS AND MUSHROOMS—STIR FRY VEGETABLE

2 red peppers (not green, but fully ripened red bell peppers, seeded, halved and sliced into ¼" strips)
1 medium or large onion (Spanish or yellow sliced into ¼" slices)
¼ lb. (approximately) mushrooms (sliced)
2-3 tbsp. peanut or other vegetable oil

SAUCE:

1 tsp. sugar
1 tsp. cornstarch dissolved in 2 tsp. water
1 tsp. soy sauce
Dash garlic powder
½ cup chicken broth

In a wok or large frying pan heat oil, add onions stirring 2 minutes. Add red peppers and mushrooms, stir 1 minute then add sauce, stir then cover on low heat for 2 minutes.

SAUCE:
Mix in order given and set aside.

CAROL THUESON

GOURMET ONIONS

6 large white onions, sliced
6 tbsp. butter
2 eggs
1 cup sour cream
Salt and pepper to taste
⅔ cup Parmesan cheese

Saute onions in butter until transparent. Place in casserole dish (9"x13" pyrex).

Beat eggs until light; add sour cream, salt and pepper. Pour over onions and sprinkle with cheese. Bake at 425° for 20 minutes.

Serves 8.

MRS. STIRLING PRICE

RITA'S HONEY ONIONS

9 medium white or yellow onions (peeled)
1 tsp. salt
½ tsp. paprika
4 tbsp. butter or margarine (melted)
½ cup tomato juice
6 tbsp. honey

Cut onions in quarters (or large thick slices). Place in well-greased large, shallow casserole. Combine salt, paprika, melted butter, tomato juice and honey. Pour over onions.

Cover dish and bake at 300° for 1 hour or until onions are tender. Serve with roast or steak.

Serves 8.

RITA LIVINGSTON

SCALLOPED POTATOES

3 tbsp. butter
3 tbsp. flour
1¾ cups milk
1 tsp. salt
¼ tsp. pepper
4½ cups potatoes
   (thinly sliced)
1¼ cups onion
   (thinly sliced)
½ cup ham, ground meat
   or grated cheese

Melt butter, add flour and stir well. Add milk, salt and pepper. Cook for 5 minutes. Arrange potatoes, onions and meat or cheese in baking dish in layers. Pour milk over potatoes. Sprinkle with paprika if desired. Bake at 400° for 45 minutes.

Serves 6.

TRACY E. GRIFFIN

STUFFED BAKED POTATOES

6 potatoes
1 16-oz. pkg. sour cream
1 lg. bermuda onion
   (chopped fine)
3 tsp. garlic salt
2 tsp. Lea & Perrins
   Worcestershire Sauce
1 tsp. Grey Poupon mustard
8 oz. sharp cheddar cheese

This recipe can be fixed ahead of time and heated just before serving. Bake 6 potatoes, let them cool; cut into halves and scoop out potato. In a separate bowl add all ingredients to potato. Use a mixer at low speed to mix all ingredients well or until potatoes are relatively lump-free. Refill potato skins and place in a baking dish. Across the top place 2 strips of cheese. Just before serving put into oven to melt cheese on top and warm.

Serves 12.

MRS. HARRY L. THOMAS JR.

SCOTTSDALE POTATO CASSEROLE

2 1-lb. pkgs. frozen hash
   brown potatoes (thawed)
¾ cup butter (melted)
¼ tsp. salt
½ cup onions (chopped)
1 can cream of chicken soup
1 pt. sour cream
2 cups cheddar cheese (grated)
TOPPING:
2 cups crushed corn flakes
¼ cup melted butter

Mix the first 8 ingredients, using just ½ cup of melted butter.
   Pour into a 7"x10" casserole. Mix corn flakes with the remaining butter and top the casserole.
   Bake for 45 minutes at 350°.

Serves 10.

ROSE B. HUFF

RATATOUILLE PROVENÇALE

Olive oil
¾ cup onions (thinly sliced)
3 cloves garlic
  (diced finely)
4 green peppers (julienned)
2½ cup eggplant (peeled,
  diced)
3 cups zucchini (½" thick)
3 cups tomatoes (peeled
  seeded, quartered)
Salt and pepper
1½ cups Jack or Romano
  cheese (shredded)

Put in a deep skillet ⅓ cup olive oil. Saute onion and garlic until golden. In deep casserole combine in layers peppers, eggplant, zucchini, tomatoes, onions, salt, pepper and cheese sprinkled. Repeat layers (approx. 3 of each item) top with cheese and dribble olive oil on top. Cover and simmer on low flame for 45 minutes to 1 hour. Uncover for 10 minutes and continue to heat to reduce liquid. Serve hot or cold.

Serves 8.

★ PETER MARSHALL
Actor, singer, TV host.
Night club performer; theatre roles include BYE BYE BIRDIE; host of HOLLYWOOD SQUARES TV series.

GREEN AND GOLD SQUASH

1 medium onion (chopped)
2 tbsp. salad oil
¾ lb. zucchini (cleaned
  and coarsley shredded)
¾ lb. yellow crook neck
  squash (cleaned and
  coarsley shredded)
2 tbsp. parsley (chopped)
½ tsp. salt
½ tsp. oregano
¼ tsp. pepper
3 eggs (slightly beaten)
½ cup milk
1 cup sharp cheese
  (shredded)
½ cup saltine cracker crumbs
  (13 single crackers)

In large frying pan, saute onion in oil until brown. Remove from heat. Stir in squash, parsley, salt, oregano, pepper and eggs blended with milk. Spoon ½ the mixture into a buttered 1½ qt. baking dish. Sprinkle ½ the cheese over first mixture. Sprinkle ½ the crumbs over cheese. Make second layer, end with cheese.

Bake uncovered at 325° for 45 minutes.

Serves 6.

JEANENE COOK

STUFFED ACORN SQUASH

Leftover lamb from leg of
  lamb
¾ slices bread (pumpernickel
  is preferred)
8-10 fresh mushrooms
  (chopped)
1 cube butter
4 tbsp. Sherry
1 tsp. fennel seeds
½ tsp. sage
1 acorn squash (butternut)
½ onion (chopped)
Salt and pepper

Grind leftover lamb and bread in a meat grinder
or with steel blade of food processor. Saute
mushrooms and onion in 3 tbsp. butter. Add
meat and bread, sherry, fennel, sage, remaining
butter (except for 2 pats), salt to taste, and lots of
fresh ground pepper. Warm through until butter
is melted and all ingredients are combined.
Meanwhile, bake at 400° a split acorn squash
face down in a little water (with seeds in) until
tender. Remove seeds and fiber and stuff with
meat mixture, mounding the top. Place pat of
butter on each half. Return to baking dish adding
a little water to keep squash moist, bake at 350°
until warmed through and slightly browned.

Serves 2-4.

KATHY PARKER

SPINACH CASSEROLE

2 10½-oz pkgs. frozen
  spinach (cooked and
  drained)
1 cup rice (cooked)
1 cup sharp cheese
  (grated)
2 eggs (slightly beaten)
2 tsp. soft butter
⅓ cup milk
2 tsp. onion (chopped)
½ tsp. Worcestershire sauce
1 tsp. salt
½ tsp. rosemary or thyme

Mix all ingredients together. Put in casserole and
bake 25 minutes at 325°.

Serves 6.

MRS. ROBERT PAGE

QUICK CURRIED CREAMED SPINACH

This is a favorite aid to preparing dinner quickly when I have been late returning home.

1 box frozen chopped spinach or equivalant fresh chopped
1 ½ cup white sauce (Aunt Penny's or made fresh)
1 tsp. Worcestershire sauce
¼ tsp. curry powder
2 tbs. fresh lemon juice
⅛ tsp. garlic powder
Salt and pepper to taste

Simmer spinach until tender (according to directions on box, if frozen) drain, stir in heated white sauce. Add seasonings and lemon juice, stir, heat quickly and serve.

★ MRS. ROBERT STACK (ROSEMARIE)
ROBERT STACK: Actor, author, sportsman. Many TV roles include star THE UNTOUCHABLES TV series (Emmy Award for Best Actor 1960); films include 1941; in Sports Hall of Fame as National Skeet-Shooting Champion.

TOMATO PIE

5-8 tomatoes (enough to fill a pie shell when sliced)
1 frozen pie crust shell
Salt
Pepper
Beau Mondo salt
1 cup mayonnaise
1 cup cheddar cheese (grated)

Remove the stem end of the tomatoes, peel and slice in ¼" thick slices. Fill a frozen pie crust shell with tomatoes. Sprinkle seasonings over the top of the tomatoes.

Blend mayonnaise and cheese together and spread on top of the tomatoes.

Bake in a 350° oven for about 45 minutes or until the top mixture is brown and bubbly.

Hint: skins of the tomatoes may be removed before slicing by immersing each tomato in boiling water for 5 seconds and then peeling.

Serves 4-6

MRS. HARRY MYNATT

TANGY BAKED TOMATOES

6 tomatoes
½ tsp. salt
½ tsp. dill weed
¼ tsp. pepper
½ tsp. minced chives
¼ tsp. Worcestershire sauce
¾ cup sour cream
¾ cup seasoned bread
   stuffing

Cut tomatoes in two thick slices. Put in shallow pan. Combine all but stuffing. Top tomatoes with mixture and sprinkle with stuffing mix. Bake at 350° for 20 minutes.

Serves 6.

MRS. THOMAS V. BERNE

VEGETABLE GUMBO CREOLE

2 pkgs. frozen okra (or 1 lb.
   fresh okra) cut crosswise
2 pkgs. frozen lima beans
2 green peppers (chopped)
4 medium tomatoes
   (sliced crosswise)
2 pkgs. frozen corn (or 8
   ears of fresh corn,
   cut off cob)
1 sm. bunch celery (coarsely
   chopped)
Bread crumbs
Butter

Partially cook lima beans in salted water and add corn. Add green pepper, okra and celery and cook until just done. Drain. Place a layer of the vegetable mixture (reserve part of okra for top layer) in buttered and crumbed baking dish. Then add a layer of tomatoes. Season with salt and pepper, dot with butter and bread crumbs.

Repeat until casserole is filled. On top place a layer of okra that has been dipped in bread crumbs and sauteed in a little butter. Cover with bread crumbs and dot with butter. Bake in 300° oven for about 1 hour. It can be cooked in the morning and reheated slowly before serving. It's even better the second day.

Serves 8-10.

★ DINAH SHORE
Actress, author, recording artist, singer, TV host. Films include UP IN ARMS; TV appearances include star CHEVROLET SHOW (numerous Emmy Awards), star DINAH! TV series; cookbook SOMEONE'S IN THE KITCHEN WITH DINAH; awarded 19 Gold Records.

"POTATOES ARE CHEAPER,
TOMATOES ARE CHEAPER,
NOW'S THE TIME TO FALL IN LOVE ..."

— *1931*

Photography by
MICHAEL JARRETT
OCB Reprographics, Inc.
Irvine, Ca.

ZUCCHINI CORN PUDDING

1 medium-size onion
½ green pepper
1 clove garlic
2 tbsp. each butter and olive oil
1 lb. zucchini (thinly sliced)
1 cup corn kernels (drained)
1 tsp. salt
½ tsp. pepper
¾ cup cheddar cheese (grated)
3 eggs (separated)

Finely chop onion, green pepper and garlic; saute in butter and olive oil until tender. Add thinly sliced zucchini; cover pot and let steam about 10 minutes. Turn fire off and stir in corn, salt and pepper and let cool.

Add cheese and well-blended egg yolks. Beat egg whites until stiff and fold into vegetables. Pour into buttered 1½ qt. casserole; place in hot water and bake 1 hour in 350° oven.

Serves 6.

CHRISTINA EMERSON

ZUCCHINI FRITTATA
(Meatless)

2 lbs. zucchini, diced
1 large onion, chopped
1 green pepper, chopped
5 tbsp. olive oil
2 oz. diced canned green chilis
¼ lb. fresh mushrooms, sliced
1 8-oz. can tomato sauce
1 tbsp. Italian herb mix
1 clove garlic, mashed
5 eggs
½ cup milk
1 cup grated cheese

Stir diced zucchini onion, green pepper, garlic and mushrooms into hot olive oil in a large heavy frying pan. Stir and cook over low heat until lightly browned and wilted. Add tomato sauce and chilies and Italian Seasoning Mix. Simmer for 20 minutes. Beat eggs with milk. Salt and pepper to taste. Pour over hot zucchini mixture. Cover and cook till eggs begin to set. Sprinkle with grated cheese, slip quickly under broiler to brown cheese. Cut into wedges.

Serves 6 people.

★ HARRY CAREY, JR.

Actor

Many films include SHE WORE A YELLOW RIBBON, GENTLEMEN PREFER BLONDES and MISTER ROBERTS.

ZUCCHINI CASSEROLE

2 or 3 lb. zucchini
   (cut in small pieces)
4 eggs
1 lb. Jack cheese (cubed)
½ cup milk
2 tsp. baking powder
1 tsp. salt
2 tbsp. flour
¼ cup parsley
1 can Ortega chiles
   (chopped)
½ cube butter
Bread crumbs

Cook squash until almost tender; drain and cool. Mix eggs, milk and remaining ingredients. Add to cooked squash. Butter pan, sprinkle crumbs on bottom and sides. Pour in squash. Sprinkle crumbs on top. Dot with butter. Bake at 325° for 30 minutes or until brown.

Serves 6-8.

★ MRS. DON RICKLES (BARBARA)
DON RICKLES: Actor, comedian.
Top nightclub headliner; TV appearances include star DON RICKLES SHOW and CPO SHARKEY TV series, and specials; films include ENTER LAUGHING and KELLY'S HEROES.

SPINACH-STUFFED ZUCCHINI

4 zucchini
1 10-oz. pkg. chopped
   spinach (frozen, cooked and
   well-drained)
2 tbsp. flour
½ cup milk
⅓ cup mild cheddar cheese
   (shredded)
Salt and pepper
4 slices bacon
   (crisp and crumbled)

Trim ends of zucchini and drop into 1 inch of boiling water. Cover and cook approximately 10 to 12 minutes.

Remove zucchini; cut into half lengthwise and scoop out center. Chop finely the scooped-out zucchini and add to spinach.

In saucepan, blend flour with milk and add spinach mixture. Add some extra grated cheese and seasoning if desired. Cook and stir until thickened.

Place zucchini halves in baking dish; salt cavities. Spoon spinach mixture into shells. Top with cheese and bacon. Bake at 350° for 20 to 25 minutes.

Serves 4.

EILEEN McCONNELL

CHEESE AND EGGS

But when I undress me
  Each night, upon my knees,
Will ask the Lord to bless me
  With apple pie and cheese

EUGENE FIELD

BAKED EGG

2 tbsp. consomme
1 tsp. cream sherry
1 egg
2 tbsp. Swiss cheese
(grated)

Butter ramekin or custard cup, etc. Put consomme and sherry in cup. Break egg into cup, top with cheese. Bake at 350° until set. Serve in cup.

Serves 1.

SUE HIRSCH

ITALIAN EGG BAKE

1 lb. sweet Italian sausage
1 tbsp. butter
½ medium red onion
(chopped)
8 fresh mushrooms
(sliced)
1 cup milk
12 eggs (beaten)
2 medium tomatoes (peeled
and chopped)
8 oz. Mozzarella cheese
(grated)
½ tsp. salt
½ tsp. pepper
½ tsp. seasoned salt

Peel and fry sausage, stirring to keep crumbly. Remove from skillet, drain off fat. In same skillet melt butter and add mushrooms and onion, saute until onion is tender but not brown. Combine all ingredients, mix well and pour into greased 9" x 13" baking pan. Bake at 400° 30 to 40 minutes or until inserted knife comes out clean.

This is a wonderful brunch dish served with a green salad, spiced peach and corn muffins. The sausage, mushrooms and onions can be prepared the day before.

Serves 8-10.

SALLY GULICK

'Why sometimes I've believed
as many as six impossible things
before breakfast,' said the Queen.
                    LEWIS CARROLL

MEXICAN CORN QUICHE

¼ cup butter
5 eggs
¼ cup flour
½ tsp. baking powder
⅛ tsp. salt
1 can cream style corn
1 cup cottage cheese
  with chives
½ lb. Jack cheese
  (grated)
1 small can green chiles
  (diced)

Using a 9"x9" pan, melt butter in it. In a large bowl beat eggs lightly. Add flour, baking powder and salt and blend. Add remaining ingredients and mix until just blended. Pour into buttered pan and bake at 400° for 15 minutes.

Reduce heat and bake at 350° for 35-40 minutes more. Can be made in larger pan and cut in small squares and used as appetizer. (Reduce baking time for larger pan.)

Serves 6.

MRS. JAMES L. KELLY (LORA)

QUICHE A LA COURANT

1 9" baked quiche or
  pie shell
½ cup ham (diced)
2 tbsp. butter
2 eggs (beaten)
1 cup whipping cream
½ cup cheddar cheese
  (shredded)
¼ tsp. ground nutmeg
½ tsp. salt
Dash pepper
½ lb. Mushrooms

Over medium flame, cook ham and mushrooms in butter until the mushrooms are tender, for 5 minutes. Set aside.

In a mixing bowl combine the eggs, cream, cheese, nutmeg, salt and pepper. Now place the mushrooms/ham combination in the bottom of the baked shell, then pour the egg mixture over it. Bake in oven at 350° for 25 minutes. Let cool for 15 minutes before serving.

Serves 6-8.

★★ VIRGINIA HEWITT and ERNST MEER
Actress; designer.
First outer-space heroine of TV, co-star SPACE PATROL TV series; with husband, Ernst Meer, top international designer of crystal chandeliers.

EASY CORNED BEEF HASH

1 can corned beef hash
¼ cup dry red wine
4 small green onions
   (chopped)
1 clove garlic (minced)
1 tomato (chopped)
1 tsp. Worcestershire sauce
1 tbsp. bacon drippings
4 poached eggs

Place hash in large bowl, add tomato, onions, wine and Worcestershire sauce. Mix well. Melt bacon drippings in skillet and add garlic and brown. Then add corned beef hash mixture and cook until it is well heated. Serve with poached eggs on top.

VIVIAN AHRENSDORF

BRIE AND BLEU CHEESE QUICHE

1 9-inch pie shell baked
   until slightly brown
1 8-oz. pkg. Philadelphia
   cream cheese
2½ oz Brie cheese
2 oz. Bleu cheese
⅓ cup + 2 tbsp. Parmesan
   cheese (grated)
½ cup + 2 tbsp. heavy cream
2 tbsp. chives (finely
   snipped)
1 tbsp. flour
¼ tsp. salt
3 eggs

Allow cheese to come to room temperature and mix well. Add other ingredients and mix thoroughly. Pour into pre-baked pie shell and bake at 350° for 30 minutes. Raise heat to 375° for 5 to 10 minutes or until puffed and lightly brown on top. Gradually reduce heat to 350° (about 5 minutes). Remove from oven and serve.

Quiche will be cooked when knife for testing comes out clean.

If using food processor put chilled cheese into bowl and process with steel blade in place until fine grained. Add remaining ingredients and process until thoroughly mixed. Pour into pie shell and proceed as instructed.

Serves 6-8.

MRS. JOHN M. NOBLE

CHEESEY-GRITTY CASSEROLE

I like this with ham and eggs for brunch.

4 cups boiling water
1 cup hominy grits
½ cup margarine
½ lb. cheese (grated)
1½ tsp. Worcestershire
5 drops hot pepper sauce
1 tsp. salt
3 eggs (beaten)
Paprika

Boil the water in a pan. Add grits. Cover and cook over low heat about 5 minutes, stirring occasionally. Add the margarine, cheese, Worcestershire and hot pepper sauce, salt and eggs, and mix well. Turn grits mixture into a 2 quart casserole and sprinkle paprika on top. Bake at 275° for 1 hour.

Serves 8.

★ JO ANNE WORLEY
Actress, comedienne.
TV roles include feature LAUGH IN and LOVE BOAT.

MONTEREY FONDUE

12 slices white bread
Soft butter or margarine
1 12-oz. can whole kernel corn
1 7-oz. can green chiles
2½ cups Jack cheese (shredded)
4 eggs (slightly beaten)
3 cups milk
1 tsp. salt

Trim crusts from bread. Spread bread with butter, then cut up each slice in halves. Arrange half the bread slices in a greased shallow 13½"x 8½" dish. Cover with half the corn. Seed chiles, cut up in strips and arrange half the chile strips over corn. Sprinkle with half the cheese. Repeat layers. Combine eggs, milk and salt and pour over ingredients in casserole. Cover and refrigerate for 4 hours. Bake at 350° for 45 to 50 minutes or until fluffy and golden brown.

Serves 6.

MRS. GARY BRONNECK

CRABMEAT QUICHE

3 eggs (slightly beaten)
1 cup sour cream
1½ tsp. Worcestershire
1 pinch salt
7½-oz. can snow crab
1 can french fried onion
   rings
1 cup Swiss cheese
1 unbaked pie shell

Mix all together, put in unbaked pie shell. Bake 55-60 minutes at 300°.

Serves 8.

MRS. JOHN KEMP

NO CRUST QUICHE

1 cup onion (minced)
1 tbsp. butter or margarine
1½ cup chicken
   (cooked and diced)
1 cup grated cheese:
   cheddar, Swiss or Jack or
   any combination
3 tbsp. canned green chiles
   (diced)
3 eggs
1 heaping tbsp. flour
½ tsp. salt
1 small can Pet milk

Cook onion in butter until golden brown. Combine onion, chicken, cheese and chiles. Toss lightly with fork.

Beat together eggs, flour, salt and milk, and stir in chicken mixture.

Spray a shallow one-quart square casserole with a non-stick spray, such as Pam. Pour mixture into prepared pan.

Bake at 375° for 30 minutes or until firm in center.

Serves 4 generously (6 smaller servings).

MRS. G. G. BAUMEN

SPINACH-SWISS CHEESE QUICHE

1 10-oz. pkg. frozen spinach
  (chopped)
1 can refrigerated biscuits
8 oz. Swiss cheese (sliced,
  cut in strips)
2 tbsp. flour
¾ cup milk
3 eggs (beaten)
½ tsp. salt
Dash pepper
Dash nutmeg

Cook spinach according to directions on package and drain very thoroughly. (You can cook it the day before.)

In a 9" ungreased pie pan, press out biscuits to form crust. Squish so all touch. Combine milk, eggs and seasonings. Add the cheese and flour and spinach. Mix well. Pour into pie crust. Bake at 350° for 1 hour. Do not cover. Serve immediately.

Also great cold or reheated.

Serves 5-6.

MRS. GREGORY PETERS (ELAINE)

CHILE SOUFFLE

1 small can green chiles
  (seeded)
2 eggs
½ cup flour
½ lb. Tillamook cheese
  (grated)
2 cups milk
1 tsp. salt

Arrange chiles in bottom of greased baking dish. Cover with cheese. Beat eggs, add other ingredients and pour over top. Bake at 350° for 45-50 minutes.

Serves 4-6.

★ MARION LEDERER
FRANCIS LEDERER: actor, educator.
Many films include BRIDGE OF SAN LUIS REY, DIARY OF A CHAMBERMAID and STOLEN IDENTITY; instructor of drama class.

EGGS SARDOU

1 cup hot creamed spinach
2 artichoke bottoms
  (warmed in salted water)
2 poached eggs
¾ cup Hollandaise sauce

Make a base of spinach on warm serving plate. Place artichoke bottoms on top. Put an egg in each and top with Hollandaise sauce.

Variation: Canadian bacon can be added.

Serves 1.

ARLEN O'HARA

EGG SOUFFLE

1 cup milk (boil 1 minute and cool)
3 egg yolks (beaten lightly)
½ tsp. dry mustard
¼ cup flour (sifted with ⅛ tsp. salt)
1 cup cottage or grated cheese
3 egg whites beaten with ¼ tsp. cream of tartar
Undiluted hot mushroom soup

Combine all ingredients except soup. Place in buttered casserole, and put this into larger pan of hot water. Bake 50 to 60 minutes at 350°, or until knife comes out clean. Serve with undiluted hot mushroom soup on top.

This is excellent dish for light supper or luncheon - such as a bridge foursome!

Serves 4.

ELLA KESSLER

SCRAMBLED EGGS WITH SHRIMP AND CHEESE

2 cups milk
¾ cup cheddar cheese (shredded)
10 eggs
½ tsp. Worcestershire sauce
½ tsp. Maggi Sauce
¾ cup pimiento (diced)
1½ tsp. salt
SAUCE:
2 cups tiny shrimp (cooked)
3 tbsp. onion (chopped)
3 tbsp. butter
2 tbsp. flour
1½ cups milk
½ tsp. salt
¼ tsp. pepper

Beat eggs in a bowl; stir in milk, cheese, salt, Worcestershire sauce and Maggi Sauce. Add pimientos. Pour into a greased baking dish; place in a baking pan with about 1 inch hot water. Bake at 325° for about 50 minutes, or until cooked. Cut and serve with sauce.

SAUCE:

Cook onions in butter; add flour, salt and pepper. Add milk and cook until sauce thickens and boils, stirring constantly. Add shrimp.

Serves 6.

★ CINDY WILLIAMS
Actress
TV roles include co-star LAVERNE AND SHIRLEY TV series.

SPANAKOPITA

2½ lb. spinach
Butter
1 small onion (chopped)
½ cup green onion
  (chopped)
2 tbsp. parsley (chopped)
2 tsp. dill weed
½ lb. feta cheese
¼ lb. Romano cheese
  (freshly grated)
7 eggs (lightly
  beaten)
Nutmeg
Salt, pepper
Filo dough

Clean, chop and blanch spinach. Drain. Melt 3 tbsp. butter in skillet, add onion and saute until tender. When almost cooked, add green onions and saute 2 minutes longer.

Mix spinach with onion, parsley, dill, feta, Romano cheese, eggs and nutmeg, salt and pepper to taste.

Melt ½ lb. butter. Lay a sheet of filo dough in a well-buttered 13"x9" baking pan and brush it with butter. Repeat filo dough and melted butter until 8 sheets have been place in bottom of pan. (Keep unused filo covered with a damp towel between additions. It dries very quickly.) Spread filling mixture over filo and pat evenly. Cover with 8 more sheets of filo and melted butter. When last sheet of filo is brushed with melted butter, cut into 2" squares through top layers of pastry and filling only. Do not cut through to bottom of pan. Bake at 350° about 50 minutes or until filo is browned and pulls away from sides of pan.

Note: To serve as an appetizer cut into smaller squares.

Serves 12.

EVELYN UNDERWOOD

TOAD IN THE HOLE

1 cup milk
1 cup flour
2 eggs
½ tsp. salt
1 tsp. baking powder
Cooked sausage

Put all ingredients (except sausage) in a bowl and beat until lumps are gone. Pour ½ of mixture into a greased 9"x9" dish and bake 10 minutes. Arrange fried sausage on top. Cover with rest of batter and bake until done, about 20 minutes, in 425° oven. Good with butter or maple syrup.

Serves 4-6.

MRS. DEAN COLBERT

ZUCCHINI CREPES

CREPES:

1 cup flour

¼ tsp. pepper

5 eggs

⅔ cup milk

2 cups zucchini
  (grated or pureed)

FILLING:

2 cups sour cream

1 cup parmesan cheese
  (grated)

1 cup Tillamook cheese
  (grated)

TOPPING:

1 cup yellow cheese
  (grated)

Cream (optional)

Prepare crepes by mixing first 5 ingredients together. Brush a 6" or 8" crepe pan with oil. Pour about 4 tbsp. of batter into pan and tilt pan so that batter covers the bottom of pan.

When edges begin to brown, turn crepe over to brown very slightly. Remove and place between paper towels. Repeat until all the batter has been used.

Mix filling ingredients. Fill each crepe generously and roll up.

Place in two 9"x13" Pyrex flat pans with edge of crepe down. Top by generously sprinkling casserole with grated cheese. (The casserole may be placed covered in the refrigerator overnight, if desired.)

When casserole is at room temperature, bake uncovered for 30 minutes at 350°.

Hints: If desired, a little cream may be poured over the stuffed crepes before baking.

Crepes may be made ahead of time and frozen flat between wax paper.

Serves 2 crepes each to 8

FRAN ARMSTRONG

The daughters of Knights, Judges, Physicians,
or others of similar conditions
had better learn the art of cooking,
though possible circumstances will not call
upon them to put it into practice.
                    BARBERINO

PASTA AND RICE

A plate of spaghetti
  Or pilaf with spice,
Oodles of noodles, potatoes and rice;

These are the dishes
  I long for the most
As I sit with my carrot sticks, yogurt and toast.

LORRAINE WOOD

FETTUCINE ALFREDO

1 lb. fettucine Noodles
½ cup Swiss or Gruyere
  cheese (grated)
6 tbsp. butter
¾ cup heavy cream
½ cup parmesan cheese
Salt and pepper to taste

Cook noodles till tender and drain. Combine butter, cream salt and pepper in saucepan and bring just to boiling. Add fettucine and simmer over low heat stirring occasionally until some of the liquid has been absorbed. Add cheese gradually, stirring constantly. When mixture is creamy, serve.

Serves 4.

MRS. D. KEITH COLWELL (DONNA)

LASAGNA

½ pkg. lasagna
1 tbsp. butter
1 lb. ground chuck (lean)
3 8-oz. cans tomato sauce
2 fresh tomatoes
½ lb. cottage cheese
1 8-oz. pkg. cream cheese
½ cup sour cream
½ cup scallions (minced)
1 tbsp. green pepper
  (minced)
2 tbsp. butter
Salt and pepper to taste

Cook noodles according to directions on package, drain. Saute chuck in 1 tbsp. butter until brown. Stir in tomato sauce, tomatoes and green pepper and simmer 10 minutes, adding salt and pepper. In a separate bowl combine cottage cheese, cream cheese, sour cream and scallions. In 2 qt. casserole spread noodles then sour cream mixture then meat in layers, ending with noodles on the top. Pour 2 tbsp. melted butter on top. Bake in 350° - 375° oven 30 minutes. For larger amount add more meat and lasagna without changing other proportions.

Serves 6.

★ JOHN HUBBARD
Administrator, author, educator, historian.
President, University of Southern California; instructor of British history.

MUSHROOM NOODLE CASSEROLE

1 lb. noodles
2 cans cream of
   mushroom soup
2 small cans mushrooms
   (with juice)
½ lb. sharp cheese
   (grated)
1 onion (diced)
1 green pepper (shredded)
2 stalks celery (diced)
Paprika
Salt and pepper to taste

Boil noodles until tender, drain and put to one side. Saute diced onions, celery and green pepper in shortening. Combine noodles, vegetables and undiluted mushroom soup. Add the mushrooms and juice and mix well. To a well-greased casserole add the noodle mixture, then a layer of cheese, until it is all used up. Salt and pepper to taste, cover and bake 1 hour at 350° Uncover-add paprika and bake ½ hour more.

Serves 8.

★ JILL ST. JOHN
Actress.
Films include COME BLOW YOUR HORN and DIAMONDS ARE FOREVER.

NOODLE PUDDING

12 oz. broad noodles
⅛ lb. butter (use ¼ lb.
   for richer pudding)
2 eggs (slightly
   beaten)
1 pt. cottage cheese
   (large curd)
½ pint sour cream
Salt and pepper to taste
3 tsp. corn flake crumbs
   (optional)
Sharp cheddar or Parmesan
   cheese (grated)
(Some grated cheddar may be
used in mixture as well as on
top, but not the Parmesan)

Boil noodles for about 8 minutes in salted water. Drain. Place in mixing bowl.

Mix butter into hot noodles and let cool. Add eggs and stir. Add cottage cheese and sour cream, salt and pepper and corn flake crumbs. Mix.

Butter a 2-qt. glass baking dish. Add mixture and cover the top with grated cheese. Bake at 350° until browned, 45 minutes to an hour.

Serves 8 generously.

MINNA SHANAHAN

MACARONI, CHIPPED BEEF AND CHEDDAR CHEESE

This is our preference for a tennis brunch.

¼ lb. sliced dried beef
2 cups cooked macaroni
2 cups white sauce
 (Aunt Penny's)
¼ lb. cheddar cheese
¾ cup crumbs
 (buttered)
Pepper

Soak the beef for ten minutes in hot water, then drain and shred. Butter a baking dish and put in a layer of macaroni, a sprinkling of shredded cheddar and pepper, then evenly cover this layer with white sauce. Repeat. Then cover with buttered crumbs. Bake in a 400° oven until the crumbs are brown.

I like this recipe because it's simple and the dried beef gives it a nice zest along with the cheese.

Serves 4.

★ LAWRENCE CASEY
Actor.
Many TV roles include co-star PEYTON PLACE and guest star ONE STEP BEYOND TV series; films include GOOD GUYS WEAR BLACK.

RIGATONI ALLA GORGONZOLA

4 oz. Swiss cheese (diced)
4 oz. Italian Gorgonzola
1½ cups milk
1 lb. small rigatoni
1 pint heavy cream
½ cup Parmigiano (grated)

In a large pan put Swiss cheese Gorgonzola and milk.

Cook rigatoni in a large pot with salted water. While rigatoni is cooking, melt cheeses on very low heat. Keep flame very low. When rigatoni is cooked, drain and pour into cheese mixture. Mix well and then add cream and Parmigiano. When blended, serve immediately.

Serves 5-6.

★ CESARE DANOVA
Actor.
Many films include TENDER IS THE NIGHT, MAIN STREET, and ANIMAL HOUSE; TV roles include star GARRISON'S GORILLAS TV series; theatre roles include co-star TIME OF THE CUCKOO at Music Center.

PASTA PRIMAVERA

1 cup zucchini (sliced)
1½ cup broccoli
  flowerets
1½ cup snow peas
1 cup petit pois
6 stalks asparagus (sliced)
1 lb. spaghetti
12 cherry tomatoes
1 cup olive oil
1 tsp. garlic (minced)
Salt, pepper
¼ cup parsley
2 tbsp. olive oil
⅓ cup pine nuts
10 mushrooms (sliced)
1 tsp. garlic (minced)
⅓ cup butter
1 cup heavy cream
½ cup Parmesan cheese
 (grated)
⅓ cup fresh basil (chopped)
1 can chicken consomme

In a medium saucepan, blanch in boiling water for 1 or 2 minutes sliced zucchini, broccoli flowerets, snow peas, petit pois, and asparagus. Drain. Refresh under cold water. Set aside.

Cook spaghetti (preferably Italian "De Cecco") in boiling salted water 8-11 minutes. Drain.

While pasta cooks saute cherry tomatoes, cut in half, in olive oil with minced garlic, salt, pepper and parsley. Set aside.

In 2 tbsp. olive oil saute pine nuts, sliced mushrooms and 1 tsp. minced garlic until brown. Add all blanched vegetables. Simmer a few minutes until vegetables are hot.

Melt ⅓ cup butter. Add heavy cream, grated Parmesan cheese and chopped fresh basil. Stir to blend and melt cheese. Add pasta and toss to coat with sauce. (If sauce gets too thick, thin with chicken consomme.) Add ⅓ of vegetables and toss again.

Divide pasta into broad soup plates and cover with remaining vegetables. Top with cherry tomatoes. Season to taste with salt, pepper and more grated Parmesan.

Serve with nice dry, robust red wine.

This is intended to be a meal in one dish, fresh fruit is a good follow-up.

DOES NOT HOLD WELL-SERVE AS SOON AS COOKED.

Serves 6.

NANCY KEMP

WORLD'S BEST SPAGHETTI SAUCE

The fruits and vegetables give this sauce a rather sweet, unusual flavor. It should be served on spaghetti cooked al dente and sprinkled with grated Parmesan and Romano cheeses or Greek Kaseri cheese. Accompany with green salad and a Chianti.

1-2 tbsp. olive oil
   (depending on fattiness
   of ground beef)
1 small clove garlic
   (chopped fine or pressed)
1 lb. ground beef
1 cup ketchup
½ cup hot chili sauce
1 tbsp. oregano
3 green olives (sliced thin)
3 black olives (sliced thin)
1 tsp. currants (dried)
1 tsp. seedless raisins
1 small red or green pepper
   (sliced)
½ roasted pepper or
   pimiento (sliced)
4-6 oz. mushrooms (sliced)
Pinch Italian red pepper
   (optional)
1½ tbsp. pine nuts
4 slices Mozzarella cheese

In a heavy pan heat the olive oil and brown the garlic. Add the meat, break it up with a fork, and brown. Add the ketchups, chili sauce, ½ cup water, oregano, and olives. Stir well and simmer slowly (use flame retarder if you have one) for at least 25 minutes. Add the currants and raisins, and simmer 5 minutes. If sauce becomes too thick, add a small quantity of boiling water. Add the green pepper and roasted pepper or pimiento, and keep simmering very slowly. When the peppers are nearly done, add the mushrooms. Stir gently. Sprinkle with red pepper if desired, and stir in pine nuts. Cover and cool. Before serving reheat slowly, stirring occasionally. Taste and correct seasoning. When sauce is hot, add the Mozzarella cheese, stirring constantly thereafter to avoid sticking. Serve as soon as cheese has melted.

Makes 3 cups.

PAULA TREHARNE

*It's a very odd thing
as odd as can be,
That whatever Miss T. eats
Turns into Miss T.*

WALTER DE LA MARE

BAKED RICE RING

3½ cups chicken or
   beef broth
1½ cups long grain rice
½ cup onion (chopped)
1 cup celery (chopped)
½ cup green pepper
   (chopped)
½ lb. fresh mushrooms
   (sliced)
½ cup margarine
1 tsp. salt
¼ tsp. pepper
¼ tsp. poultry seasoning

Bring broth to a boil in large sauce pan; add rice and reduce heat. Cook until all liquid is absorbed, about 20 minutes. While rice is cooking saute onions, celery, green pepper and mushrooms in margarine until onion is tender but not brown. Combine with cooked rice, stir in seasonings and pack into greased 9" ring mold or large casserole. Place mold or dish in a pan containing about 1" hot water. Bake at 350° for 40 minutes.

Serves 8.

EMMA L. KELLOGG

CHINESE FRIED RICE

2 cups cooked meat cut in
   fine strips (a mixture of two
   or more of the following:
   ham, lean pork, chicken or
   shrimp)
4 tbsp. oil
1⅓ cup rice (cooked)
½ cup green onion
   (finely chopped)
4 tbsp. soy sauce
2 eggs

Brown meat in oil. Add cooked rice, onion and soy sauce. Fry for 10 minutes, stirring frequently. Break unbeaten eggs over mixture, stir thoroughly. Sprinkle with chopped parsley.

Serves 6.

MRS. LEONARD WATTS

Things are seldom what they seem
Skim milk masquerades as cream.
                    SIR WILLIAM SCHWENCK GILBERT

HEFTY CASSEROLE FOR DINNER

1⅓ cups rice (salted and cooked)
1 lb. American cheese (cubed)
1 onion (finely chopped)
4 eggs (beaten)
2½ cups milk (or more)
2 tbsp. lemon juice
1 cup parsley (finely chopped)
1 cup almonds (chopped)
2 cups carrots (finely chopped)

Toss all ingredients together until well mixed. Place in buttered 9"x13" pan. Cook 1 hour at 350°. It should be firm but not dry.

Serves 8-12.

GRACE H. MC KNIGHT

RICE AND SOUR CREAM CASSEROLE

¾ lb. Monterey Jack Cheese
3 cups sour cream
2 small cans peeled green chiles (chopped)
1 small can water chestnuts (chopped or sliced)
¼ cup pimiento (chopped)
3 cups cooked rice
Salt and pepper to taste
½ cup cheddar cheese (grated) or more to taste

Cut Jack cheese in strips. Mix sour cream, chiles, chestnuts and pimientos. Butter 1½ quart casserole. Season rice with salt and pepper (while cooking). Layer rice, sour cream mixture, and Jack strips, finishing with rice. Bake at 350° uncovered for 30 minutes. Sprinkle grated cheese over rice the last 10 minutes. Can be made a day ahead and it freezes well, cooked or uncooked. Delicious with fowl.

Serves 8.

★ JOHN DAVIDSON
Actor, author, philanthopist, recording artist, singer
Many TV appearances include specials, star KRAFT MUSIC HALL, GIRL WITH SOMETHING EXTRA and JOHN DAVIDSON SHOW TV series; films include THE HAPPIEST MILLIONAIRE; night-club headliner; textbook NOTES FOR SINGERS.

PILAF

1 cube butter
1 cup vermicelli noodles
⅓ cup pine nuts
   (optional)
2 cups rice
4 cups chicken broth

Melt butter in heavy pot; add noodles and pine nuts, if desired. Brown thoroughly, stirring often. Add rice and chicken broth; stir. Cover with lid, lower heat and cook 20 to 25 minutes. Do not remove lid during this time until testing doneness in last 5 minutes.

Serves 8.

GLORIA ARNETT

WILD RICE CASSEROLE

1 lb. pork sausage
1 medium onion
1 large green pepper
1 cup celery
2 boxes long grain white
   and wild rice combination
2 cans cream of chicken soup
1 can cream of mushroom
   soup
1 large can mushrooms
   (drained)
1 can water chestnuts (sliced)
1 small jar pimiento

Brown sausage, add vegetables, onions, green pepper, celery. Cook until tender. Drain fat off. Mix remaining ingredients and pour into 3 quart casserole. Cover and bake in 325° oven for 1 hour.

This can be frozen before baking. Then bake 2½ hours.

Serves 12.

BARBARA HARRIS
President
Assistance League of Southern California

SHAHJAHANI BIRYANI
(Spiced Saffron Rice)

2 tbsp. butter
1 whole chicken breast,
    (skinned boned and cut
    into ½" pieces)
½ cup butter
4 medium onions (minced)
1 tbsp. ginger (minced)
16 whole cloves
4 4"-cinnamon sticks
2 tsp. turmeric
2 tsp. cumin seeds
1½ tsp. ground nutmeg
1½ tsp. ground mace
¾ tsp. cardamom seeds
¾ tsp.cayenne
½ cup butter
2 cups uncooked converted
    rice
4 cups chicken stock
    or broth
2 tsp. salt
1 tsp. sugar
1½ tsp. saffron threads
¼ cup butter
2 medium onions, (cut
    lengthwise into thin strips)
¾ cup dark raisins (plumped
    in water)
¼ cup light raisins (plumped
    in water)
½ cup unsalted raw cashews
    (sauteed in butter)
½ cup pistachios (shelled)
½ cup slivered almonds
    (sauteed in butter)
Silver leaf (optional garnish,
    available at Indian
    groceries)

Melt 2 tbsp. butter in 6 qt. pan. Saute chicken over medium heat until golden. Remove and set aside.

In same pan melt ½ cup butter; add minced onion and cook until soft. Stir in ginger and garlic and saute briefly.

Stir in next 8 ingredients. Add ½ cup butter. When melted, mix in rice and cook over medium heat until golden, stirring frequently. Stir in stock, salt, sugar and saffron threads. Return chicken to pan; bring to boil, cover and cook over low heat 45 to 50 minutes until liquid has been absorbed.

Melt ¼ cup butter in medium skillet. Cook onion strips until well browned. Drain on paper towels.

Arrange rice on platter. Layer in the following order: dark raisins, light raisins, cashews, pistachios, almonds, onions and silver leaf, if desired.

Note: Rice may be made a few days ahead and reheated in microwave or double boiler.

Serves 12.

★ ZUBIN MEHTA
Conductor, recording artist.
One of the world's leading symphony conductors, formerly resident Musical Director of Los Angeles Philharmonic and Director Montreal Symphony, now Director of New York Philharmonic and Musical Adviser to the Israeli Philharmonic.

SEAFOOD

*The whale that wanders round the pole
Is not a table fish.
You cannot bake or broil him whole
Nor serve him in a dish.*

ABALONE RELLENO

1 lb. Abalone steaks
1 can Ortega Green Chiles
½ lb. Monterey Jack
   Cheese
Bread crumbs
Toothpicks
Oil for frying

Dip abalone in egg. Roll in crumbs. Place 1 slice of chile and cheese in center of abalone steak. Roll up and secure with toothpick. Fry in hot oil one minute each side. Serve immediately.

Serves 4.

★ MRS. HARRY CAREY (OLIVE)
HARRY CAREY: actor, rancher.
Many films include TRADER HORN, KID GALAHAD and THE SPOILERS.

BASS FILLETS WITH DILL SAUCE

4 6-oz. bass fillets
3 tbsp. shallots (minced)
Salt and pepper to taste
¾ cup dry white wine
½ cup olive oil
4 tsp. Dijon mustard
¾ tsp. salt
4 tsp. lemon juice
2 tbsp. dill (snipped)

Flatten the skinned fillets between wax paper until they are ½" thick. Butter a flame-proof baking dish just large enough to hold the fillets. Sprinkle the bottom with the shallots.

Add the ¾ cup wine, or enough to reach halfway up the side of the fish.

Bake the fish covered with a buttered piece of wax paper in a preheated oven at 400° for 15 minutes, or until the fish flakes easily with a fork.

Transfer the fish with a slotted spatula to a warm serving dish.

SAUCE:

Reduce the pan juices over high heat to about ¼ cup. While pan juices boil, combine olive oil, mustard, salt and lemon juice. Remove the pan from the heat and add the mixture to pan juices in a stream, beating until it is well combined. Add the snipped dill.

Pour sauce over fish or serve separately from sauce boat.
Serves 4.

INGRID POLLAKOFF

CREOLE JAMBALAYA

2 tbsp. butter
1 tbsp. oil
2 onions (chopped)
1 clove garlic (chopped)
1 slice ham (cubed)
  (about 1½ cup)
3 tomatoes (chopped)
½ cup tomato juice or 1
  8-oz. can tomato sauce
Salt and pepper
Pinch of thyme
Dash of chili pepper
1 bay leaf
4 cups chicken broth
1 cup rice
1 cup raw shrimp (cleaned)
1 cup frozen or cooked
  lobster tails (cut in
  bite-size pieces)
1 cup crab meat
  (optional)
1⅓ cups cooked chicken
  (diced)
2 Italian sausages (cut in
  slices and fried until
  well done; optional but
  gives a nice flavor)
4 oz. sherry

In a large pot, saute garlic and onions in butter and oil. Add ham. When onions are brown and ham is slightly browned, add tomatoes and tomato juice or sauce. Add bay leaf and season generously with salt, pepper, thyme and chili pepper. Simmer for 10 minutes. Then add chicken broth. When mixture starts boiling, add rice. After the rice has cooked for about 15 minutes add sausages and whatever shellfish is available, such as uncooked, shelled, deveined shrimp and chunks of frozen lobster tail. Add chicken and then add crabmeat at the last minute. Stir frequently until rice is tender. Add a wine glass of sherry. Cook 5 minutes longer and serve with crusty warmed French sourdough bread, Brie cheese and a light, lovely salad.

Serves 8-10

★ DINAH SHORE
Actress, author, recording artist, singer, TV host. Films include UP IN ARMS; TV appearances include star CHEVROLET SHOW (numerous Emmy Awards), star DINAH! TV series; cookbook SOMEONE'S IN THE KITCHEN WITH DINAH; awarded 19 Gold Records.

*A man hath no better thing
under the sun,
than to eat, and to drink
and to be merry.*

BIBLE

LINGUINE WITH WHITE CLAM SAUCE

This is Andy's favorite -- everyone loves it, especially Charlie Pratt.

1½ lb. linguine
(De Cecco Brand)
½ lb. butter (2 sticks)
1 cup olive oil
3 large cloves garlic
(minced)
6 canned anchovy fillets
1 cup dry white wine
3 10-oz. cans whole baby
clams (drained and juice
reserved)
¼ tsp. red pepper flakes
(diced)
½ cup parsley firmly packed
(minced)
1 tbsp. fresh basil leaves
(minced)
2 medium fresh tomatoes
(unpeeled and chopped
coarsely)

In a dutch oven, heat butter and olive oil over medium heat. When butter is melted, add garlic and saute, stirring until it begins to change color. Rinse the anchovies gently in cold water and pat dry with a paper towel. Add them to the pan and saute, stirring, until they melt. Add the wine carefully so it doesn't splatter, then raise the heat and bring the mixture to a boil. Add the reserved clam juice and the red pepper flakes and return it to a boil. Then lower the heat and let it simmer uncovered for 2 minutes. Now, add the parsley, basil, tomatoes and the clams. Immediately turn off the heat and cover the pan. The clams have already been cooked and overheating will toughen them.

(You may refrigerate the sauce or set it slowly but do not allow it to boil. Taste it for salt. You may have to add a little. I hesitate to say how much because of the saltiness of the clams and their juice.)

In a large pot, over high heat, bring at least 5 quarts of water to a fast boil. Add 2 tbsp. salt and then the linguine. Stir it constantly until it returns to boiling. Keep heat high enough for a rolling boil but low enough to prevent boiling over. After 4 minutes keep testing the pasta, it is done when there is still firmness but the white center has disappeared (remember it will still continue to cook while you mix and serve it. Allow for that. It is better to have it underdone and let it sit in the sauce an extra minute before serving. Quickly, drain the linguine, shake the colander well to remove the water, and return the pasta to the pot. Pour the clam sauce over it and toss thoroughly. Serve immediately.

Grated cheese may be served if desired.

★ MRS. ANDY GRANATELLI (DOLLY)
ANDY GRANATELLI: Business executive, sportsman.
Owner of four INDIANAPOLIS 500 winning cars; founder of S.T.P.

SHELLFISH AND GREEN NOODLES

1 small jar button mushrooms (saute in butter)
2 tbsp. onions (minced and sauteed)
2 cans cream of mushroom soup
2 cans Pioneer minced clams (use juice)
2 cans deveined shrimp; 1 lb. fresh medium shrimp is best
2 level tsp. curry powder
Pinch of oregano
Pinch of paprika
1 cup sour cream
½ cup sherry
1 12-oz. pkg. green noodles (cooked and drained)

Mix all ingredients together, except noodles. Cook and drain noodles and place in a greased 3 quart baking dish. Pour mixture over the noodles and bake at 350° for 45 minutes.

Excellent casserole for luncheon.

Serves 12 or more.

MRS. DAVID BALDWIN HEYLER

SHELLFISH CASSEROLE

1 cup tomato juice or V-8
1 cup mayonnaise
2½ cups seafood (crab and/or shrimp)
2 cups cooked Uncle Ben's rice
⅓ cup green pepper (chopped)
Salt and pepper to taste
1 cup bread crumbs
2 tbsp. butter (melted)
½ cup almonds (slivered)

Combine in bowl, vegetable juice and mayonnaise and mix well. Add other ingredients and put in 2 quart casserole. Top with 1 cup of bread crumbs mixed with 2 tbsp. melted butter and top with ½ cup slivered almonds. Bake at 350° for 1 hour.

Serves 6.

BETTY BERRINGTON

PARTY CRAB BAIT

6 oz. shell macaroni (uncooked)
1 8-oz. pkg. cream cheese
½ pint dairy sour cream
½ pint cottage cheese
⅓ cup green onions and tops (sliced)
¼ tsp. salt
½ lb. crab meat
2 medium tomatoes (peeled and sliced)
1½ cups sharp cheddar cheese (shredded)

Cook macaroni and combine with cottage cheese, cream cheese, sour cream and onions. Combine tomatoes and crab with cheddar cheese, reserving some of the cheese for top. Bake at 350° in a king casserole for 30 minutes.

(This is so easy and quick and always gets raves.)

Serves 6.

FRANCES STEVENSON

CRAB E.B.H.

2 cups mayonnaise
2 cups half and half
8 slices white bread
1 lb. crabmeat (flaked)
6 eggs (hardboiled
  and chopped)
1 4-oz. can mushrooms
  (sliced)
1 6-oz. can water chestnuts
  (sliced)
2 tbsp. minced onion
2 tbsp. green pepper
  (chopped)
1 2-oz. jar pimientos
  (chopped)
1 tbsp. capers
½ cup sherry (dry)
Corn chips

Blend mayonnaise and half and half. Remove crusts, cut bread into cubes and mix with mayonnaise mixture until smooth. Add flaked crabmeat, eggs, drained mushrooms, water chestnuts, onions, green peppers and chopped pimientos to mayonnaise mixture. Refrigerate over-night. Stir in sherry and turn mixture into a 3-quart casserole. Top with crushed corn chips and bake uncovered at 325° for 1 hour.

Serves 8.

EDIE HILTON
Home Economist, Caterer

CRAB STRUDEL

8 oz. Philadelphia cream
  cheese
10 oz. sour cream
2 eggs
2 tsp. green onion (chopped)
¼ cup fresh dill (chopped)
1 lb. cooked crab (or
  shrimp or combination)
1 box filo dough
2 sticks butter (melted)
1½ lb. mushrooms (chopped)
1 stick butter
4 tbsp. shallots (chopped)

Mix together well the cream cheese, sour cream, eggs, onion, dill and cooked crab. Make duxelle of mushrooms, 1 stick butter and chopped shallots. Saute mushrooms and wring dry in cheese cloth, very dry.
Line a 9"x10" casserole with filo leaves, brushing melted butter on each, and have filo dough hang 3 inches over edge. Layer ¾ of a box of dough this way into casserole, brush melted butter on each sheet. Then put ½ of the duxelle and finally rest of crab mixture, then fold the filo over filling and finally the rest of the filo leaves, brushed with butter.

Bake in preheated oven for 35-40 minutes at 350°.

Serves 8-10.

KATA WARREN

CRABMEAT GRUYERE

1 cup crabmeat (cleaned)
¼ cup Swiss Gruyere cheese
  (shredded)
1 tbsp. Sauterne wine
½ tsp. salt
Mayonnaise

Mix together first 4 ingredients and use mayonnaise to hold together. Pile on rounds of white bread and bake at 450° until hot and bubbly.

Good luncheon dish.

Serves 4.

DOYNE WOOD

CRABMEAT QUICHE

3 eggs (slightly beaten)
1 cup sour cream
1½ tsp. Worcestershire sauce
1 pinch of salt
1 7½-oz. can snow crab
1 can French fried onion rings
1 cup Swiss cheese
  (shredded)
1 unbaked pie shell

Mix all together; put in unbaked pie shell. Bake 55 to 60 minutes at 300°.

Serves 8.

MRS. JOHN KEMP

CRABMEAT SOUFFLE

1 lb. crabmeat
1½ cups milk
⅓ cup ripe olives
  (cut up)
3 tbsp. butter
3 tbsp. flour
½ tsp. salt
¼ tsp. paprika
8 eggs (separated)

Melt butter, add flour, salt, paprika. Cook 2 minutes, stirring constantly. Add hot milk and cook until mixture thickens. Cool, add crabmeat, olives and well-beaten egg yolks. Fold in egg whites and pour into well-buttered dish. Put baking dish in pan of water and bake until firm. Bake 45 minutes at 375°.

Serves 6.

★ LIZABETH SCOTT
Actress.
Films include STRANGE LOVE OF MARTHA IVERS and I WALK ALONE.

SWISS CRAB CASSEROLE

2 cups cooked rice
(cooled)
3 6-oz. pkgs. frozen crabmeat
(thawed and drained)
2 cups Swiss cheese
(shredded)
2 4-oz. cans sliced
mushrooms (drained)
1 small can sliced ripe olives
⅓ cup sliced almonds
(toasted)
Parsley to garnish
¼ cup each celery, onion,
green pepper (chopped)
¼ cup butter
¼ cup flour
1 tsp. salt
2 cups milk
⅓ cup bread crumbs
3 1" x 3" slices Swiss cheese

Melt ¼ cup butter in saucepan. Saute celery, onions and green peppers. Blend in flour and salt. Remove from heat, add milk gradually, return to heat, stirring until mixture thickens.

In large bowl combine rice, crabmeat, cheese, mushrooms, olives and almonds. Add sauce and toss lightly to blend. Put in a 2 quart casserole.

Combine bread crumbs and 2 tbsp. butter and sprinkle on top. Bake 30 minutes at 350° (preheated oven). Remove from oven and arrange cheese slices on top. Let stand for 5 minutes. Garnish with parsley.

Excellent for a make-ahead meal.

Serves 6.

MRS. GEORGE B. SPEARS

WINDSOR CRAB LEGS A LA TURK

DIABLO SAUCE:
1 tsp. Lea & Perrins
2 tsp. Coleman's dry mustard
1 tsp. sherry
1 tsp. lemon juice
3 drops Tabasco sauce
Salt and pepper to taste
Bread crumbs
10 large Dungeness crab legs

Roll in sauce, roll in bread crumbs, and broil to a golden brown. Place crab legs around a mound of wild rice, topped with carved buttoned mushrooms, garnish with fresh tomatoes.

Serves 3-5.

★ THE WINDSOR RESTAURANT
Los Angeles

SPAGHETTI NEPTUNE

3-4 tbsp. oil
10 cloves garlic (sliced)
1 cube butter or margarine
3 bunches green onions
   (sliced)
1 lb. fresh crabmeat,
   flaked in large chunks
   or 2 cans
1 16-oz. pkg. thin spaghetti
or   linguini (boiled al dente)
Parmesan cheese

Heat oil in large skillet. Saute garlic until dark. Remove garlic. Add butter and onions and saute briefly. Add crab and cooked spaghetti (al dente). Mix lightly and top with grated Parmesan cheese.

Note: This is very rich and best with white wine, tossed salad and toasted French bread.

If ambitious, grate Parmesan cheese just before adding.

Serves 6-8.

RICHARD C. NELSON

CRAB TETRAZZINI

2¾ cups Mornay sauce
2⅔-oz. spaghetti
½ lb. crab meat (cooked)
1⅓ oz. button mushrooms
1⅓ tbsp. sherry
½ tbsp. lemon juice
⅔ tbsp. parsley (chopped
   fine)
2⅔ tbsp. ripe olives
   (chopped)
½ tsp. onion salt
Salt to taste.

MORNAY SAUCE

3 egg yolks
Cream (hot)
2 cups Bechamel sauce
2 tbsp. butter
2 tbsp. Parmesan or
   grated Swiss cheese

Cook spaghetti in boiling salted water.

Sprinkle lemon juice on crab. Add onion juice to Mornay sauce. Combine all ingredients well and place in well-buttered pan. Cover generously with grated parmesan cheese. Sprinkle paprika on top. Bake in 350° oven until brown and bubbly.

MORNAY SAUCE

Combine egg yolks, lightly beaten, with a little hot cream. Add 2 cups hot Bechamel sauce. Cook sauce, stirring constantly until boiling. Then add butter and cheese.

Serves 6.

★ BULLOCKS WILSHIRE TEA ROOM
Los Angeles

"JAMBALAYA
AND A CRAWFISH PIE
AND FILLET GUMBO . . ."

— 1952

Lyric and Music by HANK WILLIAMS
"JAMBALAYA (ON THE BAYOU)"
© *Copyright 1952 Fred Rose Music, Inc.*
Used by permission of the publisher
All rights reserved

Photography by
MICHAEL JARRETT
OCB Reprographics, Inc.
Irvine, Ca.

CREPES ALASKA

8 oz. butter
2 tbsp. flour
1 cup chicken stock
12 oz. fresh mushrooms
  (sliced)
12 oz. king crab meat
2 tsp. sauterne
2 egg yolks
½ cup whipping cream
8 thin, French pancakes
Salt and pepper to taste

Melt 2 oz. butter, add the flour, then chicken stock and simmer for 10 minutes. Cover and set aside. Melt 1 oz. butter and add sliced mushrooms. After mushrooms are cooked, add the crab meat. Saute together for a minute. Add the sauterne and enough of the cream sauce until you have a heavy creamed mixture. Spread this in shallow pan and let cool. In the meantime, make Hollandaise from the remaining butter and 2 egg yolks. Then add the whipping cream and set aside to keep warm. Now spread out the 8 pancakes and divide the crab meat and mushrooms on the pancakes. Roll up and lay two together in shallow baking dish. Spread glace over them and put in 450° oven until glace is golden brown. Serve at once.

Serves 4.

MRS. GRAHAM POLK

ECUADORIAN BAKED FLOUNDER

3 lbs. flounder
1 onion
1 bay leaf
1 tbsp. parsley
½ tsp. thyme
1 cup white wine
3 tbsp. butter
2 tbsp. flour
6 tomatoes (chopped
  and peeled)
½ cup cracker crumbs

Clean and wash fish. Season with salt and pepper. Sprinkle all spices evenly over the bottom of a baking pan. Place fish on top of herbs and pour wine over all. Bake at 350° for 20 minutes. Melt butter, add flour, and when flour is brown add tomatoes. Simmer 10 minutes. Pour over fish, dot with butter, cover with cracker crumbs and bake 10 minutes longer. Snapper may also be prepared this way.

Serves 6.

MRS. JAMES E. GRIFFIN

FISH STEAKS WITH HERBS

2 lbs. fish steaks (Cod,
  Haddock, Salmon
  or Halibut)
6 tbsp. butter
1 large clove garlic
  (split)
⅓ cup onion (chopped)
¼ tsp. tarragon
1 tbsp. parsley (chopped)
¼ tsp. thyme
Dash nutmeg
Dash mace
1 tsp. salt
2 tbsp. lemon juice
¾ cup fine fresh bread
  crumbs

Arrange steaks in a shallow oven-proof baking dish. Melt butter in a saucepan, add garlic and cook until tender. Remove garlic, add onion and saute a few minutes without browning. Stir in remaining ingredients except the bread crumbs. Spoon about half the mixture over the fish steaks. Bake in a preheated oven at 400° for 20-25 minutes until fish flakes easily when tested with a fork.

Makes 4-5 servings.

★ N.B.C. COMMISSARY
Julie Nemeth

BAKED LOW-CALORIE, LOW-CHOLESTROL HALIBUT STEAKS

2 lbs. Halibut steaks,
  fresh or frozen
Pepper
½ cup onion (sliced)
1 clove garlic (minced)
½ cup fresh mushrooms
  (sliced)
1 tbsp. oil
1 tbsp. lemon juice
¾ cup tomato juice
½ tsp. salt
⅛ tsp. pepper
¼ tsp. Italian seasonings
  (packaged in envelope in
  fresh produce
  departments)
2 tbsp. parsley (minced)

If frozen thaw Halibut in refrigerator. Sprinkle with salt and pepper and place in lightly-oiled baking dish. Saute onion, garlic and mushrooms in oil. Add lemon juice, tomato juice, seasonings and parsley. Spoon over halibut.

Cover and bake at 375° for 30 minutes, or until halibut flakes when tested with a fork.

This is great with steamed white rice.

Serves 6.

MRS. CLIFFORD W. LORD

COQUILLES AUX SAFRAN

2 tsp. shallots
½ lb. butter
2½ lb. sea scallops
Salt, pepper
1 tsp. saffron
½ lb. diced tomatoes
½ lb. diced fresh mushrooms
1 cup dry white wine
2 cups whipping cream
2 egg yolks

Saute shallots in butter. Add scallops and season to taste with salt and pepper. Add saffron, tomatoes, mushrooms, and white wine. Simmer for approximately 6 minutes. Remove scallops and set aside.

To stock add 1 cup of whipping cream and simmer until reduced by half. Mix remaining cup of whipping cream with egg yolks and add to the reduced sauce. Return scallops to sauce and mix.

To serve use large shell and garnish with cooked rice.

Serves 6.

★ BERNARD'S
The Biltmore Hotel
Los Angeles
Christian Gaborit-Chef Restaurateur
Bernard J. Jacoupy-Directeur de la Restauration

QUICK BARBECUED SCALLOPS

2 lbs. scallops
  (fresh or frozen)
⅓ cup butter (melted)
2 tsp. instant onion (minced)
⅓ cup brown sugar (packed)
3-5 tbsp. lemon juice
2 tsp. dry mustard
¼ to ¾ tsp. salt and dash
  of pepper
2 small jars of sliced
  mushrooms

Thaw scallops and rinse thoroughly with cold water. Cut large scallops in half. Place scallops in well-greased or foil-lined pan approximately 12"x 8"x 1½".

Combine other ingredients and pour over scallops. Broil 3" to 4" from broiler flame for 12 to 15 minutes or until lightly browned, stirring every few minutes.

Serve with rice, if desired, or arrange on platter surrounded by parsley and lemon slices.

Serves 6.

MRS. GEORGE B. SPEARS

GRAVLAKS WITH MUSTARD SAUCE

3 lbs. filet of salmon with
skin remaining on
bottom side
Salt
Crushed white peppercorns
Sugar to taste
2 bunches fresh dill
(cut up)
¼ cup aquavit, or more
to taste
1 cup vegetable oil

MUSTARD DILL SAUCE:
¼ cup brown sugar
1½ tsp. rock salt
2 tbsp. granulated white
sugar
¼ cup fresh dill
(chopped)
¼ cup red wine vinegar
½ cup salad mustard
¾ cup salad oil
Salt and pepper to taste
Tabasco sauce to taste

Place the salmon filet in a pyrex dish, skin side down. Sprinkle with salt, peppercorns and sugar. Place dill over all. Sprinkle with aquavit and then place oil on top. Lay a piece of waxed paper over the fish and press with weight. Let marinate for 48 hours, turning once if desired. To serve, slice thinly on the diagonal. Serve with plain boiled potato in its jacket and Mustard Dill Sauce.

The aquavit liquor, used to marinate the salmon, is further enhanced by a little glass of this "water of life" accompanying the specialty of the house, Gravlaks. If aquavit is too strong for your taste, try a light Danish beer instead.

Gravlaks can also be served with pumpernickel or homemade salted rye baked fresh at Scandia.

★ SCANDIA
West Hollywood
Bent Thomsen
Executive Chef

PLAKI SALONICA-A GREEK FISH DISH

1 lb. sea bass fillet
(about ½" to ¾" thick)
¼ cup olive oil
1 medium tomato (sliced)
¼ cup parsley (chopped)
2 cloves garlic (crushed)
1 tsp. salt
½ tsp. pepper (white)
1 lemon

Preheat oven to 425°. Cover bottom of shallow 3 qt. baking dish with half of the olive oil. Place fish fillet in baking dish and cover with tomato slices. Sprinkle with parsley, garlic, salt and pepper. Add the juice of one lemon and the remaining olive oil. Bake covered for 25 minutes or until fish flakes with fork.

Serves 2.

TOM BROCKMILLER

MUSHROOM SHRIMP SUPREME

I have many favorites but this one both Rusty and I love.

2 lbs. shrimp (cooked
   and deveined)
2 cups rice (cooked)
½ lb. fresh mushrooms
   (sliced)
1 cup mayonnaise
2 cups cream of chicken
   soup
1 pkg. green onion dip mix
2 cups cheddar cheese
   (grated)

Combine all ingredients except cheese and mix well. Pour into a lightly greased casserole and top with cheese. Bake at 350° for about 30 minutes, or until bubbling.

Serves 6.

★ FAY DRAPER (MRS. RUSTY DRAPER)
RUSTY DRAPER: recording artist, singer.
Top country-pop singer; nightclub headliner; star SWINGING COUNTRY TV series; many film and theatre roles; awarded six Gold Records.

SHRIMP SOUFFLE CASSEROLE

6 slices white bread (French
   or Sourdough, crusts
   removed)
1 lb. cooked shrimp
   (small or medium)
½ lb. sharp cheddar cheese
   (shredded)
4 tbsp. onion (chopped)
¼ cup butter or margarine
   (melted)
2 tbsp. (or more) sherry
3 eggs (beaten)
½ tsp. dry mustard
1 pint milk

Break bread into bite-size pieces. Layer bread, shrimp and cheese in buttered 2-quart casserole. Top with onion. Repeat these layers.

Pour melted butter and sherry over layers.

Pour combined milk, eggs and dry mustard over all.

Cover and refrigerate 8-24 hours. Bake covered one hour at 350°. Serve immediately.

Serves 6.

MRS. MORRIS A. DENSMORE

SHRIMP CREOLE

1 large onion (chopped)
1 small bell pepper
  (slivered)
½ cup celery (sliced)
2 tbsp. cooking oil
½ lb. okra (washed
  and cut in pieces)
6 medium-size fresh
  tomatoes
½ lb. shrimp (more if you
  like)
Salt and pepper to taste
1 tbsp. cornstarch
Rice

Saute onion, bell pepper and celery in cooking oil. Peel and slice tomatoes and add to mixture. Add okra and cook until okra is tender. Add shrimp and cook 3 minutes until the shrimp changes color. Salt and pepper to taste. Mix cornstarch in 2 tbsp. of juice from pan and add to thickened sauce. Serve over hot white steamed rice.

Serves 4.

MRS. G. G. BAUMEN

MICROWAVE STEAMED SHRIMP

1 lb. fresh shrimp (may be
  shelled before or after
  cooking)
½ tsp. cayenne pepper
½ lemon (sliced)
½ onion (sliced)
1 rib celery (sliced)

Place all ingredients in glass baking dish and cover with wax paper. Microwave 4 minutes on HIGH. Add 1 teaspoon salt, stir and recover; return to microwave for additional 3 minutes. Let steam, covered, for 2 minutes then test for doneness. Do not overcook or shrimp will be tough. Serve hot with dip or chill for salad, etc.

Serves 4.

JEANNE ROUSSELLOT

SAVORY SALMON LOAF

1 1-lb. can salmon
3 cups fine bread crumbs
1½ tbsp. parsley (chopped)
1 tbsp. lemon juice
1¼ tsp. salt
3 tbsp. butter (melted)
2 tbsp. white onion
  (grated)
2 eggs (well beaten)
¾ cup liquid (saved from
  salmon)

Combine everything except the eggs and liquid. Place in greased loaf pan. Add enough milk to liquid to make ¾ cup. Combine with eggs. Pour over salmon mixture. Bake 45 minutes at 350°.

Serves 4.

LILLIAN DANIELSON

SAUTEED SALMON STEAK

6 salmon steaks
2 tbsp. Grey poupon mustard
¼ cup apple juice
2 tbsp. butter

Spread fish with mustard. Melt butter in skillet. Add juice. Saute fish 20 minutes on each side. You may need to add a bit of apple juice as salmon simmers.

SUE HIRSCH

SALMON STEAK TERIYAKI

4 salmon steaks
¼ cup cooking oil
3 tbsp. lemon juice
2 tbsp. soy sauce
½ tsp. dry mustard
½ tsp. ground ginger
⅛ tsp. garlic powder

Place salmon in glass baking dish. Combine marinade ingredients and pour over. Let stand for 2 hours (or more) or all day in refrigerator. Drain, reserving marinade. Place on broiler. Broil 3" from heat for 5 minutes. Brush, turn. Cook for another 5 minutes (more or less depending on intensity of broiler heat). Serve with lemon wedges.

Serves 4.

JEANNE HAYES

FILET OF SOLE WITH SHRIMP

1½ lbs. filet of sole
1 tbsp. lemon juice
⅛ tsp. paprika
Dash cayenne pepper
½ lb. raw shrimp, (shelled)
SAUCE:
2 tbsp. butter
2 tbsp. flour
1 cup milk
1 tsp. salt
TOPPING:
¼ cup bread crumbs
1 tbsp. parsley (chopped)

Season filets with lemon juice, paprika and cayenne. Fold in half with shrimp in center and place in shallow glass baking dish.

Cover with sauce and top with bread crumbs mixed with parsley. Cover with saran and microwave on MEDIUM 15 minutes, or until fish will flake.

SAUCE: Microwave butter in 4-cup glass measure for 1 minute on HIGH. Add flour, salt, and stir in milk. Microwave on HIGH for 2 to 3 minutes until thick.

Serves 4.

JEANNE ROUSSELLOT

MYSTERY SOLE AU GRATIN

The following recipe belonged to a founder member who traveled the world extensively during the 20's and 30's. She was a good cook and enjoyed collecting recipes. If you were around then perhaps you can convert the amounts to today's prices. If you like to solve puzzles...have fun.

10¢ worth of tomatoes
Butter
Pepper
Salt
5¢ worth of mussels
Garlic
1 red pepper
Soup stock
10¢ worth of shrimps
2 onions, chopped
Bread crumbs
Sole

Broil tomatoes with a little butter, pepper and salt. Steam mussels in butter, garlic, parsley, pepper and one red pepper. Add a little soup stock by degrees. Shell shrimps and put them into a dish. Chop onions, some parsley, butter and some bread crumbs together and set aside. Then take a large pan and put in the sole which have been previously salted. Sprinkle over them first the chopped onions, parsley, butter and crumbs, then mix and throw the mussels, shrimps and the juice of the tomatoes and mussels gravy and let bake 45 minutes.

MRS. MAURICE S. HELLMAN
(Submitted by Lucille Hellman Walsh)

PAUPIETTES OF SOLE-MUSHROOM SAUCE

A favorite of mine I could eat every day!

8 filets of sole (small)
2 oz. pkg. frozen shrimp
1½ oz. butter
2 oz. button mushrooms
½ pt. milk
1 oz. flour
Salt and pepper

Roll up filets with 2 or 3 shrimp inside each. Stand upright in oven proof dish, top each with thin pat of butter, cover with waxed or grease-proof paper and bake at 350° for 20 minutes. While fish is baking, wash mushrooms and steep gently in the milk with salt and pepper for 10-15 minutes. Drain and save liquid. Melt 1 oz. butter in saucepan, add flour gradually, and milk drained from mushrooms and liquid that has accumulated around fish. Bring to boil, stirring until thick, add mushrooms, pour over fish.

Serves 2 for main course or 4 for first course.

★ CARY GRANT
Actor, business executive.
Countless films include SUSPICION, THE PHILADELPHIA STORY, NORTH BY NORTHWEST; Honorary Academy Award 1965; Faberge executive.

FILET OF SOLE-TARRAGON CHIVE BUTTER

2 lbs. filet of sole
½ cup butter or margarine (melted)
2 tbsp. lemon juice
2 tbsp. tarragon (chopped) (more if desired)
1 tbsp. chives (snipped)
Salt and pepper to taste

Brush filets with ¼ cup butter. Sprinkle with lemon juice. Put in baking dish and cover with foil. Bake at 350° for 25-30 minutes or until fish flakes with fork. Combine rest of butter with tarragon, chives, salt and pepper. Heat slightly and pour over fish.

Serves 6.

MRS. R. KENNETH COLLINS
San Mateo Assistance League

WHITEFISH ITALIENNE

**PERINO'S SAUCE
ITALIENNE:**
4 beefsteak tomatoes
  (peeled)
2 tbsp. tomato paste
½ medium onion
  (diced fine)
⅓ cup (2⅔ fl. oz.) clarified
  sweet butter
⅓ tsp. ground black pepper
2 tsp. granulated sugar
1 tsp. salt
Pinch of nutmeg

**WHITEFISH FOR
POACHING ITALIENNE:**
4 lbs. of whole whitefish
  or equivalent of 2 lb. 10
  oz. of whitefish filets
1 tbsp. clarified sweet butter
2 tsp. shallots
  (diced fine)
4 oz. jumbo mushroom caps
  only (peeled, cleaned and
  sliced fine)
5 drops lemon juice
Pinch of salt
½ cup (4 fl. oz.) Chablis
  white wine
Garnish of chopped parsley

SAUCE:

To prepare clarified butter, melt about 3 ounces of sweet butter. The pure butter will tend to surface and the undesired disposable whitemilk solid particles will tend to remain at the bottom of your pan. Transfer the clarified pure butter to a separate cup.

When preparing sauce, preheat the butter in a 13" or 14" aluminum or stainless steel skillet. Then hold on medium fire and attend constantly. Add onions, but do not permit to brown.

Cut tomatoes in half horizontally, squeeze out and discard seeds and juice, then dice tomato pulp. Add to skillet and stir. Add tomato paste. Stir again.

Add all other ingredients. Allow to simmer for 15 minutes.

WHITEFISH FOR POACHING ITALIENNE:

1 lb. of whole whitefish yields 10½-oz. of filet of whitefish per person served. If starting with whole fish, remove head, tail and center bone. From resulting filets remove all remaining individual bones, either with small pliers, large tweezers or with fingers alone. Lay filet, skin down, on flat surface, and with a sharp knife separate skin from the flesh. Hold one end of skin under slight tension as knife is applied, and it should separate from the fish in one piece. Carefully trim off any skin section which remains unseparated. Cut filets into portions of either 1 piece of 10 to 10½-oz. or 2 pieces of 5 to 5¼-oz. per person to be served.

Apply clarified butter to surface of a 13" or 14" aluminum or stainless steel skillet. Do not preheat the skillet. Place shallots into skillet, then add all of the fish. Place mushrooms over fish. Add lemon juice, salt and wine. Cover either with wax paper or skillet lid in a very careful manner in order to prevent escape of steam while cooking. Place skillet on top of range at medium heat. Permit to cook slowly, always making certain steam does not escape. Do not exceed 10 minutes cooking time. Temporarily remove skillet from fire.

With large spatula transfer the fish and its covering mushrooms from the skillet to a separate warmed platter or serving tray. Keep the original skillet uncovered with its remaining poaching liquid. then replace skillet on the same fire, leaving it there until the liquid reduces to about ½ of its volume. This should take about 2 to 3 minutes time. If steam has escaped, there may not be adequate liquid for reduction, or if there is too much liquid, the resulting sauce will be too thin.

To this poaching liquid, add the separately prepared Italienne Sauce. Stir and simmer for an additional 2 to 3 minutes.

Pour this completed sauce over the fish and serve hot with boiled potatoes and any desired green vegetables. Garnish with chopped parsley.

Serves 4.

★ PERINO'S RESTAURANT
Los Angeles
Chef Miguel Olmeda

PAELLA VALENCIANA

2 to 3 oz. sweet red peppers
(cut in strips)
Oil
½ chicken (cut in small
pieces)
½ lb. pork ribs or sausages
2 large onions (chopped)
8 cloves garlic (minced)
1 tbsp.parsley (chopped)
1 large tomato (peeled and
cut in small pieces)
6 large shrimp (cleaned with
heads off, shells on)
½ lb. squid (cleaned and
cut in pieces)
36 small mussels (cleaned)
Salt and pepper to taste
1½ cups converted rice
½ cup cooked peas
Pinch of saffron (optional)

Fry the pepper in oil in a paella pan until soft; remove. Brown the chicken, pork or sausages and remove. In the same fat, put the onion, garlic and parsley; cook until golden brown, stirring constantly. Add peeled tomato and mash with a fork; stir well. Add shrimp, squid and mussels and a little water, if necessary. Cook until mussels open and shrimp are almost cooked. Remove shrimp and mussels, leaving all juices in the paella pan, together with the squid. To this, add one quart of water, bring to the boil and add the browned chicken. Cover and simmer until chicken is almost done. Add the salt, pepper and rice for last 20 minutes. When this is ready, again add the shrimp, peas, sausage or pork and cook a little longer.

To serve decorate with the mussels in their shells and strips of pimientos. Serve from the same pot, or paella, in which it was cooked, placing it on a tray and wrapped in a white napkin.

Serves 4.

★ ALICE MARBLE
Sportswoman.
National Singles and Mixed Doubles Tennis Champion four times; winner of World's Women's Tennis Championship at Wimbledon, 1939; Top-ranking Woman Tennis Player in United States, 1936-1940; now tennis instructor in Palm Desert.

POULTRY

Sing a song of sixpence, A pocket full of rye,
Four and twenty blackbirds, Baked in a pie;
When the pie was opened, the birds began to sing;
Was that not a dainty dish to set before the king?

TOM THUMB'S PRETTY SONG BOOK

CHICKEN ALMOND VERMICELLI

2 whole chicken breasts (skinned and boned)
2 tbsp. butter
1 cup mushrooms (sliced)
1 cup celery (diagonally sliced)
1 large onion (sliced)
2 tbsp. imported soy sauce
1 tbsp. cornstarch
1½ cups chicken broth
1 tsp. salt
⅛ tsp. freshly ground black pepper
½ cup water chestnuts (sliced)
2 cups broccoli spears or asparagus (cooked, drained and diagonally sliced)
8 oz. vermicelli, or thin spaghetti (cooked and drained)
2 tbsp. toasted slivered almonds

Cut the chicken breasts into ¼" strips and saute in the butter until just tender, about 5 minutes.

Remove the chicken from the pan. Add the mushrooms, celery and onion into the liquid remaining in the pan. Cook 2 or 3 minutes, stirring constantly. Blend the soy sauce and cornstarch together and gradually add the broth, salt and pepper. Add to the vegetables and heat, stirring long enough to thicken the mixture. Add the water chestnuts, reserved chicken and the broccoli or asparagus. Reheat the mixture to the boiling point. Serve over the vermicelli and sprinkle almonds over the top.

Serves 4.

★ MILLICENT AND ROBERT WISE
ROBERT WISE: director, film editor, producer.

Edited CITIZEN KANE; many films include EXECUTIVE SUITE, I WANT TO LIVE, WEST SIDE STORY (Academy Award 1961) and SOUND OF MUSIC (Academy Award 1965).

A little peach in an orchard grew,
A little peach of emerald hue;
Warmed by the sun and wet by the dew,
It grew.

    EUGENE FIELD, 'THE LITTLE PEACH'

APRICOT CHICKEN

For us working ladies who also like to entertain with a minimum of kitchen work and hysteria, this is foolproof.

1 bottle Wish Bone Russian Dressing
1 pkg. of onion soup mix
1 jar of apricot preserves
1 whole chicken (cut up)

Mix all together, and marinate chicken when you leave for work. Before cooking, turn pieces (pyrex dish, pot, whatever) and then cook at 350° for 1 hour. Try chicken, and if it is loose from the bone, you've done it. Basting a few times while cooking will help. If you want more juice for gravy (it's great served with rice) add more preserves or some water about half way.

Serves 4.

★ NANETTE FABRAY MacDOUGALL
Actress, comedienne.
Film roles include BLOOMER GIRL, BANDWAGON, A CHILD IS BORN, and early OUR GANG COMEDIES.

CHICKEN BURGER BISTRO

2 lbs. chicken breasts (boned and skinned)
1 lb. lean veal
1 medium onion
¼ lb. mushrooms
Butter
Parsley (chopped)
3 whole eggs
Salt and pepper
Worcestershire sauce
M.S.G.
4 oz. white bread crumbs.

Grind chicken and veal together. Saute onion and mushrooms in butter until golden brown. Cool. Grind with meat. Mix all ingredients together. Add salt, pepper, Worcestershire sauce, and a dash of M.S.G.

Form patties (like hamburger), dip in white bread crumbs. Saute in butter until golden brown. Finish in oven for 10 minutes at 325°. Serve with mustard sauce.

Serves 6-8.

★ THE BISTRO
Beverly Hills

CHICKEN CACCIATORE

4 large chicken breasts
   (split and boned)
Flour
6 oz. marinated artichoke
   hearts (drain and save oil)
½ lb. mushrooms
3 tbsp. reserved artichoke oil
½ tsp. oregano
½ tsp. basil
½ tsp. pepper
Parsley (minced)
1 1-lb. can tomatoes
1 clove garlic
1¼ tsp. salt
1 tsp. M.S.G.
½ cup sherry

Brown in reserved oil the flour-coated chicken. Put in 8 x 11" casserole. Mix all other ingredients except sherry and artichokes and pour over chicken. Cover.

Bake at 350° for 1 hour. Add sherry and artichokes and bake 10 minutes more.

Serves 8.

PAT THORNBURGH

CHICKEN CASSEROLE

WHITE SAUCE:
3 cups milk
1 cup canned milk
1½ cubes butter
3 tbsp. flour
½ tsp. salt
½ tsp. onion salt
½ tsp. pepper
½ tsp. celery salt

4 cups chicken (diced) or
   1 lb. pkg. frozen crab meat
1 cup Minute Rice (measure
   uncooked and then cook)
2 cans mushroom soup
½ small can pimiento
1 2½-oz. splintered pkg.
   sliced almonds
1½ cups bread crumbs
   (buttered)

Make white sauce. Combine with balance of ingredients. Cover with 1½ cups buttered bread crumbs. Bake at 350° for 1 hour. (Pan approximately 9 x 13".)

Serves 16.

★ MARILYN STAGGS
JACK STAGGS: Administrator
Executive Director, Motion Picture & Television Country House and Hospital.

CANTONESE CHICKEN

1 cup celery (chopped)
1 cup onion (chopped)
¾ cup almonds (slivered)
2 tbsp. butter
¼ tsp. salt
4 cups cooked chicken
  (diced)
1 can water chestnuts
  (chopped)
2 tbsp. cornstarch
1 cup pineapple juice
2 cups pineapple chunks
1 cup cooked (but crisp)
  carrots (sliced small)
2 tbsp. soy sauce
2 tsp. lemon juice

Saute celery, onions and almonds in butter. Add salt and chicken. Combine cornstarch with pineapple juice, soy sauce and lemon juice and cook until thickened, stirring constantly. Just before serving, combine sauce and chicken mixture, add carrots, pineapple chunks and heat through. Serve over Chinese noodles.

Serves 8.

BARBARA SELDA BRASNICK

JOY'S CHICKEN BREASTS

½ onion (chopped fine)
8 chicken breasts
  (skinned and boned)
2 tbsp. parsley (chopped
  fine)
¼ lb. Swiss cheese (strips)
Salt and pepper
Flour
2 eggs
Cracker crumbs
¾ cup chicken broth
¾ cup sherry wine
3 tbsp. flour
Sweet white grapes
  (Thompson seedless)

Saute onion until tender. Fill each chicken breast with mixture of sauteed onion, parsley, Swiss cheese, salt and pepper. Pull the breast together and hold with toothpick.

Dip stuffed breasts in flour, then into beaten and seasoned eggs and finally into cracker crumbs. Put on wax paper and refrigerate overnight.

Saute chicken in butter, then place in casserole. Add chicken broth and sherry wine. Bake at 325° until tender (about 45 minutes).

Remove chicken breasts and thicken broth with flour into gravy before returning breasts to casserole. Reheat.

Add sweet white grapes to chicken just before serving.

Serves 8.

DOYNE WOOD

PHYLLIS DILLER'S CHICKEN CHARISMA

6 chicken breasts (skinned
  and boned)
Lots of butter
¼ lb. fresh mushrooms
  (sliced and not too thin)
3 small cans of artichoke
  hearts (or 2 large ones)
Flour
Chicken stock or bouillon
White wine to taste
1 can chicken gravy

Saute breasts until brown in butter. Remove the breasts from the pan and put in a baking dish.

Add fresh mushrooms to the skillet you just browned the breasts in--add more butter before you saute the mushrooms. Sprinkle mushrooms over the chicken in the baking dish. Place artichoke hearts with chicken ARTISTICALLY in baking dish (allow about 2 hearts per person).

In skillet where you sauteed mushrooms, add flour to the drippings, plus chicken stock (or bouillon) to make gravy. (Make about 4 cups of gravy. If you don't have enough drippings for this, add 1 can of chicken gravy.) Salt and pepper to taste. Add NO GARLIC. Add white wine to taste. Pour gravy over the entire casserole. Cover and bake about 1 hour at 350° or until chicken breasts are tender. Uncover the casserole the last 15 minutes of baking.

Serves 6.

★ PHYLLIS DILLER

Actress, author, comedienne, pianist, model.
Top nightclub headliner, many TV appearances include star PRUITTS OF SOUTHAMPTON and BEAUTIFUL PHYLLIS DILLER TV series; Films include BOY, DID I GET A WRONG NUMBER!; theatre appearances include star HELLO DOLLY on Broadway; several books include PHYLLIS DILLER'S HOUSEKEEPING HINTS.

WOOD'S WORLD CHAMPION WHITE CHICKEN CHILI

8 chicken breasts (stewed in hot water with salt and pepper) shredded into relatively small pieces (3/16")

1 dozen corn tortillas

2 lbs. Monterey Jack cheese (shredded)

1 7-oz. bottle green taco sauce

1 4-oz. can Ortega diced green chile peppers

1 large can Mexican corn (drained) You can buy at any grocery store and it has red and green chiles in it)

½ pint whipping cream

Put the chicken in a two-quart casserole. Salt and pepper.

Cut the tortillas into strips about ⅜" wide and from 1 to 2 inches long. Put a few at a time in a skillet of hot grease at least ½ inch depth. 3-5 seconds is as long as you need to leave them in the grease. You do not want them to get crisp, just soft and tender.

Put ⅓ of the tortillas in the bottom of the casserole. Cover this with ½ of the shredded cooked chicken. Cover the corn with ½ of the taco sauce and green diced chile mixed together. Cover this with ½ of the shredded cheese. Then repeat all the layers, and put the remaining third of the tortilla strips on the top. Then cover the top with a semi-generous amount of grated Parmesan cheese.

At this point you can keep it in the icebox all day if you want to make this part of it ahead of time.

Just before you put it in the oven, pour the ½ pint of whipping cream slowly over the top and distribute as evenly as possible. Put in a 325° oven uncovered for 45 minutes to an hour. This will easily serve eight. With it you can have refried beans and guacamole.

Serves 8-10.

★ JOANNE DRU WOOD

Actress, dancer, model.

Former Powers model; many Broadway musicals and films include RED RIVER, SHE WORE A YELLOW RIBBON, and JOLSON STORY; GUESTWARD HO! TV series.

CONFETTI CHICKEN

6 breasts, (boned and
   halved)
Bread crumbs
½ lb. sharp cheddar cheese
⅔ cup mayonnaise
1 green pepper (chopped)
½ cup scallions
   (chopped)
8 slices bacon
   (fried and crumbled)
3 egg whites (beaten)

Season chicken to taste before browning. Saute in oil until faintly browned. Mix together cheese, green pepper, scallions, bacon crumbs and mayonnaise and fold in 3 egg whites beaten until frothy. Dip chicken in batter and bake for 40 minutes in baking dish.

Serves 12.

★ MALA POWERS
Actress.
Films include co-star CYRANO DE BERGERAC.

CURRIED CHICKEN CASSEROLE EXTRAORDINAIRE

4 chicken breasts
   (skinned & boned)
1 apple (chopped)
1 onion (chopped, med. fine)
1 can cream mushroom
   soup
½ pint sour cream
1 tbsp. curry powder
Salt
Pepper
1 tbsp butter

Saute onions and apple in butter in skillet, add curry powder, stir in mushroom soup and sour cream. Arrange chicken breasts in bottom of casserole. Sprinkle with salt and pepper . Pour ingredients of skillet over chicken. Bake in 350° oven approximately 45 min. Covered. Serve with chutney, chopped peanuts, raisins, coconut and mandarin oranges.

★ JANE KEAN
Actress, comedienne, dancer, singer.
Nightclub and theatre appearances as one of Kean Sisters; co-star JACKIE GLEASON SHOW TV series.

CHICKEN CURRY

1 cup shortening
4 onions (finely chopped)
1 cup flour
4 pts. chicken broth
1 cup milk
3 tsp. curry powder
4 apples (finely chopped)
4 tbsp. pickle relish
4 tbsp. raisins
4 tbsp. catsup or
   tomato sauce
4 lbs. chicken breasts
   (boned, cooked and diced)
5 tsp. salt (or to taste)
3 eggs, hard-boiled and
   sliced
Juice of one lemon
Cooked rice

GARNISHES:

1 egg (hard-boiled
   and grated)
1 large jar chutney
½ cup parsley (chopped)
½ can coconut (grated)

Heat fat. Fry onions until transparent. Sprinkle flour over onions and stir until brown. Lower heat. Stir in broth and milk. Simmer until thick.

Add curry powder, apple, relish, raisins and catsup. Stir. Simmer 20 minutes. Stir. Add chicken and salt. Simmer 10-20 minutes again. Add 3 eggs. Before serving, add lemon juice.

Serve over rice with individual side dishes of garnishes.

Serves 25.

GRACE H. McKNIGHT

*"Oh, where are you going to,
all you Big Steamers,
With England's own coal,
up and down the salt seas?"
"We are going to fetch you
your bread and your butter,
Your beef, pork, and mutton,
eggs, apples and cheese."*

RUDYARD KIPLING

CHICKEN CZARINA

3 lbs. boneless chicken
  breasts
Butter
1 bunch green onions
  (chopped with tops)
1 lb. mushrooms (chopped)
1 tbsp. (or more) garlic
  powder
1 4-oz. can black olives
  (chopped)
½ cup (or more) dry
  white wine
2 cups sour cream
Salt and pepper to taste

Brown and cook chicken breasts in a small amount of butter. Remove to platter and keep warm.

Saute onions and mushrooms with garlic powder until tender; add olives, wine and sour cream (do not boil). Season to taste. Pour cream over chicken and serve with rice.

Serves 6.

JANICE VOGEL ACKELS

CHICKEN FLORENTINE

2 10-oz. pkgs. frozen spinach
  (chopped)
3 whole chicken breasts
  (boned skinned and
  quartered)
¼ lb. butter (melted)
Flour
1½ cups whipping cream
Salt, pepper and paprika
Parmesan cheese (grated)

Cook spinach according to package directions. Drain well and place in bottom of buttered baking dish (7 x 11"). Dredge chicken pieces in melted butter, then flour. Lay pieces single layer over spinach. Sprinkle with salt, pepper and paprika. Pour whipping cream over chicken. Sprinkle with Parmesan cheese. Bake in preheated 400° oven for 20 minutes. (It really only takes 20 minutes.)

Serves 3.

KATHY CARR

HONEY CHICKEN

2 2-lb. broiler-fryers
  (cut up)
½ cup butter (melted)
⅛ cup prepared mustard
½ cup honey
1 tsp. salt
1 tsp. curry powder

Place chicken pieces in shallow baking dish, skin side up. Mix together butter, mustard, honey, salt and curry powder. Pour over chicken. Bake at 350° for 1¼ hours, basting every 15 minutes until chicken is tender and nicely browned.

Serves 4 to 6.

MRS. A. F. OSTERLOH, III

CHICKEN JUBILEE

8 chicken breasts (boned
  halved and skinned)
1 cup + 2 tbsp. flour
2 tsp. salt
½ tsp. garlic salt
¼ tsp. white pepper
1 cup vegetable oil
1½ cups dry white wine
1 large can pitted dark
  sweet cherries, (reserve
  the liquid)

Shake chicken breasts in 1 cup flour, salt, garlic salt and pepper in brown bag two at a time. Heat oil in large skillet and add chicken to brown on all sides. Remove and put in 13½ x 8"baking dish. Pour wine over, cover with aluminum foil and bake 25 minutes.

Add cherries (drained) to chicken. Bake uncovered for about 20 to 30 minutes. Arrange in chafing dish or serving platter (keep warm). Pour wine liquid into saucepan. Dissolve 2 tbsp. flour in reserved cherry liquid and bring to boil, stirring constantly until thickened. Pour some over chicken and serve rest in gravy boat. Warm brandy just before igniting and pour over chicken and ignite. Avert face to avoid flames.

Serves 8-10.

MRS. CHANDLER HARRIS
President
Assistance League of Southern California

BREAST OF CHICKEN WITH GRAPES

4 chicken breasts (split,
  boned and skinned)
½ cup butter
2 tbsp. onion (grated)
1½ cups whipping cream
2 tbsp. brandy
2 tbsp. sherry
2 tbsp. cornstarch
½ tsp. salt
¼ tsp. pepper
1 cup green seedless grapes

Saute chicken in butter on low heat for 20 minutes; turn several times. Remove chicken. Simmer onion in butter for 5 minutes. Add cream slowly.

Blend brandy, sherry and cornstarch until smooth. Add to cream. Cook, stirring constantly until thickened. Add seasoning, grapes and chicken. Heat through and serve.

Serves 4.

LEA ANN KING

CHICKEN MARCHAND DE VIN

1 2½ to 3 pound chicken (disjointed)
½ cup chicken fat or vegetable oil
2 cups Marchand de Vin Sauce

MARCHAND DE VIN SAUCE

¾ cup butter
½ cup mushrooms (finely chopped)
½ cup ham (minced)
⅓ cup shallots (finely chopped)
⅓ cup onions (finely chopped)
2 tbsp. garlic (minced)
2 tbsp. flour
½ tsp. salt
⅛ tsp. pepper
Dash cayenne
½ cup red wine
¾ cup beef stock

Dredge chicken pieces in seasoned flour. Heat oil or chicken fat in large skillet and fry chicken until golden brown and tender. Place chicken pieces in a casserole and cover with hot Marchand de Vin sauce. Bake in preheated 350° oven (moderate) 20 to 25 minutes.

MARCHAND DE VIN SAUCE:

In a 9" skillet melt butter. Lightly saute the mushrooms, ham, onion, shallots and garlic. When the onion is golden brown, add flour, pepper, salt and cayenne. Brown well, about 7 to 10 minutes. Blend in the wine and stock and simmer over low heat for 35 to 45 minutes. Yields 2 cups.

Serves 2-3.

ARLEN O'HARA

OREGANO CHICKEN

2½-3 lb. broiler-fryer cut up (I use breasts and legs)
1½ tsp. salt
½ cup flour
⅛ tsp. pepper
¼ cup shortening
1 can (6 oz.) frozen orange juice (thawed)
1 juice can of water
2 tbsp. dark brown sugar
½ tsp. oregano
½ tsp. nutmeg

Sprinkle chicken with 1 tsp. salt. Mix flour, remaining salt and pepper in bag. Add chicken and shake to coat pieces. Brown chicken in shortening - spoon off fat. Combine remaining ingredients and add to chicken. Cover pan. Simmer ½ hour, turning several times. If sauce is too thick, add water. Accompany with hot, cooked rice.

Serves 4.

JACKIE HALLAIAN

CHICKEN MARENGO ROYAL OAKS

½ cup seasoned bread crumbs
1 tsp. salt
½ tsp. freshly ground pepper (black)
1 3-lb. roasting chicken (disjointed)
¼ cup olive oil
½ cup butter or margarine
1 cup dry white wine
2 cups tomatoes (freshly peeled and quartered)
1 clove garlic (finely chopped)
½ lb. mushrooms (sliced)
½ cup parsley (chopped)

Preheat oven to 350°. Take commercially seasoned bread crumbs, pour into paper bag and shake chicken until well-coated. Reserve remaining bread crumbs.

In a large skillet heat olive oil and butter, add the chicken and brown on all sides. Remove chicken to a buttered casserole. Add reserved crumbs to the oil remaining in the skillet and stir in the wine. When the sauce is thickened and smooth, pour over the chicken, adding the garlic, tomatoes, and mushrooms. Cover the casserole and bake until chicken is tender, about 45 minutes. Before serving remove lid and sprinkle with chopped parsley.

Serves 4.

★ JAYNE MEADOWS ALLEN & STEVE ALLEN
Actress — actor, author, composer, pianist, raconteur, TV host.
Her many TV guest appearances include MEDICAL CENTER and co-star MEETING OF THE MINDS TV series — His songs include SOUTH RAMPART STREET PARADE, THE START OF SOMETHING BIG and film title song PICNIC; films include star BENNY GOODMAN STORY; TV appearances include original host of NBC TONIGHT SHOW (Sylvania Award), star STEVE ALLEN SHOW, and star MEETING OF THE MINDS TV series; books include THE GIRLS ON THE TENTH FLOOR.

When I demanded of my friend
what viands he preferred,
He quote: 'A large cold bottle,
and a small hot bird!'

EUGENE FIELD

CHICKEN MOGHLAI

8 whole chicken breasts
  (skinned, boned and
  halved)
Salt and pepper
Flour
½ cup butter
4 medium onions (chopped)
4 garlic cloves (minced)
1 tbsp. minced ginger
½ tsp. cumin powder
½ tsp. turmeric
¼ tsp. cumin seeds
¼ tsp. caraway seeds
¼ tsp. cayenne
1 can whole green chiles
  (minced)
1 1-lb. can whole peeled
  tomatoes, (undrained)
2 cups chicken stock
  or broth
2 pints sour cream
1½ cup brown sugar
1 tsp. saffron threads
½ tsp. cardamom powder
¼ tsp. ground cloves
¼ tsp. nutmeg
2 tbsp. catsup
2 to 3 tsp. dried red
  pepper flakes
Chopped cilantro (garnish)

Place chicken on cookie sheet. Season very generously with salt and lightly sprinkle with pepper. Dust thoroughly with flour. Melt ¼ cup butter in 14" skillet. Brown the breasts until golden on both sides. Remove and set aside. Add onions to skillet and saute over medium heat until soft. Stir in garlic and ginger and cook 2 minutes.

Add cumin powder, turmeric, cumin seeds, caraway seeds, cayenne and chile. Stir in tomatoes, mashing with a wooden spoon. Blend in chicken stock or broth. Return chicken to pan and bring to boil. Reduce heat and simmer uncovered for 8 to 10 minutes. Combine remaining ingredients except cilantro. Slowly stir into chicken mixture. Cook covered over low heat 30 minutes. Uncover and cook 45 minutes more, stirring frequently. Season to taste with salt and more red pepper flakes, if desired. Place in serving bowl and garnish with cilantro.

Note: The sauce will have a curdled appearance, which is proper with this recipe. The texture will be smooth to the taste, however.

Excellent cooked in advance and reheated.

Serves 12 to 16.

★ *ZUBIN MEHTA*
Conductor, recording artist.
One of the world's leading symphony conductors, formerly resident Musical Director of Los Angeles Philharmonic and Director Montreal Symphony; now Director of New York Philharmonic and Musical Adviser to Israeli Philharmonic.

CHICKEN L'ORANGE

1 chicken (cut up)
½ butter and ½ oil
Salt and pepper
¾ cup orange juice
⅓ cup Triple Sec
1 heaping tsp. crushed
   rosemary
Orange sections (fresh
   or canned)

Brown cut up chicken in half butter and half oil. Season with salt and pepper. When nicely browned pour ¾ cup orange juice mixed with ⅓ cup Triple Sec over the chicken. Sprinkle with rosemary. Cover and simmer slowly until done-about ½ hour. Orange sections can be added last 5 minutes. Serve with rice or plain buttered noodles.

Serves 4.

★ MRS. WILLIAM SHOEMAKER (CINDY)
WILLIAM "SHOE" SHOEMAKER: Sportsman.
One of world's top jockeys; won Kentucky Derby 3 times, Belmont Stakes 4 times; Preakness twice; winner of over 700 stakes races, first jockey to have 7,000 wins; won 5 national riding championships with record 388 winners, 1950; record 485 winners, 1953; title "World's Winningest Jockey" with winner #6,033, 1970.

PAPRIKÁS CHICKEN

3 tbsp. butter
3 medium sized onions
   (chopped finely)
4 chicken breasts
   (boned, leave skin)
2 tsp. good paprika
1 tsp. salt
½ cup chicken stock (MBT)
1 cup sour cream
1½ cup mushrooms (sliced)

Brown the onions in the butter. Add chicken and brown thoroughly. When brown add paprika and salt. Add stock and cream. Cover and SIMMER (never boil) for 40 min. Saute mushrooms in extra butter, add last ten minutes, remove chicken skin at this time. add more cream if desired. sprinkle with parsley before serving. Can be prepared ahead and frozen.

★ MRS. HENRY TEMIANKA (EMMY)
HENRI TEMIANKA: Author, conductor, educator, lecturer, recording artist, violinist.

International soloist and guest conductor; co-founder and conductor Paganini Quartet, founder and leader California Chamber Symphony; books include FACING THE MUSIC.

CHICKEN PARISIENNE

4 whole chicken breasts,
  (halved, boned and
  skinned)
Salt and pepper
Garlic powder
Flour for dusting
3 tbsp. butter
5 scallions, white part
  only
1 cup sour cream
2 cups fresh mushrooms
  (sliced)
1 10-oz. can cream of
  mushroom soup
¾ cup cream sherry
1 tsp. tarragon
Paprika
Parsley

Season chicken with salt, garlic powder and pepper. Dust with flour. Melt butter in large skillet. Brown chicken on both sides and then arrange in ovenproof dish. Mix remaining ingredients, except parsley and paprika, together. Pour over chicken. Can be refrigerated at this point.

Bake uncovered in 400° oven for 40 to 50 minutes. Last 10 minutes of baking, sprinkle with paprika. Garnish with parsley.

Serves 4-6.

MRS. BURTON WARD

POULET EN COCOTTE

3-3½ lbs. chicken (whole)
3 tbsp. butter
Salt and pepper
12 tiny onions
2 turnips (thickly sliced)
2 carrots (thickly sliced)
2 or 3 slices bacon (cut up)
Pinch of thyme, oregano
8 mushrooms

Melt butter in casserole (casserole must have tight cover and can be used on top of stove.) Brown chicken on all sides thoroughly. Sprinkle with salt and pepper and herbs. Arrange vegetables which have been boiled 10 minutes around chicken. Arrange bacon on top of chicken, then add whole washed mushrooms (uncooked). Cover and cook in 375° oven 25 or 30 minutes.

Note: I sometimes add about 6 partially cooked new potatoes (skins on) with the other vegetables.

Serves 4.

MRS. ARTHUR ARMSTRONG

CHICKEN ROLLS

4 large chicken breasts
  (split, boned, skinned
  and salted)
8 slices Swiss cheese,
  (cut in halves)
½ cup blue cheese
  (crumbled)
⅓ cup flour
2 eggs (well beaten)
¾ cup seasoned bread
  crumbs
⅓ cup butter

Pound each chicken breast with mallet to ⅛ inch thickness. Sprinkle lightly with salt. Place 2 slices Swiss cheese on each breast and top with about 1 tsp. blue cheese, roll up, tucking in ends. Secure with wood picks. Coat chicken with flour, dip in egg, then coat with bread crumbs. Cover and chill for an hour.

Melt butter in skillet. Cook chicken over medium heat, turning to lightly brown all sides. Transfer chicken to shallow baking pan. Bake at 375° 20 to 30 minutes. Remove wood picks.

Serves 8.

MRS. CARL KANE

SPICED CHICKEN

1 3 lb. broiler-fryer
  (quartered)
2 tsp. salt water
Water
½ tsp. pepper
1 tbsp. flour
1 tsp. paprika
3 medium onions
  (thinly sliced)
Spice Sauce

SPICE SAUCE:
½ tsp. pepper
1½ cups tomato juice
¼ tsp. cayenne
½ tsp. dry mustard
1 bay leaf
1½ tsp. Worcestershire sauce
¾ cup vinegar
2 tsp. sugar
3 cloves garlic (minced)
3 tbsp. butter or corn oil

Soak chicken in 1 tsp. salt and enough water to cover for 15 minutes. Rinse and pat dry with paper towels. Sprinkle with remaining salt, pepper, flour and paprika. Arrange flesh-side down in a shallow baking dish. Arrange onions on chicken and pour on Spice Sauce. Bake at 350° for 1 hour, basting often.

SPICE SAUCE:

Combine pepper, tomato juice, cayenne, mustard, bay leaf, Worcestershire, vinegar, sugar, garlic and butter in a saucepan. Simmer, uncovered, for 10 minutes. Use immediately, or cool and refrigerate.

Serves 4.

JACKIE HALLAIAN

CHICKEN A LA SHELLEY

2 small chickens (cut up)
1 cup soy sauce
1 cup clover honey
1 tsp. of garlic
½ cup of lemon juice
1 cup water

Marinate chicken for ½ hour in mixture of soy sauce, honey, garlic, lemon juice and water. Barbecue over hot coals or in oven. Cook 40 minutes (until brown) turn over often. Serve over wild rice.

Serves 8.

★ SHELLEY WINTERS
Actress
Many films include POSEIDON ADVENTURE, DIARY OF ANNE FRANK (Academy Award 1959) and A PATCH OF BLUE (Academy Award 1965).

CHICKEN IN SHERRY

1 cup mushrooms (sliced)
¼ cup butter
4 chicken breasts
1 tsp. salt
⅛ tsp. pepper
⅛ tsp. garlic powder
½ tsp. paprika
¼ tsp. crushed rosemary
¾ cup dry sherry
¼ cup water
1 tsp. cornstarch
¼ cup green onions (sliced)

Brown mushrooms in 2 tbsp. butter. Remove from pan. Wipe chicken dry and brown. Sprinkle with seasonings. Add wine and simmer for 30 or 40 minutes until tender. Blend water and cornstarch. Stir into pan liquid. Cook, stirring until thickened. Add mushrooms and green onions.

Serves 4.

DR. SHERRIE ATKINSON

CHICKEN BREASTS IN SOUR CREAM

2 chicken breasts, (split boned and skinned)
Salt and pepper to taste
½ pt. sour cream
1 cup cheese cracker crumbs
¼ lb. margarine or butter (melted)

Season chicken. Roll each piece of chicken in sour cream, then cracker crumbs and then in melted margarine. Place in shallow baking dish. Pour remaining margarine over chicken. Bake at 375° for 45 minutes.

Serves 4.

MRS. B. G. RAMOS

STICKY CHICKEN

1 frying chicken (cut up)
Flour
Oil
1 pkg. onion soup mix
1 1-lb. can stewed tomatoes
1 cup dry white wine
Pepper
8 oz. Jack or Mozzarella
   cheese (shredded)

Coat chicken in flour. Brown in oil, then place in shallow baking dish. Blend soup mix, tomatoes, wine and pepper; pour over chicken. Bake at 325° for 1 to 1½ hours. Sprinkle shredded cheese over chicken 15 minutes before chicken is done.

Serves 6.

BETTY KEMP

CHICKEN VENEZUELA

4 chicken bouillon cubes
   (dissolve in broth)
1½ cups rich chicken broth
2 cups light cream
   (or canned milk)
Corn oil for frying
12 or more corn tortillas
½ cup onion (chopped)
3 tbsp. butter or margarine
3 to 4 cups chicken (chopped
   and cooked)
1½ cups chili salsa (may
   use canned)
1½ cups sour cream
2 tbsp. capers
Salt to taste
2 to 3 cups Monterey Jack
   cheese (grated)

Dissolve bouillon cubes in broth. Stir in cream. Set aside. Heat oil in skillet and dip tortillas into it for a few seconds to make them hot and pliable. Then dip each into cream and broth mixture. Reserve remaining broth mixture.

Make filling by sauteing onion in butter. Stir in chicken, chili salsa, capers and sour cream. Spread filling on tortillas; roll and place seam side down in a baking dish. Pour reserved liquid (broth and cream) over top of placed tortillas. Sprinkle with cheese.

Bake 25 to 30 minutes in 350° oven.

Hint: This casserole may be made ahead and frozen.

Serves 6-8.

★ JODY JACOBS
Columnist, editor, writer.
Society Editor for Los Angeles Times.

ARROZ CON POLLO
(Chicken with Rice)

This is an authentic Panamanian favorite.

1 2½ lb. frying chicken
  (cut up)
1 tbsp. oil
¼ lb. pork or 3 bacon slices
  (diced)
1 large tomato or 1 small can
  tomato (diced)
1 medium onion (diced)
1 small red or green pepper
  (diced)
1 clove garlic (diced)
1 8-oz. can tomato sauce
1 can sweet peas
  (reserve the liquid)
1 small jar green olives
  (pitted)
1 lb. long grain rice
1 tbsp. capers
1 4-oz. jar sliced pimiento
2 cups water
Salt and pepper to taste

Heat oil in heavy skillet. Brown chicken, pork or bacon together. Remove the meats and set aside.

In the same skillet saute the tomatoes, onion, peppers and garlic for 3 minutes. Return the chicken to skillet, add the water, tomato sauce, salt and pepper and cook covered for 45 minutes. Remove the chicken, add the reserved liquid, capers and rice to skillet. Add more water if needed to cover the rice. Cook uncovered at medium high heat until all liquid is absorbed, turn heat to low, cover tightly and cook for 15 minutes.

Bone and dice chicken, discard skin. Stir rice, add chicken and olives. Blend. Add peas and pimiento. Cover and let stand 15 minutes or until rice is tender.

Serves 4.

★ MRS. LAFITTE PINCAY, JR.
LAFITTE PINCAY, JR.: Sportsman.
Leading jockey nationally in money and races won in 1979; National Riding Champion 1971; given Eclipse Award as Nation's Leading Rider 1973, 1974; in Racing's Hall of Fame 1975.

CORNISH HENS POLYNESIAN

1 pkg. brown rice mix
¼ cup dry sherry
½ cup drained, crushed
  pineapple
  (reserve juice)
½ cup seedless raisins
3 hens (cut in half)
2 tbsp. honey
½ cup pineapple juice

Cook rice as directed on package. Add sherry, crushed pineapple and raisins. Make mounds of rice and lay halves of hens over them. Bake at 325° for 2 hours. Baste after 1 hour with honey and pineapple juice.

Serves 6.

MRS. LESTER B. DAVES

PREGNANT CORNISH HENS

4 Cornish Hens
4 Russet potatoes
Butter
Salt and pepper

Wash and dry hens. Peel potatoes and pare to proper shape to insert in cavity of each hen. Boil potatoes until they are half cooked. Insert in cavity and close with skewers. Truss hens. Arrange close together in roasting pan. Coat with melted butter. Put in 400° oven for 40 minutes. Baste with lots of butter several times (about every 15 mins.) Serve with gravy made from pan drippings.

Serves 4.

MRS. ARTHUR ARMSTRONG

ROAST DUCKLING

3 5-to 6-lb. ducklings
2 apples
3 stalks celery
2 onions
2 tbsp. salt
Dash pepper

BING CHERRY SAUCE:

1 16-oz. can Bing cherries
   (reserve juice)
1 small jar currant jelly
1 tbsp. cornstarch
½ cup Burgundy
Dash cinnamon
Dash nutmeg
1 tbsp. sugar

Wash ducks thoroughly. Pat dry with paper towels. Rub ducks with salt and pepper inside and out. Cut up apples, celery and onions. Fill cavities of ducks with vegetables. Place on oiled cookie sheets and roast at 325° for 3½ hours.

Take out of oven and pour off all fat. Let ducks cool completely for at least 2 hours.

30 minutes before serving split ducks in half with poultry scissors. Put halves - wing side up - back on cookie sheet and roast at 350° for 30 minutes.

Especially good accompanied with bing cherry sauce and wild rice.

BING CHERRY SAUCE:

Drain cherries, reserving juice. Combine juice from cherries, currant jelly, cornstarch, Burgundy, cinnamon, nutmeg, and sugar. Cook until thickened. Add cherries. Serve over duck.

Serves 6.

YVONNE LEFKOWITZ

CHICKEN LIVERS SUPREME

1 large onion (chopped)
1 bell pepper (chopped)
6 slices bacon (fried)
2 pkgs. frozen chicken livers
Flour
Salt and pepper
1 can artichoke hearts
½ cup burgundy wine
4 English muffins

Fry onions, bell pepper and bacon. Dust chicken livers with flour and season with salt and pepper. Add to pan. Add artichoke hearts and wine and warm. Serve over toasted muffins cut in half.

Variation: Instead of English muffins, substitute brown rice.

Serves 4.

MRS. GILBERT NUÑEZ (BETTY)

TURKEY PIE WITH CORN BREAD

3 tbsp. butter
4 tbsp. flour
1 chicken bouillon cube
1 cup boiling water
1 cup evaporated milk
½ tsp. salt
¼ tsp. paprika
¼ tsp. garlic or onion
    salt
Dash pepper
1½ cups potatoes (diced
    and cooked)
1 cup peas, carrots or
    mushrooms (cooked)
1½ cups turkey (cooked
    and diced)

CORN BREAD TOPPING:
½ cup sifted flour
½ tsp. salt
1½ tsp. baking powder
2 tsp. sugar
½ cup yellow cornmeal
2 tbsp. shortening
1 egg (beaten)
½ cup milk

Melt butter in sauce pan; thicken with flour. Dissolve bouillon cube in water and then stir in evaporated milk. Add this to flour and butter; stir until smooth and thickened. Add salt, pepper, garlic (or onion) salt, paprika, turkey, potatoes and vegetables. Mix well; turn mixture into 2 quart greased casserole. Bake at 425° for 10 minutes.

CORN BREAD TOPPING:

Sift together flour, salt, baking powder and sugar. Stir in cornmeal; cut in shortening until mixture resembles coarse meal. Combine eggs and milk. Add to dry ingredients; stir until moistened. Spread corn bread topping over turkey casserole. Continue to bake 20-25 minutes, or until topping is browned.

Serves 4-6.

MAUDE TOUHEY

TURKEY AND DRESSING

If you have ever heard him on television describing the preparation of this recipe, you will know what happens to the other ½ bottle of brandy!

Turkey
Bread stuffing and corn
  bread stuffing (Pepperidge
  Farm)
Celery
Onion
Pecans
Walnuts
Sage
Mushrooms
Jones Country sausage
  (broken)
½ large jar applesauce
½ large can crushed pineapple
1 small jar orange marmalade
½ bottle of brandy

Cook turkey in 250° oven for several hours until done. Best test is when legs can be moved freely. Cook under a heavy duty aluminum foil tent. Baste occasionally in the early hours and frequently the last hour or two to get the turkey brown.

DRESSING:

Mix equal portions of a prepared bread stuffing (Pepperidge Farm) and a corn bread stuffing. Add to taste: celery, onion, pecans, walnuts, sage, mushrooms, and sausage. Add to taste: applesauce, crushed pineapple, orange marmalade and brandy.

★ ED McMAHON

Actor, announcer, raconteur, singer, TV host, nightclub performer, straightman.
NBC TONIGHT SHOW TV series, host WHODUNNIT!; films include FUN WITH DICK AND JANE.

TURKEY ORIENTAL

4 tbsp. butter
½ lb. mushrooms (sliced)
1 cup water
¼ cup soy sauce
¼ cup sherry wine
1½ tbsp. cornstarch
1½ tbsp. onion (chopped)
1 tsp. monosodium glutamate
½ tsp. garlic powder
3 cups turkey (cooked and
  chopped)
1 6-oz. can water chestnuts
  (coarsely chopped)
2 tbsp. pimiento (slivered)
¼ lb. Chinese peas
White rice

Melt butter in skillet. Add mushrooms and cook until tender about 3 minutes. Add water, soy sauce, and sherry. Dissolve cornstarch completely in a little water and add to mushrooms. Cook, stirring, until the sauce thickens. Add onion, monosodium glutamate, garlic powder, turkey, chestnuts and pimiento. Cover and simmer over low heat 8 to 10 minutes. Wash and string Chinese peas, add to skillet. Cook covered, for 3 minutes more. Serve over hot white rice.

Serves 6.

MRS. G. G. BAUMEN

TURKEY FILETS WITH PISTACHIOS

1 cup butter
6 turkey filets (cut from breast, approx. 6 oz. each)
Salt and pepper to taste
4 shallots (finely chopped)
4 large mushrooms (sliced)
2 tsp. flour
⅓ cup dry white wine
⅔ cup chicken broth
2 egg yolks
½ cup heavy cream
⅓ cup pistachios (chopped and shelled)
¼ tsp. dried tarragon
1 tbsp. lemon juice

Melt ¼ cup of butter in a large skillet. Saute the turkey on both sides until golden. Season with salt and pepper. Remove from pan and set aside.

Add shallots to pan and saute for 5 minutes. Add the mushrooms and cook for another 5 minutes, adding more butter if needed. Sprinkle in the flour and cook for about 3 minutes. Add the wine and broth, stirring until slightly thickened.

Return the filet to the pan and cover and cook for 15 minutes on low heat. Beat the cream and the egg yolks together. Add some of the hot sauce to cream mixture, then stir in to the hot sauce. Stir until thickened. Add pistachios, tarragon and lemon juice. Correct seasoning.

Serves 6.

★ CAROL BURNETT
Actress, comedienne, dancer, singer.
Many TV appearances include GARRY MOORE SHOW and star CAROL BURNETT SHOW (countless Emmy Awards); theatre roles include ONCE UPON A MATTRESS on Broadway.

TURKEY TETRAZZINI

8 oz. thin noodles
1 lb. fresh mushrooms (sliced)
3 tbsp. butter
3 tbsp. butter
5 tbsp. flour
2 cups chicken broth
1 cup all-purpose cream
4 tbsp. sherry
Salt and pepper to taste
½ large turkey breast (cubed and baked)
Parmesan cheese
½ cup blanched slivered almonds

Cook noodles in boiling water 6-7 minutes and drain. Saute mushrooms in butter and add to noodles.

Make a sauce with second 3 tbsp. butter, flour, chicken broth and cream. Add sherry, salt and pepper to taste. Mix with turkey and noodle mixture.

Place in greased casserole and sprinkle with Parmesan cheese mixed with almonds. Bake in 375° oven until crumbs are brown.

Serves 6.

HARRIET KEAST
New York City, New York

MEATS

She likes it hot, he likes it sweet
And a little tart if it's for meat;
A dash of salt, of spice and of pepper,
Tomato sauce, the very best ever!

ANONYMOUS

BARBEQUED BEEF BONES ANTONIO

1 lb. beef rib bones per
   serving
MARINADE:
4 tbsp. soy sauce
¼ cup red wine vinegar
¼ cup salad oil
1 cup dry red wine
⅓ cup plum jam
1 medium onion (chopped)
2 cloves garlic (mashed)
Zest of 1 lemon
1 tsp. thyme leaves (crushed)

Combine marinade ingredients in a saucepan over medium heat until well blended. Allow to cool.

Place beef bones in a large plastic bag and put bag in a rimmed pan. Pour cooled marinade into bag. Refrigerate and allow to marinate at least 6 hours of overnight, turning bag occasionally. Then remove from bag and reserve marinade. Prepare bed or charcoal in barbeque, place beef bones on grill, and allow 45 minutes for medium doneness. Turn and baste often with reserved marinade.

MRS. S. DARYL PARKER

BEEF BELMONT

3 lbs. brisket of beef
1 bay leaf
6 peppercorns
1 small onion
1 carrot (peeled)
1 stalk celery
8 carrots
Pinch salt
1 box frozen Fordhook baby
   lima beans
4 oz. wide noodles
8 matzo balls (from a
   delicatessen or make them
   yourself from matzo meal)
HORSERADISH SAUCE:
½ pint sour cream
3 tbsp. horseradish,
   drained well
Fresh ground pepper

Cover beef with cold water. Add bay leaf, peppercorns, onion, carrot and celery. Bring to a boil. Simmer 2½ hours or until tender. Remove beef.

Strain broth into another pan. Reserve 1 cup of broth in the original kettle. Put beef back in the 1 cup of broth. Turn heat low to keep hot. Scrape 8 carrots. Slice in half lengthwise. Cut in 1½" pieces.

Put salt, carrots and lima beans into strained broth. Boil until almost tender. Add noodles. Boil until noodles are tender.

Add 6 matzo balls and heat until warmed through. Serve soup first. Each serving contains 1 matzo ball, 2 lima beans, 2 pieces celery, 2 pieces carrot, 2 noodles and broth. On dinner plate, serve the beef sliced, noodles, lima beans, celery, carrots and horseradish sauce.

HORSERADISH SAUCE:

Mix all ingredients.

NOTE: The reason for 2 extra matzo balls is that hopefully you will have enough soup, noodles and vegetables to serve soup for lunch the next day with your extra matzo balls. If you have beef left, you can serve it for dinner with noodles and cheese and a vegetable, or for lunch with horseradish sauce on a Kaiser roll.

Serves 6-8.

★ GRETCHEN ADAMSON
(MRS. HAROLD ADAMSON)
HAROLD ADAMSON: Author, lyricist.
Many stage musicals, hit songs include HEIGH-HO, THE GANG'S ALL HERE and IT'S A MOST UNUSUAL DAY; film scores include AROUND THE WORLD IN EIGHTY DAYS.

CABBAGE BORSCHT

4 lbs. lean flanken
   (short ribs)
2½ quarts beef stock
   (or water)
2 onions (sliced)
1 16-oz. can whole tomatoes
3-4 marrow bones
2 heads of cabbage
   (shredded coarsely)
Lemon juice to taste
Ginger snaps (about 6-8)
Salt and pepper to taste
Sour cream garnish

Combine meat, stock, onions, bones, tomatoes and bring to boil, skim foam, add cabbage and reduce heat and simmer about 2 hours until meat is tender. Blend in lemon juice and sugar, salt, pepper and ginger snaps to thicken. Broth should have a sweet/sour taste. Preparing a day ahead enhances the flavor. Can be stored in freezer. Meat can be served with horseradish sauce (horseradish combined with sour cream).

Serves 10-12.

★ MRS. LOUIS NYE (ANITA)
LOUIS NYE: Actor, comedian.
TV appearances include STEVE ALLEN SHOW TV series; films include THE LAST TIME I SAW ARCHIE.

BEEF A LA BOURGUIGNONNE
(Beef Burgundy)

3 lbs. Sirloin tip
(preferably prime beef)
Seasoned flour (salt, pepper
and paprika)
4 tbsp. oil
4 tbsp. butter
⅓ cup pork (diced,
small cubes)
Cognac
3 carrots (chopped)
4 shallots (chopped)
1 large onion (chopped)
2 stalks celery (chopped)
1 clove garlic
¼ tsp. oregano
½ tsp. thyme
1 bay leaf
Sprigs of parsley
1 tbsp. tomato puree
½ cup Burgundy wine
2 cups brown stock or
canned beef consomme
Roux (butter & flour to
thicken sauce)
24 small white onions
18-20 small mushrooms
Sugar to taste
Lemon to taste

Cut beef into 1½"x1" cubes, roll in seasoned flour.

Heat oil and butter in large skillet. Saute diced pork until browned well, take out and save. Brown meat and put in heavy casserole.

Heat the cognac and pour over the meat, ignite cognac and let it flame for a few seconds.

Saute the chopped carrots, celery, onion and shallots for a few minutes, add the pressed garlic, put over the meat in the casserole. Add the thyme, bay leaf and parsley. Add the Burgundy wine and brown stock and tomato puree to skillet and simmer for about 5 minutes. Strain the sauce and add to the casserole. If needed, add a little water to cover. Sprinkle a few of the browned diced pork to the casserole.

Cover casserole and bake in slow oven at 300° for about 1½ hours. Take out and thicken with Roux, return to slow oven for about 1 hour. Brown onions in butter, add little sugar, cover and cook until done about 20 minutes. Saute mushrooms in little butter. Add lemon juice. When ready to serve add onions and mushrooms and sprinkle with parsley. Serve with rice pilaf, crisp French bread and green salad.

Serves 4-6.

MRS. HENRY C. ALEXANDER

BRISKET

1 4-or 5-lb. brisket (fat off)
2 oz. sweet Vermouth
3 cans beef bouillon
(use water from rinsed
cans)
2 cans tomato soup
Salt and pepper
Parsley
Bay leaf
4 carrots
2 stalks celery
Small onions
Marjoram
Thyme
Peanut oil
Butter
Powdered ginger mixed with
flour

Put vegetables in Cuisinart or food grinder. In a sauce pan put bouillon, tomato soup and water from rinsed cans. Add ground vegetables and herbs. Simmer till vegetables are tender. Add salt and pepper and sweet Vermouth. Reserve. Rub meat with flour mixed with ginger. Put ½ peanut oil with ½ butter at bottom of dutch oven. Brown meat on all sides in dutch oven. Pour all grease out. Pour vegetable sauce on bottom of dutch oven about ½ inch. Place meat on top of sauce. Cover. Bake in 250° oven for 3 or 4 hours. Test for doneness. Baste every hour. If sauce around meat diminishes add some reserved sauce. When meat is done, remove.

Pour liquid into a covered bowl. In a glass, enamel or Corning ware container, put ½" of sauce over bottom. Place meat on top. Cover. Refrigerate meat liquid and reserved sauce. All this can be done 2 or 3 days before dinner party. Remove meat from refrigerator. Slice, cut off any fat. Remove any particles of fat from meat liquid sauce, add the meat liquid to reserved sauce and mix. Place ½ inch of sauce over bottom of shallow serving casserole. Place slices of meat on sauce. Pour sauce over meat slices. Thoroughly heat covered in 350° oven 20 to 25 minutes. Serve heated reserved sauce on side.

Serves 6 to 8 people.

★ EILEEN RUBY (MRS. HARRY RUBY)
HARRY RUBY: author, composer, lyricist, pianist, publisher.
Many songs include WHO'S SORRY NOW, NEVERTHELESS, and themes of GROUCHO MARX and THE REAL McCOYS TV series

MADAME WU'S BEEF SADEA

This is a favorite dish of Robert and Lola Redford's two children. They always order it when they come in and love to do the barbecuing.

1 lb. flank steak
1 tsp. Indian curry powder
1 tsp. light Chinese soy sauce
1 tsp. red cooking wine
1 tsp. sugar
16 6" barbecue bamboo
   skewers
1 tbsp. vegetable oil

Prepare the flank steak the night before, removing all gristle and fat. Cut about 1½ inches from one end, and about 1 inch from the other-- you will be left with mid-section of the steak. Store in freezer overnight so that it will cut more easily.

Cut across the grain of the frozen steak into 32 strips 1/16 inch thick. Lace two strips like peppermint ribbon candy on a skewer, one following the other.

Mix the curry powder, soy sauce, red wine and sugar into a marinade and pour it into a shallow pan. Roll the skewered beef in the marinade and place with the skewer over the side. Pour the remaining marinade over the beef, and marinate for 3 to 4 hours.

Lightly grease your stove top grill or skillet with vegetable oil and preheat. Before placing each beef skewer on the grill, let the excess marinade drip into pan. Grill just long enough to brown both sides. When ready to serve, bring individual mini preheated hibachis (with charcoal or Sterno) and allow guests to barbecue their beef to their own tastes. Makes 16 skewers.

Serves 8.

★ MADAME WU
Author, lecturer, restaurateur
Book MADAME WU'S ART OF CHINESE COOKING.

BEEF WELLINGTON
OR BREAST OF TURKEY WELLINGTON

5 lb. New York strip or whole
　filet; or ½ breast of
　turkey
Carrots
Celery stalks
½ onion
Puff pastry or Pepperidge
　Farm patty shells
1 lb. mushrooms
2 shallots (chopped)
Dash of brandy
Squeeze of lemon
Egg (slightly beaten)

MADEIRA SAUCE

2 tbsp. butter
½ lb. mushrooms (halved)
4 tsp. flour
1 cup condensed beef broth
1 tsp. Worcestershire sauce
1 tbsp. chives (minced)
3 tbsp. Madeira wine
Kitchen Bouquet to color

Trim away fat on meat and tie with twine to make a compact roll. Slice carrots into ½" pieces; celery into 1" pieces. Chop onion coarsely.

Place carrots, celery and onions in the bottom of pan with the meat on top. Cover with foil. Cook at 350°; beef about 35 minutes, turkey about 1½ hours. Let cool.

Chop finely and saute mushrooms and shallots. Add dash of brandy and a squeeze of lemon. Set aside. Roll out puff pastry or defrosted patty shells. Brush pastry with egg. Place mushrooms and shallots on the rolled-out pastry. Put meat (or turkey breast) on top with the top of the meat on the bottom.

Draw up pastry to completely encase meat. Seal by moistening edges with water and pressing together. Brush with egg.

Bake at 350° until brown.

HINT: This can be made ahead of time. Brown before serving.

MADEIRA SAUCE

Melt butter, add mushrooms and saute 3 to 4 minutes until golden. Push to side of pan. Blend in flour slowly; then add broth slowly. Cook stirring until thickened. Add remaining ingredients and cook 3 to 5 minutes. Makes 1¾ cups.

Serves 8.

JANIE WILEY

INDIVIDUAL BEEF WELLINGTONS

4 8-oz. beef filets
½ cup fresh mushrooms
  (sliced)
Butter
2 pkg. refrigerated crescent
  rolls
1 egg (beaten)
1 tsp. milk

MADEIRA SAUCE:

2 tbsp. butter
2 10-oz. cans consomme
1 tsp. beef extract
2 tbsp. flour
2 tbsp. tomato paste
½ cup Madeira wine

Brown filets on both sides in butter. Remove from skillet and cool on wire rack.

Saute mushrooms in butter.

Flatten dough into rectangles and using a cup cut 8 circles. Flatten second package of dough and cut strips approximately 2" wide. Place a filet on each circle, top with ¼th of the mushrooms and another circle of dough. Carefully seal the steak using strips around the sides.

This may be done several hours ahead, refrigerated and covered, until 30 minutes before cooking time.

Brush all sides with mixed egg and milk. Bake in 400° oven 15 minutes. Serve with Madeira Sauce.

MADEIRA SAUCE:

Brown butter and flour together, add consomme, tomato paste, and beef extract. Simmer 20 minutes. Add wine and simmer 10 minutes more. Sauce may be done ahead and reheated. Serve sauce in gravy boat.

Serves 4.

BOBBI McCORMICK

GREEK BEEF

1½ lb. beef cubes
  (stewing beef)
1 6-oz. can tomato paste
½ cup wine vinegar
1 bay leaf
1½ cans beef broth
2 lbs. small white onions
1 cup walnuts
½ lb. Feta cheese
  (cubed)

Brown meat in small amount of oil. Add tomato paste, vinegar, bay leaf and broth. Cover and simmer 1½ hours. Add onions; cook until tender. Add walnuts. Add cubed cheese before serving.

Serves 4.

MRS. ALAN W. MURDOCH (INEZ)

MY OWN GOOD "HOT" CHILI

4 lbs. lean ground beef
2 lge. onions (chopped)
2 cloves garlic (minced)
2 12-oz. cans tomato paste
4 cans water
3 15-oz. cans tomato sauce
2 tbsp. dry mustard
4 tbsp. Worcestershire
1 tsp. cinnamon
1 can chili powder (to taste)
2 tbsp. cayenne pepper
Salt
2 tbsp. ground cloves
1 tbsp. rosemary
2 tbsp. oregano
2 tbsp. cumin seed
2 tbsp. paprika

Brown ground beef slightly, add chopped onion and garlic. Saute until soft, add tomato paste, tomato sauce, cans of water and all seasoning. Simmer several hours and adjust seasonings to suit your taste. Start with light touch as you add chili powder and cumin seed.

★ MRS. SID GILLMAN
SID GILLMAN: Sportsman
Former coach of Chicago Bears, Los Angeles Rams and San Diego Chargers football teams.

CHILI BEEF CASSEROLE

2 lbs. ground lean beef
½ cup onions (diced)
Salt and pepper to taste
1 8-oz. pkg. wide noodles
1 10-oz. can cream of
   mushroom soup
1 10-oz. can cream of
   celery soup
½ cup ripe olives (sliced)
2 cups fresh zucchini (sliced)
1 cup bell pepper (sliced)
1 cup celery (sliced)
1 cup fresh mushrooms
   (sliced)
4 oz. Mozzarella cheese
   (grated)
4 oz. cheddar cheese
   (grated)
1-2 tsp. chili powder

Saute beef with onion, chili powder, salt and pepper.

Cook noodles per package directions. Combine soups. Layer meat, olives, zucchini, pepper, celery, and mushrooms in one large or two square casseroles. Sprinkle cheeses on top.

Bake at 350° for 40 minutes.

Can be frozen before baking.

Serves 8-10.

BETTY CUNNINGHAM

POLLY BERGEN'S CHILI

6 medium onions (finely chopped)
6 medium green peppers (finely chopped)
2 cloves garlic (minced)
Cooking oil
4 lbs. ground round or chuck
4 16-oz. cans Italian-style tomatoes
4 to 6 16-oz. cans kidney beans (drained)
2 6-oz. cans tomato paste
1 cup water
Salt and pepper
1 tsp. red wine vinegar
3 whole cloves
2 bay leaves
2 tbsp. chili powder, or more to taste
4 drops Tabasco sauce
Sugar

In a large skillet brown onion, peppers and garlic in oil until golden.

In a separate skillet brown ground meat in batches. Separate meat with a fork and cook until all meat is browned. Drain off excess oil.

Place onion, green pepper, garlic and meat in a large pot. Add tomatoes, kidney beans, tomato paste, water, salt and pepper to taste, vinegar, cloves, bay leaves, chili powder and Tabasco sauce. Cover and simmer over low heat for 1 hour. Add sugar to taste. Simmer uncovered for another hour. Remove cloves and bay leaves before serving.

LEFTOVER IDEA: Mix 3 parts chili to 2 parts rice in a casserole. Cover with parmesan cheese, bake in 350° oven 45 minutes.

Serves 12 or more.

★ POLLY BERGEN
Actress, business executive, singer.
Many TV and film roles include PLAYHOUSE NINETY presentation HELEN MORGAN STORY (Emmy Award Best Actress 1958); founder Polly Bergen Cosmetics.

SOUTH OF THE BORDER CASSEROLE

½ lb. ground beef
1 cup onions (chopped)
½ tsp. salt
1 tbsp. hot chili sauce
½ cup milk
1 egg
2 tbsp. flour
1 4-oz. can whole chiles
1 cup cheddar cheese (grated)

Brown beef and onions. Season with salt. Mix in hot sauce.

Beat milk, egg and flour in blender. Drain chiles and remove seeds. Layer half chiles, all the beef, and half the cheese. Pour in milk, flour, egg and mix. Top with remaining chiles and cheese. Bake at 375° for 30 minutes.

Serves 2.

MRS. VINCENT ROSSI

BUDDY HACKETT'S CHINESE CHILI

His famous "Chinese Waiter" must have been helping him in the kitchen!

2 lbs. chili meat with 5% suet
  (can use ground chuck)
1 large onion (diced)
1 tsp. chili powder
2 tsp. Farmer's Ground
  California dry chili
1 pinch oregano
½ tsp. granulated garlic
1 tsp. salt
1 #5 can beef consomme
Vegetable oil
3 cups celery (diagnoally
  sliced)
1 cup onion (sliced)
1 cup water chestnuts
  (sliced)
1 cup bamboo shoots
  (sliced)
1 cup bean sprouts
½ tsp. salt

Saute the meat along with the diced onion, chili powder, ground dry chili, oregano, garlic and 1 tsp. salt. When well cooked add enough flour to take up the fat. Simmer for 20 minutes. Add the can of beef consomme to chili and simmer for 2 hours, stirring frequently.

In separate saucepan, saute the celery and sliced onions in a small amount of vegetable oil. Then add water chestnuts and bamboo shoots. Keep stirring so that the vegetables will cook fast and evenly. While still hot, drain all liquid from the vegetables. Add the chili to the vegetables and you will have Buddy Hackett's personal creation of Chinese chili.

Serves 6.

★ BUDDY HACKETT
Actor, comedian, collector.
Top nightclub headliner, TV appearances and films include THE MUSIC MAN and ITS A MAD, MAD, MAD, MAD WORLD.

CORN CHIP CASSEROLE

2 onions (chopped)
oil
1 lb. ground round steak
1 can Las Palmas chili
  sauce
1 can water
1 pkg. regular Fritos
1 lb. American cheese
  (grated)

Fry onions in small amount of oil, add meat and brown, add chili sauce and water. Simmer 15 minutes.

Place a layer of meat mixture in a greased casserole, then a layer of Fritos, then a layer of cheese. Continue, ending with a layer of Fritos, topped with a layer of cheese. Bake at 350° for 30 minutes.

Serves 4.

MRS. GLEN H. MITCHEL
Past President
Assistance League of Southern California

CORNED BEEF AND CABBAGE WITH RED POTATOES

3¼-4 lb. corned beef brisket
Water
1 tsp. mustard seed
1" stick of cinnamon
6 red potatoes (scrubbed)
1 large onion
1 tbsp. butter
1 head cabbage, medium-size
  (finely shredded)

Place meat in 4 qt. (or larger) pressure cooker, cover with water and bring up to 10 pounds pressure. Remove from heat immediately, reduce pressure and drain off water.

Add 3 cups water, mustard seed and cinnamon. Cover, bring to 10 pounds pressure and cook 1 hour and 15 minutes. Reduce pressure. Remove meat and keep warm in oven.

In the meantime, bake the potatoes at 400° for 1 hour.

Cook onion in butter until soft in large frying pan. Add 1 cup liquid from corned beef to onion, add shredded cabbage and cook on high heat, stirring for about 10 minutes until limp but slightly crunchy. Serve with remaining liquid for potatoes.

Serves 8.

MRS. THOMAS O. BROWN

STUFFED FLANK STEAK

1 flank steak
Salt, pepper and flour
3 cups rice (cooked)
½ lb. mushrooms
2 small onions (chopped)
½ tsp. sage
3 tbsp. butter
Water or red wine

Have flank steak scored lightly, sprinkle with salt, pepper and flour and pound well, (or have butcher put through meat tenderizer several times and then score in diamond pattern on both sides.)

Combine rice, mushrooms, onions, sage, butter, season with salt and pepper. Mix and spread stuffing over flank steak. Roll up and tie or secure with toothpicks. Brown in oil and add ½ cup water or red wine.

Cover and cook in oven at 350° or on top of stove for 1½ hours until tender. Baste occasionally.

Serves 6.

MRS. EDWARD L. SMITH

EGGPLANT ITALIANO

1 medium sized eggplant (peeled)
1½ lbs. ground round steak
1 large carton cottage cheese
2 eggs
2 pkg. Mozzarella cheese (sliced)
1 large can tomatoes
1 can tomato paste (small)
1 pkg. prepared spaghetti sauce mix
2 tbsp. olive oil
Parmesan cheese (grated)

Prepare meat sauce by browning ground round in olive oil. Add tomatoes, tomato paste and spaghetti sauce mix.

While sauce is simmering, mix together cottage cheese and eggs. Cover bottom of rectangular baking dish with ½ of the meat sauce. Place ½ of cottage cheese mixture over sauce and top with ½ of the Mozzarella cheese slices. Add a layer of eggplant sliced ½" thick. Cover with remainder of meat sauce, cottage cheese and Mozzarella slices. Sprinkle with grated Parmesan cheese. Bake in 350° oven for 45 minutes. Remove from oven and let stand for 10 minutes before serving.

Serves 4-6.

★ MRS. JONATHAN WINTERS
JONATHAN WINTERS: Actor, comedian TV appearances include star JONATHAN WINTERS SHOW; films include IT'S A MAD, MAD, MAD, MAD WORLD.

FLORENTINE CASSEROLE

1 6-oz pkg. noodles
1 lb. ground beef
⅓ cup mushrooms (sliced)
3 cups spaghetti sauce
1 pkg. chopped frozen spinach (thawed and drained)
1 cup sour cream
½ cup grated Parmesan cheese

Cook noodles as package directs. Drain. Brown meat until brown and crumbly. Add mushrooms and saute until tender. Drain off fat.

Mix spaghetti sauce and noodles with meat and mushrooms. Layer noodle mixture, spinach and sour cream in a 2½ qt. casserole. Top with cheese.

Bake uncovered for 30 minutes at 375°.

Serves 5 to 6.

MRS. G. G. BAUMEN

HAMBURGER STUFFED FRENCH BREAD

1 lb. loaf French bread
1½ lbs. ground beef
¾ cup onions (chopped)
¾ tsp. oregano
½ tsp. salt
¼ tsp. pepper
1½ cups bread crumbs
¼ tsp. mustard
⅓ cup parsley (chopped)
1 egg (slightly beaten)
1½ cups cheddar cheese
 (shredded)
Butter (melted)

Cut off ends of bread and save. Hollow out center, leaving thick crust. Reserve 1½ cups crumbs.

Combine beef, onions, oregano, salt and pepper in skillet and brown. Remove from heat. Add bread crumbs, mustard, parsley, egg and cheese. Blend well. Fill loaf with mixture, replace ends of loaf with toothpicks. Brush with butter and wrap in aluminum foil.

Bake at 400° for 10 minutes. Slice and serve. Serves 4-6.

MRS. ROBERT LEAMY

ITALIAN MEAT SAUCE FOR SPAGHETTI

1 cup onion (chopped
 fine)
1 clove garlic
 (chopped fine)
1 cup celery (chopped
 fine)
2 tbsp. olive oil
1 1 lb. 4-oz. can Italian-style
 tomatoes
2 6-oz. cans tomato paste
1½ tsp. salt
1 tsp. granulated sugar
¼ tsp. nutmeg
½ tsp. oregano
⅛ tsp. pepper
¼ cup parsley (chopped)
¼ cup Parmesan cheese
 (grated)
1 lb. ground round (browned
 and drained)
1½ cups fresh mushrooms
 (sliced and sauteed about
 5 minutes)

Fry onions, garlic, and celery in oil about 5 minutes. Crush tomatoes and add with tomato paste to onion, garlic and celery. Add all other ingredients (except ground round and mushrooms) and simmer in a covered saucepan at least 4 hours. Stir often to prevent scorching. Add browned ground round and simmer covered about 30 minutes longer. Mushrooms may be added for last 15 minutes of cooking. Serve over spaghetti and pass extra Parmesan cheese.

Serves 6.

SUE EHLERS

KOULIBIAC
(A Russian Entree)

PASTRY:

1 egg yolk
½ lb. butter
⅓ cup water (approx.)
2½ cups flour
Salt
A pinch of sugar

STUFFING:

1 pound ground beef
½ cup mushrooms
   (finely sliced)
⅛ pound butter
2 tbsp. fresh parsley
   (chopped)
2 hard boiled eggs (chopped)
1 egg
Salt and pepper
3 scallions (sliced)

Work all the ingredients together adding water a little at a time, working quickly until smooth and pliable. Let pastry rest in refrigerator, if possible, for 24 hours.

STUFFING:

Saute the meat in butter. Pass the meat a second time through the chopper. Mix all the ingredients and bind with egg.

Roll the pastry (at room temperature) into a rectangle. Arrange the stuffing in the middle, wrap the koulibiac up and turn it over on an oiled baking tray (this is done in order to hide the seam). Bake at 350° for 30-35 minutes. Serve with HOME MADE gravy and mushrooms poured over each sliced piece.

Serves 5-6.

MRS. HENRY F. SIMMS

CALF'S LIVER
WITH ONIONS AND APPLES

1 tbsp. bacon drippings
1 tsp. butter
1 lb. calf's liver, sliced
Salt and freshly ground
   pepper
2 onions (thinly sliced)
2 apples (peeled, cored
   and thinly sliced)
¼ cup consomme
1 tsp. wine vinegar
Parsley (freshly chopped)

Heat the bacon fat and butter in a frying pan and add the calf's liver which has been seasoned with salt and pepper.

Saute until nicely browned on both sides and remove it from the pan. Keep warm. Place onions in pan and saute until lightly brown. Add apples and saute for another 3 minutes, covered. Add the consomme and vinegar and bring to a boil. Put liver back into the pan and simmer for 2 minutes. Remove liver and arrange on a preheated serving platter. Surround it with the apples and onion slices. Pour the pan gravy over it and sprinkle with freshly chopped parsley.

Serves 4.

GLORIA DAHL

LASAGNE

2 lbs. ground lean beef
1 large onion, (chopped)
2 cloves garlic, (minced)
2 tbsp. parsley, (chopped)
2 tbsp. olive oil
1 28-oz. can tomatoes
2 6-oz. cans tomato paste, water
1 bay leaf, sweet basil, oregano, peppermint to taste
1 tsp. salt, pepper
8 slices or more of lasagne pasta
1½ lbs. Ricotta cheese
2 eggs
Fresh parsley
1½ lbs. Mozzarella cheese
½ cup or more Romano cheese

Brown beef, onion, garlic and parsley in olive oil. Add tomatoes, tomato paste, water, bay leaf, sweet basil, oregano, peppermint, salt and pepper. Simmer covered slowly for 2 hours.

Cook 8 or more slices of pasta for 10 minutes only and put into cold water.

Mix Ricotta cheese, beaten with eggs and fresh parsley. Pour meat sauce into buttered flat casserole, arrange Lasagne noodles, then three kinds of cheese, repeating layers. Top with Romano. Bake at 375° for 20 minutes.

Serves 8-10.

DOYNE WOOD

MEAT LOAF

1½ lbs. ground beef
1 small onion (grated)
4 slices bread (crusts removed and soaked in water and squeezed dry)
1 egg
⅛ tsp. garlic powder
⅛ tsp. fines herbes
Salt and pepper to taste
1 tbsp. parsley (finely minced)
1 1-lb. can Hunt's herbed tomato sauce

This is a favorite for cold sandwiches the next day.

Combine all ingredients and ½ cup tomato sauce. Mix thoroughly. Place meat mixture into 9 x 5" loaf pan. Pour remaining sauce over top. Bake in 350° oven for 1 hour.

Serves 6.

★ WALTER MIRISCH
Producer
Many films include SOME LIKE IT HOT, MAGNIFICENT SEVEN, THE APARTMENT (Academy Award Best Picture 1960), WEST SIDE STORY (Academy Award 1961) and IN THE HEAT OF THE NIGHT (Academy Award 1967); Irving Thalberg Award for Outstanding Achievement (1978); former president, Motion Picture Academy of Arts & Sciences.

VEG-MEAT LOAF

1½ lbs. lean ground meat
1 medium onion (peeled
  and cut up)
1 medium carrot (peeled
  and cut up)
1 medium stalk celery
  (peeled, cut up and leaves
  removed)
1 egg
1 piece sprouted wheat bread
¼ cup water
Pinch of dill weed, tarragon,
  marjoram, thyme, garlic
  powder

Cut up carrot, celery, onion in small pieces. Put in blender with water. Turn on blender until it is mixed well.

Mix meat with egg and crumbled bread. Add the contents from the blender to the meat. Knead together. Add spices. Mix well. Shape into loaf in Pyrex dish and bake in 350° pre-heated oven for 1 hour.

Serves 6.

★ RHONDA FLEMING
Actress

Many films include SPELLBOUND and A CONNECTICUT YANKEE IN KING ARTHUR'S COURT; theatre roles include star KISMET.

GEOFF EDWARDS' PIZZABURGER PIE

1 lb. lean ground beef
½ cup dry bread crumbs
½ tsp. oregano
1 tsp. salt
1 8-oz. can tomato sauce
1 7-oz. pkg. frozen French-
  fried onion rings
1 2½-oz. jar sliced
  mushrooms (drained)
1 cup Mozzarella cheese
  (shredded)

In bowl combine ground beef, bread crumbs, oregano, salt and ½ cup tomato sauce. Mix gently but firmly. Spread evenly in 10" pyrex pie plate to form crust. Bake ½ hour at 350°. Drain the fat and spread the rest of the ingredients on top and bake 15 minutes at 400°. If you like it crispy, put it under broiler for approximately 2 minutes. OPTIONAL: Add sliced Pepperoni.

Serves 4 to 6.

★ GEOFF EDWARDS
Actor, author, radio and TV host, sportsman.
Star GEOFF EDWARDS SHOW on KMPC radio; TV appearances include TREASURE HUNT and JACKPOT TV series; voice of World Team Tennis, Los Angeles Strings tennis team local coverage; book, GEOFF EDWARDS' YOU'VE GOT TO BE KIDDING cookbook.

POT ROAST AU VIN

3 lbs. chuck, round bone
or 7-bone boned roast
2 tbsp. flour
1 tsp. Lawry's Seasoned Salt
1 tsp. Lawry's Seasoned
Pepper
½ tsp. garlic salt
1 16-oz. pkg. sour cream
1 cup dry red wine
1 onion (grated)
Bacon drippings

Combine dry ingredients and dredge into all sides of meat.

In a heavy skillet melt 2 tbsp. bacon drippings. Heat over low fire and grate onion into fat (sometimes more fat is needed). Brown pot roast in this until brown on all sides. Place in oven at 300° for 2 hours. Drain off fat. Cover meat and fill pan with sour cream and red wine. When adding red wine to sour cream slowly blend it together. Cook 1 more hour.

Serves 6.

MRS. HARRY L. THOMAS, JR.

FRED MacMURRAY'S FAVORITE SUPER FLEMISH POT ROAST

4 to 5 lbs. beef chuck roast
1 tbsp. salad oil
4 medium sized onions
(sliced)
2 tbsp. butter or margarine
2 tbsp. flour
1 12-oz. can of beer
1 tbsp. brown sugar
1 tbsp. vinegar
1 bay leaf
2 cloves garlic
½ tsp. salt
2 tbsp. parsley (chopped)

Using heavy Dutch oven pan brown meat in oil on both sides. Remove from pan and saute onions in butter until golden color. Then sprinkle with flour and cook 2 minutes, stirring all the time. Add beer, sugar, vinegar and rest of ingredients. Put meat back in pan and cover with sauce, using a lid, and simmer two hours on stove or in oven at 350°. Has own delicious gravy.

Serves 8.

★★ JUNE HAVER AND
FRED MacMURRAY
Actress, dancer, singer — actor, saxaphonist.
Her films include HOME IN INDIANA and DOLLY SISTERS — His many films include DOUBLE INDEMNITY, THE CAINE MUTINY, and THE APARTMENT.

PERFECT RARE ROAST BEEF

Rolled roast of beef, cross rib or standing

Start roasting time before noon. Set temperature at 525°.

Place meat on a rack and put rack in a roasting pan. Add 1 cup water to the roaster. Bake 45 minutes.

Turn off oven. DO NOT OPEN OVEN DOOR until dinner time. Reheat meat for ½ hour at 350° just before serving.

FLORENCE LEIGH

BETTY'S WILD RICE CASSEROLE

3 tbsp. butter
1 stalk celery
(cut into pieces)
2 green peppers
(cut small)
4 med. onions (cut small)
1 lb. lean ground beef
½ lb. fresh mushrooms
(sliced)
½ cup wild rice (washed)
½ cup white rice (uncooked)
1 can mushroom soup
3 oz. soya sauce
2 cups water
½ cup red wine
Garlic powder to taste

Saute in butter: celery, green peppers, onions, beef and mushrooms.

Mix both rices with mushroom soup. Mix all ingredients with water, wine and garlic powder. Bake in buttered casserole for 1½ hours at 350°. (NO SALT).

Serves 6-8.

DOYNE WOOD

SHABU-SHABU

800 gms. or 2 lbs. beef sliced as thin as bacon
½ head of Chinese cabbage into 3" pieces
1 bunch spring onions including green tops cut into 2" lengths
3 cups bean sprouts
10 mushrooms (sliced in half)
10 pieces of bamboo shoots
1 square of Tofu (bean curd) (cut into 1½" squares)
2 quarts of soup stock*
Harusame, Konnyaku and sliced cabbage if available

DIPPING SAUCES:

1.
Peanut-Sesame sauce (meat)
¼ cup roasted and ground sesame
¼ cup peanut butter (smooth, creamy of any American brand)
1 tbsp. sake
1 tbsp. sugar
2 tbsp. Mirin (1 each of sake and sugar)
3 tbsp. soy sauce
Optional grated garlic and ginger
Put all ingredients into blender and add ½ cup soup stock. This sauce will keep in refrigerator 3-4 days.

A winter food cooked at the table in a large pot while eating.

Heat the soup stock in a large pot and keep it slowly boiling.

Provide each guest with chopsticks or fondue forks, bowls for the two dipping sauces and a bowl of hot rice. Each guest dips a slice of the beef or vegetables into the soup stock and cooks it until it is done.

Then it is dipped into either sauce and eaten immediately.

* Hot water can be substituted, or chicken stock.

2 bouillon cubes and quarts of water to make soup stock also can be used.

Serves 5.

MRS. TSUNEKO BAN
Past President
Nagoya International Ladies Club, Japan
Sister Club to Assistance League of Southern California

2. Lemon, soy sauce and vinegar (vegetables)
½ cup of rice vinegar
¾ cup soy sauce
Juice of ½ lemon
Mix and add touch of Accent.

CHINESE SHORT RIBS

2 tbsp. shortening
Short ribs of beef
½ cup water
1 tsp. soy sauce
½ tsp. ground ginger
3 medium white onions
  (sliced)
2 large green peppers
  (sliced)
1 cup mushrooms (sliced)
1 cup celery (sliced)
¼ cup water
2 tbsp. cornstarch
2 tbsp. liquid from
  sweet pickles
1 #2 can pineapple chunks
  (drained)
5 more tsp. soy sauce
1 can water chestnuts (sliced
  and drained)
½ cup sweet pickles (sliced)
1 can Chinese noodles

In hot shortening brown ribs on all sides. Add ½ cup water, soy sauce, ginger, and simmer until tender. Add onions, peppers, mushrooms, celery and simmer until vegetables are tender, but CRISP.

Mix the ¼ cup water, cornstarch, soy sauce and liquid from pickles until smooth. Add to hot meat mixture until it thickens. Stir in pineapple, water chestnuts and pickles. Heat more.
Serve on large platter with noodles.

GRACE SEMER

CUBE STEAK ITALIAN STYLE

2 cube or round steaks
2 tbsp. corn oil
¾ cup fine bread crumbs
3 tbsp. Parmesan cheese
  (grated)
2 tsp. parsley (minced)
1 clove garlic (minced)
½ tsp. dried or fresh basil
½ tsp. salt
⅓ tsp. pepper

Dip meat in oil on both sides. Combine remaining 7 ingredients and cover oiled meat with crumb mixture. Let stand 20 minutes.

Pan fry or pan broil in greased pan 5 minutes each side.

Serves 2 people as written. Can be increased for as many as needed.

MRS. JOSEPH KEMP

BAKED STEAK

1 green pepper (cut in
  small strips)
1 Bermuda onion
  (sliced)
Sirloin steak (1½-2" thick)
1 cup catsup
1 cup water
½ tsp. sugar
2 tsp. Worcestershire sauce
Pepper and salt

Line the baking pan with green pepper cut in small strips and one sliced Bermuda onion. Put steak on top of vegetables.

Make sauce of the catsup, water, sugar and Worcestershire sauce mixed together. Pour in corners of pan. Sear steak well underneath the broiler for a few minutes without turning; then put in 450° oven for 25-60 minutes, depending on thickness of steak. Keep uncovered, do not baste or turn. Season with salt and pepper when almost baked.

MRS. ERNEST ACH

TOM KENNEDY'S SKIER'S STEAKS

2 lbs. lean ground beef
1½ cups onion (minced)
1½ cups green pepper
  (finely diced)
1½ cups tomato (chopped
  and peeled)
¼ cup stuffed olives
  (minced)
2 cups cheddar cheese
  (shredded)
1 tsp. salt

Thoroughly mix ground beef, onion, green pepper, tomato, olives, cheese and salt. Shape into thick patties and place on a platter or tray and refrigerate 2 or 3 hours. When ready to cook, again press together each meat patty firmly to prevent crumbling while cooking. Grease a hot grill or heavy skillet, add "steaks." Brown on each side. Turn heat low and cook until done as desired, about 10 minutes on each side for medium rare. Serve with pilaf or poppyseed noodles.

Makes 6-8 servings.

★ TOM KENNEDY
TV host.
Host of NAME THAT TUNE and WHEW! TV series.

JOHN WOODEN'S FAVORITE SWISS STEAK

1½ inch thick beef cut off
   the round (cut in serving
   size pieces)
Flour
Salt and pepper to taste
Oil or Crisco
2 onions
2 cups water

Flour, salt and pepper to taste serving-size pieces of steak. Brown in oil or Crisco. Remove to heavy roasting type pan with lid.

Cut onions for four to six servings, dust with flour, and brown in frying pan. Add more oil if necessary. Add water, blend and pour over Swiss steak.

Cover roaster and bake at 275° for 2 hours or more. Gravy will be brown and ready to serve.

Serves 4-6.

★ MRS. JOHN WOODEN (NELL)
JOHN WOODEN: Sportsman
Head Basketball Coach Emeritus of U.C.L.A. All American basketball player 1930, 1931, 1932; into National Basketball Hall of Fame as player 1960, and as coach in 1972, the only one in both categories; College Coach of the Year 1964, 1967, 1969, 1970, 1972, 1973; coached U.C.L.A. teams won NCAA Championships 10 years 1964-75.

FOUR-HOUR STEW

1 lb. stew meat (lean)
1 onion (cut up)
4 carrots (cut up)
3 stalks celery (cut up)
3 or 4 mushrooms (cut up)
2 potatoes (cut up)
¼ cup brown rice
1 can peas (drained)
1 can (large) peeled tomatoes
   (cut up)
2 cups water
1 cup red wine (Burgundy)
5 or 6 large bay leaves
Salt to taste

Place ingredients in large 5-quart pot in the order given. (Meat first - bay leaves last). Cover tightly. Cook 4 hours at 275° (start in cold oven). Last ½ hour remove bay leaves.

Serves 8.

BETTY WELBOURN

CHUCK WAGON STEW

2 lbs. stew meat
1 tbsp. shortening
1 large onion
(chopped)
2 cloves garlic (minced)
1 small can tomato sauce
1 cup rice (uncooked)
Salt and pepper to taste

Melt shortening in Dutch oven and brown meat. Add onion, garlic, salt and pepper. Cover with boiling water and cook until almost done. Add rice, tomato sauce and sufficient water to cover and cook until done.

Serves 6.

★ BUCK AND DELL JONES
Actor, sportsman --- sportswoman.
He was star of countless Western films, stunt rider, rancher, hero of Coconut Grove fire in Boston, Massachusetts.---She is former stunt rider, awarded World's Trick Riding Championship, 1917.

FLEMISH BEEF STEW

4 lbs. boneless beef
(cubed)
Flour
¾ cup butter
8 medium onions
(thinly sliced)
4 cloves garlic
(crushed)
2 16-oz. cans of beer
2 cups beef broth
¼ cup brown sugar
¼ cup parsley
(minced)
4 tsp. salt
1 tsp. thyme
1 tsp. marjoram
1 tsp. pepper
¼ cup vinegar

Dredge meat in flour. Brown in one-half the butter. Sprinkle ½ cup more flour over meat. Saute garlic and onion in separate skillet in remaining butter. Combine with meat and add remaining ingredients, EXCEPT FOR VINEGAR. Cover and bake 2 hours at 325°. Add vinegar shortly before serving. Serve with rice or noodles.

Serves 6-8.

MARGARET JOHNSON

TACOS AND SAUCE

TACOS:

1½ lbs. ground beef
1 medium sized onion
   (chopped finely)
Salt
Pepper
Bay leaf
Oregano
Garlic salt
2 pkgs. cheddar cheese
   (grated)
Oil
1 dozen thin tortillas

SAUCE:

1 can Ortega green chile
   salsa
1 can Ortega diced green
   chiles
1 regular can of whole
   peeled tomatoes
1½ medium onions
   (chopped finely)
Salt
Pepper
Garlic salt
¼ cup red wine vinegar

Brown meat in cast iron skillet with onion, salt, pepper, bay leaf, oregano and garlic salt. Stir with fork and make the meat into small pieces. Remove bay leaf. Drain in colander.

Grate cheese.

Put about ⅜" oil in bottom of skillet until medium hot. Hold tortillas in hand and put spoonful of meat mixture and handful of cheese in tortillas. Lay tortillas in the oil and hold spatula on top so the tortilla won't open. Tortilla takes about 2 minutes to turn golden, then flip it over for 2 or more minutes (can cook about 3 at a time). Take tortillas out and set them on end in baking dish lined with paper towel. To keep warm, put them in the oven at 250°.

SAUCE:

Mash the tomatoes. Add all ingredients except vinegar. May be stored for a couple of weeks or more.

Make tossed green salad with oil and vinegar dressing and put on the table with sauce.

TO SERVE:

Before serving the tortillas open with a spoon. Put spoonful of salad and sauce on top of meat and cheese in tortilla.

Makes 1 dozen.

MR. R. E. BAUM
MR. MICHAEL BAUM

TAMALE PIE

2 XLNT tamales (sliced)
1 small can ripe olives (chopped)
1 lb. ground round
1 small can Ortega diced chiles
1 bunch green onions (chopped)
2 8-oz. cans tomato sauce
Parmesan cheese

Place in buttered casserole in order named: tamales (sliced); olives, ground round, browned; chiles; green onions, including some tops; add tomato sauce. Sprinkle cheese generously over casserole and bake at 350° for 30 minutes covered, and 30 minutes uncovered.

Serves 4.

★ HOWARD W. KOCH
Director, producer.
President, Academy of Motion Pictures Arts & Sciences; TV films include THE OSCARS special, THE UNTOUCHABLES and JOHNNY RINGO TV series; films include MAN FROM TEXAS and ANGELS IN THE OUTFIELD.

TAMALE PIE

1 cup yellow cornmeal
1½ cups milk
2 tbsp. chili powder
¼ cup salad oil
1 large onion (diced)
1½ lb. ground beef (lean)
1 can tomato sauce
1 can water
1 can whole kernel corn
1 tbsp. salt and pepper
Garlic salt, if you like
Cheese (grated)

Mix cornmeal, milk, chili powder, garlic salt and let stand.

Fry onions in salad oil until limp. Add meat and brown. Add tomato sauce and corn (I use Niblets) and cook well. Add cornmeal mixture. Pour into a greased baking dish. I use a large Pyrex. Bake 45 minutes at 350°. Sprinkle with grated cheese and bake 10 minutes longer. This is served with pinto beans and a lettuce salad.

Serves 8.

★ DEBBIE REYNOLDS
Actress, dancer, philanthropist, recording artist, singer.
Many films include SINGIN' IN THE RAIN, THE RAT RACE and THE UNSINKABLE MOLLY BROWN. Theatre roles include star IRENE revival; Founder of Thalians.

VAQUERO PIE

1½ lbs. ground beef
2 tsp. salt
3 med. onions (sliced)
2 cups hot water
¼ of a bell pepper (diced)
½ cup flour
⅓ cup tomato sauce
3 medium potatoes (peeled)
Paprika
Cheese (grated)

Boil potatoes with 1 tsp. salt. Drain and mash.

Fry sliced onion until brown in butter. Set aside.

Fry the ground beef in a skillet with fat. Stir while browning to prevent lumping. Cook until rawness disappears. Sift in flour and scrape from bottom of skillet as it browns.

When the meat and flour are well browned, add the browned onion, 1 tsp. salt, chopped bell pepper, tomato sauce and water. Stir rapidly, simmer about ½ hour, stirring frequently, adding water if necessary. When done it should be only slightly thick.

Pour into a shallow baking pan or dish. Cover the top with the mashed potatoes. Sprinkle with paprika and grated cheese. Bake until well heated about ½ hour in 400° oven.

Serves 4.

★ NICHOLAS S. FIRFIRES
Artist, sportsman.
Renowned member Cowboy Artists of America; portraits and action paintings hang in many museums, including Cowboy Hall of Fame in Oklahoma.

TONGUE IN RAISIN ALMOND SAUCE

Sliced, cooked tongue
SAUCE:
1 cup sugar
1 cup red wine
1 cup raisins
2 tbsp. butter
3 tbsp. lemon juice
½ tsp. Worcestershire sauce
½ tsp. salt
⅛ tsp. pepper
¼ tsp. cloves
Few grains of mace or nutmeg
1 cup currant jelly

Cook sauce ingredients together until jelly dissolves, stirring constantly. Arrange tongue in dish, add sauce and sprinkle with almonds.

Serves 8.

GRACE SEMER

STUFFED BEEF TENDERLOIN

¼ lb. fresh mushrooms
  (chopped)
1 medium onion (chopped)
¼ lb. butter
1 pkg. frozen spinach souffle
  (thawed)
4 oz. seasoned bread stuffing
2 tbsp. lemon juice
Salt and pepper
2 beef tenderloins
6 strips of thick bacon

Saute mushrooms and onion in butter. Stir in uncooked spinach souffle, bread stuffing, lemon juice, 3 tbsp. butter (melted) and salt and pepper to taste.

Slice into beef tenderloin the long way to make a pocket, being careful not to slice all the way through. Fill pocket with spinach mixture and tie roast up with kitchen twine if desired, although it is not necessary. Top each roast with 3 slices of bacon and roast the meat at 350° for approximately 30-40 minutes or to desired doneness.

Cut roasted meat into thick slices. NOTE: One beef tenderloin may be used for small number of people, but stuffing recipe will not divide. Leftover stuffing may be preserved for another use.

Serves 8-10.

KATHY PARKER

VEAL CORDON BLEU

8 veal scallops
8 thin slices ham
4 slices Swiss cheese
  (⅛ to ½" thick)
½ cup flour (approx.)
3 eggs (beaten with 3 tbsp.
  milk)
Salt
Pepper
1½ cups fine bread crumbs
Butter
Cooking oil

Pound veal flat. On 4 of the scallops, place 1 slice of ham, 1 slice of cheese, 1 slice of ham and another veal scallop. Press edges together firmly with tines of fork. Coat each with flour, dip in seasoned egg mixture; coat with bread crumbs, place on waxed paper and refrigerate at least 1 hour.

In a large, heavy skillet melt 4 to 6 tbsp. butter with ½ cup of oil over moderate heat until foam subsides and fat colors slightly. Add the scallops turning occasionally. Brown for 15 to 20 minutes until golden and crisp on both sides. Serve on heated platter with thin slice of lemon.

Serves 4.

MRS. GEORGE B. SPEARS

*"YOU'RE THE CREAM IN MY COFFEE,
YOU'RE THE SALT IN MY STEW . . ."*

— 1928

BREADED BABY VEAL CUTLET "A LA SUISSE"

4 6-oz. each veal cutlets
Salt
Black pepper, freshly ground
1 egg
1 tsp. water
1 cup fresh bread crumbs
¼ cup butter
16 slices avocado
   (1 large, peeled)
16 slices tomato (2
   medium peeled, sliced
   vertically, 8 slices each)
8 slices Swiss cheese
   (⅛" thick)
Flour for dredging
Lemon for juice
Paprika
Tomato sauce for serving

Pound cutlets until thin. Sprinkle lightly on both sides with salt and pepper. Dredge lightly, but thoroughly with flour. Beat egg lightly with water and dip floured cutlets in mixture. Shake excess egg from meat and coat with bread crumbs. Press cutlets with palm of hand so crumbs will adhere well to meat. (When preparing bread trim crusts from slices of fresh white bread, cut bread into cubes, blend a few at a time in electric blender. If no blender available, day old bread may be rubbed through a sieve.)

Heat butter in large skillet. Saute cutlets in it until golden brown on both sides. Do not overcook. Remove pan from stove and with cutlets still in pan, alternate slices of tomato and avocado on cutlet, 4 pieces of Swiss cheese, sprinkle with paprika. Put pan under broiler, not too close to heat so tomato and avocado can heat thoroughly, and melt and brown cheese. Remove gently from pan with a spatula. Put on warm platter to serve.

Serve with tomato sauce.

Serves 4.

★ HOTEL BEL-AIR
Beverly Hills
Horst Joehnk, Executive Chef

VEAL MARENGO

3 lbs. veal stew meat
  (2" pieces)
4 tbsp. olive oil
1 cup onions (minced)
1 tsp. salt
¼ tsp. pepper
2 tbsp. flour
2 cups dry white wine or
  white vermouth
1 cup canned crushed
  tomatoes or 1 cup tomato
  puree (canned or fresh)
½ tsp. basil
½ tsp. thyme
Julienne strip of orange peel
2 cloves garlic (minced)
Salt and pepper
¾ lb. fresh mushrooms
  (buttons if small, quartered
  if large)
1 pkg. petit pois (frozen
  peas defrosted)
½ cup parsley (minced)

Heat oil in skillet until very hot. Brown meat and transfer to casserole. Add extra oil if necessary and saute onions for 5 minutes.

Coat the meat with flour, salt and pepper. Over medium heat cook meat until lightly browned.

Add wine to skillet with the browned onions. Cook for 2 minutes then add the tomatoes, herbs, garlic, salt and pepper. Bring to a simmer. Add orange strip. Add to casserole and simmer mixing the flour and liquid together. Cover and bake in 325° oven for 1½ hours. (The meat should be tender when pierced with a fork.)

Add the mushrooms, cover and return to oven for 15 minutes more.

Pour contents into a sieve over a saucepan. Remove the strip of orange peel and return meat and vegetables to the casserole. Skim the fat off the sauce and boil the sauce down rapidly until it reduces to 2½ cups. (If too thin add 1 tsp. cornstarch diluted in 2 tsp. water). Season to taste and pour sauce back into casserole. Add peas and mix well. They will cook by the heat of the sauce. Serve on a bed of noodles.

NOTE: May be frozen.

★ MRS. ROBERT S. FINKEL (JANE)
ROBERT S. FINKEL: Director, producer.
Many TV specials include Julie Andrews, Pearl Bailey, Bing Crosby, also THE OSCARS, THE EMMYS, MISS UNIVERSE; TV series include PEARL BAILEY SHOW and PEOPLE'S CHOICE; winner of 3 Emmys, 2 Sylvania Awards, George Foster Peabody Award, and French Silver Rose d'Or Montreaux.

MARINATED VEAL CHOPS

4 1-inch thick veal chops
⅓ cup olive oil
2 tbsp. vinegar
¼ tsp. pepper
2 large cloves garlic
   (crushed)
3 tbsp. soy sauce

Trim chops. Arrange in shallow dish. Prepare marinade: Blend oil, vinegar, pepper, garlic and soy sauce. Pour over veal. Let stand at least 4 hours, turning occasionally. Preheat broiler. Remove veal from marinade. Reserve marinade. Arrange veal in broiler pan; broil 4 to 5 inches from heat for about 10 minutes on each side, brushing frequently with reserved marinade.

Serves 4.

ILAMAY TALLAKSON

VEAL MOZZARELLA

About 4 lbs. of veal cutlets
   (trimmed of fat and
   pounded well)
Flour
Seasoned egg
Soda cracker crumbs
Oil
Thin slices of ham
Mozzarella cheese (sliced)
   (about 1½ lbs.)
SAUCE:
4 8-oz. cans tomato sauce
2 garlic cloves (mashed)
2 tsp. basil
2 tsp. oregano
1 tsp. salt
½ tsp. pepper
Romano cheese (grated)

Flour veal cutlets, dip in seasoned egg and then in soda cracker crumbs. Fry quickly. Arrange cutlets in shallow pan, single layer, and top with thin slice of ham and nice slice of Mozzarella cheese. Cover with sauce. Sprinkle with Romano cheese. May be refrigerated at this point until baking. Bake at 350° 45 minutes.

Excellent served with green noodles and a vegetable such as snow peas.

Serves about 10.

CAROLYN PADDEN

OSSO BUCCO

⅓ cup flour
1 tsp. salt
¼ tsp. pepper
4 veal shanks
2 tbsp. bacon drippings
1 tbsp. olive oil
1 cup onions (coarsely
  chopped)
1 cup carrots (coarsely
  chopped)
1 cup celery (coarsely
  chopped)
2 cloves garlic (crushed)
1 cup tomatoes (coarsely
  chopped)
1 cup white wine
1 tsp. dried basil leaves
1 tsp. dried thyme leaves
1 bay leaf
3 tbsp. parsley (chopped)

Dredge veal shanks in flour, salt and pepper. Heat bacon fat and olive oil in a dutch oven. Saute the veal shanks, turning them until all sides are nicely browned. Remove from pot. Add onions, carrots, celery and garlic and saute for about 5 minutes. Add tomatoes, wine, basil, thyme, and bay leaf. Mix well and bring to a boil. Return veal shanks and simmer covered for 2 hours. Just before serving, add the parsley. Serve the Osso Bucco with rissoto.

Serves 4.

GLORIA DAHL

VEAL PARMIGIANA

6 veal cutlets (steaks
  cut in half)
1 egg (beaten)
Salt and pepper
¾ cup bread crumbs
3 tbsp. Parmesan cheese
  (grated)
Olive oil
½ lb. fresh mushrooms
  (sliced)
1 cup tomato sauce
Wine
Mozzarella cheese (sliced)

Dip pieces of·veal in seasoned beaten egg (salt and pepper), then in mixture of ¾ cup bread crumbs and 3 tbsp. grated Parmesan cheese. Saute in hot olive oil until golden brown. Put in shallow baking pan. Saute mushrooms.

Pour 1 cup tomato sauce and enough wine to just about cover meat. Place mushrooms on top. Bake in 350° oven for 1 hour. Last 15 minutes place slices of Mozzarella cheese on each slice of meat.

Serve with rice or noodles, Italian green beans, French bread, white or rosé wine.

Serves 6.

FORNIA HORSLEY

KALVFILET OSKAR (VEAL OSKAR)

This meat and seafood combination, adapted from a dish made for King Oskar II in 1905, has been the most successful dish we've ever had, so much so that Scandia has been called "the house that Oskar built," says Manager-Consultant Ken Hansen.

4 5-oz. slices of veal loin (trimmed, pounded and flattened to ¼" thickness)
Salt and pepper
Flour
4 large asparagus (peeled)
2 tbsp. butter
4 pieces Dungeness crab legs (cooked)
SAUCE ESPAGNOLE
SAUCE BERNAISE

Sprinkle the veal on both sides with salt and pepper and gently dust with flour.

Bring a skillet of salted water to a boil, add the peeled asparagus and cook until tender, 10-12 minutes depending on the diameter of the stalks. Drain and set aside.

Heat the butter in a skillet and brown the floured veal about 1 minute on each side. Remove the veal to a warm platter.

Top each piece of veal with an asparagus spear and on top of that a crab leg. Pour some Sauce Espagnole over each and then a little Sauce Bernaise. Serve with pomme frites (French fried potatoes) on the side.

Serves 4.

★ SCANDIA
West Hollywood
Bent Thomsen, Executive Chef

This dish of meat is too good for any but anglers, or very honest men.

IZAAK WALTON

SAUCE ESPAGNOLE

¼ lb. veal (minced)
¼ lb. cooked lean ham (minced)
1 carrot (diced)
1 small onion (diced)
¼ cup butter
¼ cup flour
4 cups beef broth
2 sprigs parsley
1 bay leaf
Pinch thyme
Salt and pepper to taste

Place veal, ham, carrot, onion and butter into a saucepan and cook over moderate heat, stirring for 8 to 10 minutes or until ingredients are lightly browned. Add flour and cook mixture over moderately low heat, stirring for 5 minutes or until mixture is a rich brown.

Remove pan from heat and add beef broth, stirring until well combined. Add bouquet garni made from parsley, bay leaf and thyme tied in cheese cloth bag. Simmer sauce, stirring occasionally for 30 minutes or until reduced to 3 cups. Strain sauce through a fine sieve into a bowl and season with salt and pepper.

★ SCANDIA
West Hollywood
Bent Thomsen, Executive Chef

SAUCE BEARNAISE

½ cup white wine
4 tbsp. tarragon vinegar
1 tbsp. finely chopped shallots
Pinch chopped tarragon
Small pinch coarse black pepper
Pinch salt
3 egg yolks
¾ cup softened butter
Cayenne pepper
Chopped tarragon
Chopped chervil

Place first 6 ingredients in the top of a double boiler and boil over direct heat until reduced by half. Remove from heat, strain and cool.

Put wine sauce in double boiler placed over moderate heat and add egg yolks and softened butter a little at a time, beating constantly until well blended. Season with cayenne, tarragon and chervil.

★ SCANDIA
West Hollywood
Bent Thomsen, Executive Chef

PASTA WITH VEAL

PART ONE:
1 cup parsley (chopped and packed)
1 tbsp. dried sweet basil
½ tsp. salt
⅛ tsp. pepper
2 cloves garlic (crushed)
½ cup olive oil
2 tbsp. butter
2 tbsp. boiling water
3 oz. Parmesan cheese (grated)
¼ cup walnuts (finely chopped)
8 oz. cooked hot spaghetti

PART TWO:
2 lbs. white veal
2 tbsp. butter
1 oz. Parmesan cheese (grated)
½ cup chicken broth
Salt and pepper

Combine all ingredients of Part One except spaghetti very thoroughly. Saute veal in butter after cutting in bite size strips. Mix veal and Part One together, then mix in with hot spaghetti very gently. (Hands do the best job.) Pour into a bake and serve dish. Add chicken broth and butter to moisten and enrich if mixture is dry. Correct seasoning. Sprinkle with additional Parmesan and bake until heated thoroughly and cheese browned-325°-350°.

Flavors marry when prepared early in day or the day before serving.

Serves 4.

MRS. KELLY STUMPUS

A Book of Verses underneath the Bough
A Jug of Wine, A Loaf of Bread—and thou
Beside me urging in the Wilderness—
Oh, Wilderness were Paradise enow!
EDWARD FITZGERALD

PAPRIKA SCHNITZEL

6 veal cutlets (cut ½"
  thick)
¼ cup all-purpose flour
1 tsp. seasoned salt
¼ tsp. pepper
1 egg (beaten)
2 tbsp. milk
¾ cup fine dry bread
  crumbs
1 tsp. paprika
3 tbsp. shortening
¾ cup chicken broth
1 tbsp. all-purpose flour
¼ tsp. dried dillweed
½ cup dairy sour cream

Pound veal to ¼" thickness. Cut small slits around edges to prevent curling. Coat meat with mixture of ¼ cup flour, seasoned salt, and pepper. Combine egg and milk. Place cutlets in egg mixture, then in mixture of crumbs and paprika. In a large skillet, cook 3 cutlets at a time in hot shortening 2 to 3 minutes on each side. Remove from pan to platter; keep warm. Pour broth into skillet, scrape to loosen drippings. Blend the 1 tbsp. flour and dillweed into sour cream. Stir sour cream mixture into broth. Cook and stir until mixture is thickened. Do not boil. Pass sauce with cutlets.

Serves 6.

GLENDA GRIBBEN

VEAL PICCATA

1 veal tenderloin
½ lemon
2 tbsp. parsley chopped)
Salt and pepper
Flour
½ lb. mushrooms
Butter

Partially freeze veal tenderloin and slice ¼" thin. Dredge with flour.

Heat large fry pan until the butter (about ½ stick) is sizzling hot. Be generous with butter. Put in veal slices. Turn almost immediately and brown other side. Should be in pan only a few seconds. Remove from pan to warm platter.

Add more butter if needed and saute sliced mushrooms. Spread mushrooms over meat. Turn off heat. Add a little more butter and deglaze pan with lemon juice. Pour from pan over the mushrooms and meat. Sprinkle with chopped parsley and serve.

Recipe can be doubled but 1 lemon may be too much. I serve with poppy seed noodles and a green vegetable.

Serves 3 or 4.

MRS. ARTHUR A. ARMSTRONG

VEAL SAUTÉ

2 lbs. of veal (sliced thin)
(remove connective tissue
so it won't curl)
3 tbsp. salad oil
2 tbsp. butter
1 tsp. salt
¼ tsp. pepper
2 tbsp. flour
1 cup white wine
1 tomato (peeled
and chopped)
1 onion (peeled and
chopped)
2 tbsp. parsley
(chopped)
1 cup mushrooms (sliced)
4 oz. Mozzarella cheese (thin
sliced)

Heat the oil and butter together. Dust the meat with flour and brown a few pieces at a time (don't crowd the pan or the meat won't brown). Remove slices as they brown and hold aside. To the remaining fat in pan add the seasonings, wine, tomato, onions and parsley. Arrange meat back in pan and cook 15 minutes. Add mushrooms and cook 10 more minutes. Top with Mozzarella cheese and melt briefly under the broiler.

Serves 4-5.

NANCY COCHRAN

ITALIAN VEAL STEW

2 lbs. shoulder of veal
(boneless)
1 cup onion (diced)
1 cup green pepper (diced)
3 tbsp. olive oil
2 cups tomato sauce
2 tsp. salt
1 tbsp. parsley (fresh,
chopped)
1 clove garlic (minced)
2 tsp. oregano leaves
(crumbled)
¼ tsp. fresh ground black
pepper

Cut veal into 1" cubes and set aside. Saute onion and green pepper in hot oil until onion is transparent. Add meat and brown on all sides. Stir in tomato sauce and spices. Cover and simmer 1 hour or until tender. Serve hot over rice.

Serves 6.

LORA KELLY

VITELLO TONNATO

3-4 lbs. of lean veal
  cut from the leg and
  rolled and tied
1 large onion (sliced)
1 2-oz. can tuna with oil
2 cups dry white wine
Few peppercorns
2 cloves garlic (chopped)
Several stalks of celery
  with tops (coarsely
  chopped)
Pinch thyme
Few sprigs of parsley
Chicken broth
Jar of capers
Several lemons

SAUCE:

1 pint mayonnaise
Cooled strained broth
1 lemon

Have your butcher bone and roll the veal, eliminating as much fat as possible and tie securely. Place the meat with all the ingredients in a heavy kettle with enough chicken broth to cover. Bring to boil, then simmer until meat is tender when pierced with the point of a small sharp knife. Cool the meat in the broth.

When meat is cold, remove, wrap securely in foil and refrigerate overnight.

Place the kettle with all the ingredients still in it over high heat and bring to a rolling boil. Boil until you have approximately 1 pint rich broth. Strain and cool.

SAUCE:

Combine mayonnaise with enough of the cool strained broth to make a smooth sauce the consistency of a thin cream sauce. Combine well with the juice of a lemon. At this point taste the sauce for seasoning. To serve, mound cool, cooked rice on a large serving platter. Sprinkle generously with finely chopped parsley. Slice the cold veal very, very thin and arrange, overlapping down the center of the platter, leaving a ring of rice all around. Spoon the sauce over the meat only, covering it completely, and scatter well-drained capers in the sauce. Serve remaining sauce in a sauce boat on the side with a few capers on top.

This is an excellent dish for a hot summer night. I serve sliced tomatoes sprinkled with dill and a cold broccoli ring mold filled with marinated carrots. Good Italian or French bread and a dry white wine round out an excellent summer menu.

Serves 8.

CARLEEN M. KEMMERLING

VEAL VERONIQUE

Tenderloin of veal
(8 medallions)
3 oz. butter
½ cup dry white wine
½ cup sour cream
1 jigger cognac
1 cup Thompson seedless
grapes
8 artichoke bottoms

Saute the veal in butter until tender. Add white wine and simmer. Remove meat and add sour cream, cognac and grapes. Blend well. Serve the medallions on artichoke bottoms and top with the sauce.

Serves 4.

MRS. GRAHAM POLK

LAMB AND ARTICHOKE HEARTS

2 lbs. lamb meat (cubed)
1 onion (chopped)
1 clove garlic (chopped)
2 tbsp. oil or butter
4 #2 cans artichoke hearts
1 large can whole button
mushrooms
Juice of 1 lemon
Season to taste

Braise lamb cubes, mushrooms, onion, and garlic in 2 tbsp. oil or butter. Let simmer until lamb is done, about 30 minutes.

Rinse artichokes in cold water and pour over cooked lamb mixture. Add juice of lemon. Heat all, slowly. Serve with steamed rice.

Serves 6.

★ MRS. JOE MOSHAY (JOSEPHINE)
JOE MOSHAY: Conductor
Founder and leader of Southland's top   society orchestra.

BARBEQUED "BUTTERFLY" LAMB

1 leg of lamb, (boned
   and laid out flat)
1½ cups dry red wine
2 tbsp. parsley (snipped)
2 tbsp. chives (chopped)
½ tsp. Worcestershire sauce
¼ tsp. ground black
   pepper
⅛ tsp. marjoram
⅛ tsp. rosemary
⅛ tsp. thyme
2 cloves garlic (mashed
   with 1 tsp. salt)

Combine all ingredients to make a marinade. Pour over lamb and marinate overnight in refrigerator.

Barbecue lamb about 20 minutes per side, basting frequently with marinade. This time is for "very rare". Cook longer for rare or medium.

1 5-lb. boneless leg of lamb will serve 6 to 8.

MRS. RICHARD LINDGREN

LAMB CURRY

2 cooking apples (peeled
   and sliced)
1 green pepper (chopped)
2 onions (sliced)
1 clove garlic (crushed)
2 tbsp. olive oil
½ tsp. marjoram
½ tsp. salt
½ tsp. thyme
1 tbsp. curry powder
   (for mild)
2 tbsp. flour
½ cup dry red wine
1 cup consomme
1 lemon (juice and rind)
½ cup seedless raisins
2 whole cloves
2 cups cooked lamb (diced)
½ cup shredded coconut
1 tbsp. sour cream

Saute apples, green pepper, onions and garlic in oil. Sprinkle with marjoram, salt, thyme, curry powder and flour. Mix well and cook 5 minutes.

Add wine and consomme, lemon juice and rind, raisins and cloves. Allow to simmer about half an hour. Then add lamb and coconut. Cook an additional 15 minutes. Just before serving, add sour cream, blending well. Serve with rice and condiments.

Serves 4-6.

VIVIAN AHRENSDORF

INDONESIAN CURRY DINNER
Lamb Curry

¼ cup safflower oil
1 cup onions (chopped)
1 cup celery (chopped)
3 lbs. lamb (cut in small
    pieces)
3 sour apples (chopped)
1 tsp. salt (or more,
    to taste)
1 tbsp. peanut butter
½ tsp. pepper (ground)
1½ cups chicken broth
1 tsp. thyme
2½ tbsp. curry powder
1 tsp. parsley
½ tsp. sugar
½ cup sherry

CONDIMENTS

1 cup raisins
1 #2 can crushed pineapple
1 small pkg. coconut
1 small jar ginger bits
1 jar chutney
1 cup ground or chopped
    peanuts
4 hard boiled eggs
    (separated)
1 cup chopped green onions
1 lb. bacon (fried crisp)

DELIGHT

1½ quarts ice cream
1 can lichee nuts
1 can mandarin oranges
8 tbsp. Amaretto liqueur

Saute onions and celery in oil, add meat and toss over high flame until all pink has disappeared. Sprinkle curry powder and seasonings, add apples and peanut butter. Moisten with broth to desired thickness, simmer about an hour or until tender. Add sherry. Bring to sharp boil and remove from fire. Place meat in center of boiled rice and pour gravy over. Serve extra gravy in boat, if desired.

INDONESIAN DINNER CONDIMENTS

Boil raisins to plump; drain crushed pineapple; separate yolks and whites of hard boiled eggs, put through a fine sieve and serve separately; dry fried bacon with paper towels and crumble. Serve each condiment in a separate bowl, group on a tray or in center of table.

INDONESIAN DELIGHT

Place lichee nuts and mandarin orange wedges around ice cream in individual bowls. Pour Amaretto over. For best result, use "mandarin chocolate," coffee or chocolate ice cream.

Serves 8.

LORRAINE WOOD

LAMB DOLMA

The basic Dolma stuffing to serve a family of 4-6.

1½ lbs. lamb or beef
  (both mixed, ground)
½ cup rice
3 large onions (chopped
  fine)
½ bunch parsley (chopped)
1 can tomato paste
Salt and pepper to taste
Juice of ½ lemon

Mix all ingredients well by hand in bowl. Vegetables commonly used are as follows: Tomato, green pepper, zucchini, squash, Japanese eggplant, cabbage, grape leaves. Clean vegetables, remove tops and insides, stuff with meat mixture. Put tops back on, pour tomato sauce over all. Add 1" water in bottom of pan. Place in preheated oven (350°) covered for 1½-2 hours. Baste from time to time. Over top squeeze remaining half lemon.

JACKIE HALLAIAN

LAMB AND EGGPLANT BAKE

1 medium eggplant
2 tbsp. flour
⅓ cup margarine
1 lb. ground lamb
¼ cup onions (chopped)
½ tsp. salt
Dash pepper
1 8-oz. can tomato sauce
¼ cup Parmesan cheese
  (grated)
½ lb. Mozzarella cheese
  (sliced)

Slice eggplant crosswise ½" thick. Dip in flour to lightly coat both sides. Melt margarine in large skillet. Brown eggplant slices over medium high heat on both sides. Place in shallow 2 quart casserole.

In same pan, cook lamb and onion, salt and pepper until the lamb is crumbly and brown. Spoon meat over eggplant, cover with tomato sauce and Parmesan cheese. Bake at 350° for 20 minutes. Remove and cover top with Mozzarella cheese and bake 10 minutes longer.

Makes 4-6 servings.

MARY MELONE

SPRING GARDEN LAMB

6 round-bone or shoulder
  lamb chops
Butter, salt and pepper
1 can condensed consomme
½ tsp. thyme
½ cup celery (chopped)
½ cup green onions (sliced)
  and tops (reserve some of
  the tops for serving)
1 3-oz. can broiled sliced
  mushrooms
3 tbsp. flour
1 tbsp. parsley flakes
1 cup sour cream

Slowly brown lamb in small amount of butter or margarine. Sprinkle with salt and pepper.

Add consomme, thyme, celery and green onions. Cover, simmer 40 minutes. Stack chops to one side.

Drain mushroom liquid slowly into flour and blend until smooth, stir into consomme and cook, stirring constantly until thick. Add mushrooms and parsley.

Top chops with sour cream; cover and heat 3 minutes. Sprinkle with chopped onion tops.

Serves 6.

EDIE BARTLETT

PARSLEYED LEG OF LAMB

7 lb. leg of lamb (all
  fat removed)
Garlic cloves
¼ tsp. each sage, savory,
  marjoram, thyme (mix
  together)
Salt
M.S.G.
Freshly ground pepper
1 cup bread crumbs
¼ lb. butter (melted)
1 bunch parsley (chopped)
6 mushrooms (sliced)
1 tsp. sherry or bourbon

Cut gashes all over lamb and insert in them thin slivers of garlic and a pinch of the seasonings. Pinch edges together to seal. Rub lamb all over with salt, pepper and M.S.G. Roast at 350°, 20 minutes per pound for rare, or 30 minutes per pound for well done.

Twenty minutes before lamb is done remove from oven, pour off and reserve the drippings. Coat the lamb with a paste made from the bread crumbs, butter and parsley. Add a little of the drippings if the mixture is too dry. Cook at 400° for 20 minutes. Make gravy from the pan drippings and the mushrooms. Add sherry or bourbon to season.

Serves 12.

MRS. JOSEPH KEMP

MOUSSAKA

1 large eggplant
½ cup olive oil
1 large onion, (chopped)
1 lb. ground lamb
2 cloves garlic, (minced)
1 8-oz. can tomato sauce
1 tsp. cinnamon
Salt and pepper to taste
4 egg yolks
2 tbsp. butter
1½ tbsp. flour
1½ cups milk
⅓ cup Greek or Parmesan
   cheese (grated)

Sprinkle salt on eggplant slices, let stand 10 minutes, blot dry. Brown in oil and drain on towels. Arrange half the eggplant in a shallow, greased baking dish.

Cook onions in oil until tender. Remove and set aside, add lamb and cook stirring until redness disappears. Drain. Add onion, garlic, tomato sauce, cinnamon, salt, pepper and 2 egg yolks. Stir and pour over eggplant. Arrange remaining eggplant over lamb.

Heat butter in small saucepan, add flour and stir constantly until brown. Add milk a little at a time, stirring until it thickens. Let cool. Add remaining egg yolks, stir and pour over meat and eggplant. Sprinkle with cheese. Bake at 350° for 45 minutes. Cut in squares to serve.

Serves 6 or 4 hearty eaters.

LEE BOTSFORD

ROAST LAMB WITH HERBS

SAUCE:
1 clove garlic (crushed)
1 tsp. salt
1 tsp. pepper
½ tsp. ginger (powdered)
1 bay leaf
½ tsp. each thyme, sage and
   marjoram
1 tbsp. soy sauce
1 tbsp. olive oil
1 5-7 lb. leg of lamb
   (trimmed)

Combine all ingredients. Make deep slits in the lamb and rub the sauce thoroughly over and into the meat.

Place meat on rack in a roasting pan and roast uncovered at 350° about 1½ hours or until thermometer registers 140° for rare-175° for well done.

PAULA TREHARNE

CROWN RACK STUFFED WITH EGGPLANT

½ cup oil
3 cloves garlic
½ cup flour
½ tsp. salt
½ tsp. pepper
1 eggplant (cubed and unpeeled)
2 tbsp. butter
3 onions (diced)
1 lb. ground pork or meat loaf mix
1 cup bread crumbs
1 tbsp. parsley (freshly chopped
1 tsp. mixed herbs
Salt and pepper
Crown rack of lamb or pork depending on number being served

Heat oil and saute 2 peeled garlic cloves. Stir flour with salt and pepper and coat eggplant. Saute eggplant in oil; remove and drain on paper towels. Discard almost all oil and add 2 tbsp. butter. Saute onion until golden and add ground pork and brown. Drain excess fat and blend meat with eggplant, crumbs, parsley, herbs and ½ tsp. salt and ¼ tsp. pepper. Let cool.

Preheat oven to 350°. Rub salt on crown. Mince remaining garlic clove and rub on meat. Rub oregano or marjoram on meat. Fill crown with stuffing. Put foil over stuffing and on ends of ribs. Roast on metal rack in open roasting pan. Roast 35 minutes per pound.

The eggplant stuffing is also good with a breast of veal or turkey.

CARLEEN M. KEMMERLING

SPICY LAMB SHANKS

4 lamb shanks
1 tsp. dill weed
1 large onion (sliced thinly)
½ tsp. oregano
1 tsp. rosemary
1 large can tomato sauce
1 large clove garlic
½ cup brown sugar
1 cup white wine

Brown shanks. Put all ingredients in an oven roaster. Cover and cook for 3 hours in 300° oven. Uncover and continue cooking 30 minutes.

Serves 4.

MRS. SPENCER LAWSON

LAMB RAGOUT

2 lbs. lamb stew meat
2 tbsp. fat
2 tbsp. flour
1 clove garlic (minced)
2 tbsp. tomato paste
Salt and pepper
6 sprigs parsley
½ tsp. thyme
1 bay leaf
20 tiny onions, (peeled)
2 turnips, (chopped in large chunks)
3 carrots (chopped in large chunks)
3 tbsp. butter
1 tbsp. sugar
6-8 small new potatoes

Use a heavy metal 5 or 6 qt. casserole. Sear meat in fat and brown thoroughly. Sprinkle with flour and continue browning. Add garlic. Then add enough water to cover meat. Add tomato paste, salt and pepper and herbs tied in bouquet garni. Cover and cook gently on top of stove for 45 minutes.

Meanwhile peel onions. Scrape carrots and turnips and cut in good size pieces. Saute in butter until they begin to brown. Sprinkle with sugar and continue browning stirring all the while until they are very brown and carmelized. This gives the ragout color and flavor. Add vegetables and whatever butter remains in pan to lamb and cook 45 minutes longer.

Peel potatoes and cook them with ragout until tender. This will take 20-30 minutes. Skim off fat and taste for seasoning. May be prepared a day ahead.

Serves 6-8.

MRS. FRANCES ARMSTRONG

SWEET AND SOUR LAMB SHANKS

4 lamb shanks
½ cup red wine
½ cup yellow mustard
½ cup currant jelly
Salt and pepper
Bay leaf

Place lamb shanks in oven pot. Pour wine over them.

Mix together mustard and jelly. Spread over shanks. Add salt, pepper and bay leaf. Cover with lid or foil.

Bake 1½ hours at 325°. Uncover last 20 minutes if needs browning.

Serves 4.

JANIE WILEY

GREEK STYLE LAMB SHANKS

4 lamb shanks, ¾-
  1 lb. each
Salt and pepper
1 large onion (thinly sliced)
1 medium sized green pepper
  (seeded and cut in strips)
1 8-oz. can tomato sauce
1 clove garlic (minced
  or pressed)
⅓ cup dry white wine or
  regular strength chicken
  broth
½ tsp. each salt and oregano
  leaves
¼ tsp. each sugar, ground
  cinnamon, and dry
  rosemary
1 tsp. lemon peel (grated)
1 tsp. parsley (chopped)
1 tsp. or more Feta cheese
  (crumbled) (optional)

Sprinkle lamb shanks lightly with salt and pepper and arrange in a 4-5 quart casserole or Dutch oven. Scatter onion and green pepper over top.

Stir together the tomato sauce, garlic, wine, salt, oregano, sugar, cinnamon, and rosemary; pour over meat.

Cover and bake in a 350° oven for 2½-3 hours or until lamb is very tender when pierced.

Remove meat to a warm serving platter; keep warm. Skim fat from cooking liquid then pour liquid over lamb.

Garnish with lemon peel, parsley and cheese.

Serves 4.

MRS. CHARLES K. MAIR

LAMB RIBLETS

3-4 lbs. of lamb ribs
  (Marinate for 1 hour or
  more at room temperature
  in any oil and vinegar
  type of salad dressing
  or in this ginger and
  lime marinade)

MARINADE:
½ cup olive oil
½ tsp. salt
4 tbsp. lime juice
1 tbsp. grated lime rind
1 tbsp. fresh ginger
  (grated) or ½ tsp.
  powdered ginger

Combine all ingredients. Pour marinade over ribs, turn to coat evenly, then turn again after half hour or so.

Heat oven to 375°, drain ribs of marinade and place on rack in roasting pan with a little (1-2 cups) water in pan below. Sprinkle ribs with ½ tsp. garlic powder, ¼ tsp. fresh ground pepper, ½ cup parsley (chopped). Bake for 45 minutes OR transfer after 30 minutes to barbecue grill to finish OR add 4 medium potatoes (quartered), 8 small white onions (parboiled) and 1 (1 lb. 12 oz.) can tomatoes and bake covered another 45 minutes.

Serves 6.

JACKIE HALLAIAN

KERN COUNTY CASSOULET

Jack is fond of casseroles, preferring them to huge slabs of meat that need to be carved. (!) This is a recipe from the collection of my sister-in-law in Bakersfield where I spent my childhood and where the Basque influence is strong.

6 small lamb shanks
2 carrots (peeled and diced)
4 stalks of celery (diced)
1 medium onion (chopped)
2 bay leaves
2 ounces of garlic sausage (sliced)
2 cups navy beans
6 cups chicken broth
1 tbsp. salt
1 tsp. white pepper
1 tsp. garlic salt
½ cup flour

Soak navy beans in water overnight. Trim excess fat from shanks and brown on all sides in broiler of oven. Place in Dutch oven and add all ingredients except flour. Cover and bring to a boil, then turn to low heat and simmer for 1½ to 2 hours. Make a thin paste of the flour with water and stir into shank mixture, mixing well. Cook, stirring constantly, until slightly thickened.

Serves 6 generously.

★ DENISE SMITH, (MRS. JACK SMITH)
JACK SMITH: Author, columnist, humorist, savant. Writes daily JACK SMITH column for national syndication; books include GOD AND MR. GOMEZ and SPEND ALL YOUR KISSES.

ROAST LAMB WITH CURRANT SAUCE

1 6-lb. leg of lamb
1 tbsp. gin
2 tsp. salt
½ tsp. prepared mustard
¼ tsp. white pepper

CURRANT SAUCE:
Pan juices
½ cup currant jelly
1¼ cups water
¼ tsp. salt
¼ cup gin
2 tbsp. flour

Wipe lamb well and place on a rack in a shallow roasting pan fat side up. Blend gin, salt, mustard and pepper to make a paste. Spread over lamb. Roast in a preheated 350° oven for approximately 3 hours or desired time. Serve with currant sauce.

To make sauce: Remove excess fat from drippings. To drippings add currant jelly, add 1 cup water, heating until jelly is melted. Add salt and gin and stir to blend. Blend flour with the remaining ¼ cup water and stir into sauce. Cook, stirring constantly, until mixture thickens and boils. Remove from heat and serve with lamb.

Serves 8.

INGRID POLLAKOFF

LAMB SHISKABOBS

2 lbs. lamb (trimmed and
    cut in 1" cubes)
Mushroom caps
Onions (quartered)
Cherry tomatoes
Green pepper squares

MARINADE:

½ cup lemon juice
2 tbsp. olive oil
2 tbsp. crushed oregano
1 tsp. salt
1 tsp. fresh ground pepper

Marinate lamb chunks 6-8 hours or overnight. Skewer alternately with mushrooms, onions, tomatoes, and green pepper. Broil or charcoal until green pepper is tender.

Marinade is great for lamb chops, also.

Serves 6.

LINDA SMALDINO

FRENCH LAMB STEW

3 tbsp. olive or salad oil
2 lbs. lean stewing lamb
    (cut into 1" cubes)
1 medium onion (peeled
    and chopped)
1 clove garlic (peeled
    and chopped)
2 tbsp. flour
1 cup chicken broth
1½ tsp. salt
⅛ tsp. pepper
1 bay leaf (crumbled)
¼ tsp. marjoram
2 tbsp. lemon juice (or ½
    cup dry white wine)
1 8-oz. can tomato sauce
2 cans baby onions
3 carrots (scraped and sliced)
1 tbsp. parsley (finely
    chopped)

Heat oil in heavy 4-quart kettle. Trim the fat from the lamb. Brown lamb on all sides over high heat. Remove and reserve. Pour off most of the remaining oil, leaving about 1 tbsp. Saute onion and garlic until golden.

Return meat. Sprinkle flour over meat. Add chicken broth, salt, pepper, bay leaf, marjoram and lemon juice (or white wine). Mix well. Add tomato sauce. Cover and simmer over low heat for ½ hour. Skim off fat. Add onions and continue simmering for 15 minutes. Add vegetables, cook until tender.

Serves 6.

JAN MOORE

NATURAL LAMB STEW

3 cups chicken broth
3 lbs. lamb (cubed)
2 large baking potatoes
  (peeled and shredded)
3 large onions (quartered)
1 tsp. parsley
1 tsp. thyme
1 tsp. onion salt
½ tsp. ground black pepper
1 bay leaf
4 "white rose" potatoes
  (peeled and quartered)
1 bunch carrots (peeled and
  cut in chunks)
8 turnips (quartered)
Fresh parsley
½ cup sherry

Poach meat in broth for 15 minutes, stirring occasionally. Strain off broth, cool and skim off fat. Add shredded potatoes, onions and seasonings to meat. Cover with broth and simmer about 2 hours, stirring regularly to keep stew from sticking to bottom of pot. Remove bay leaf, add quartered potatoes, turnips and carrots cut into chunks. Simmer about 1 hour, covered, until vegetables are tender. About ½ hour before completion, add a few sprigs of parsley and the sherry.

Serves 8.

MRS. ALLEN K. WOOD

PORK CHOP A LA DIXIE

4 pork chops
2 tbsp. salt
Brown sugar
2 tbsp. flour
1-1½ cups hot water
1 tsp. vinegar
1 small box raisins
1 apple (peel, core and slice)
Drippings from chops

Brown pork chops sprinkled with salt. Sprinkle brown sugar over pork chops.

With drippings mix flour, hot water and add vinegar. Boil until thick. Sprinkle raisins over chops, core apple, slice in apple rings, put in between pork chops as you layer. Put in oven at 375° for 30 minutes or 350° for 45 minutes. Serve with rice and corn muffins.

Serves 4.

DR. SHERRIE ATKINSON

HUNGARIAN GOULASH

3 strips of bacon (chopped)
1 tbsp. butter
2 medium onions (chopped)
2 tbsp. paprika (preferably
  Hungarian)
2 lbs. lean pork
1½ cans consomme
2 lbs. sauerkraut (rinsed
  and drained)
2 tbsp. tomato paste
½ tsp. caraway seeds
Salt and pepper
Sour cream

In heavy 4 quart Dutch oven heat bacon and butter, When bacon browns remove and reserve. Add onion and cook until golden. Lower heat, add paprika stirring constantly. Add pork and broth. Cover and simmer 1 hour. Add sauerkraut, bacon, tomato paste and caraway seeds. Cover and bake at 300°. Add salt and pepper. Serve with dollops of sour cream. Freezes beautifully.

Serves 8.

MRS. JOHN ALCANTARA

PORK RAGOUT

2 lbs. lean boneless pork
  shoulder
3 tbsp. butter or oil
3 tbsp. flour
2 garlic cloves, mashed
½ cup parsley, chopped
Salt and pepper to taste
2 cups water
1 cup red wine
1 lb. small white onions
4 carrots, sliced
1 cup black olives
4 small potatoes, sliced

Cube pork and brown in a heavy skillet or Dutch oven. Sprinkle flour over the meat and cook until flour has browned. Add parsley and garlic. Season with salt and pepper; add liquids. Cover and bring to the boiling point. Simmer 1½ hours. Add vegetables and cook ½ hour more or until vegetables are tender. Adjust seasonings and if necessary thicken gravy.

Serves 6.

JEAN MALONEY

CANTONESE ROAST PORK

4-6 lbs. lean loin of pork
   (usually 2 loin roasts)
   or 4 or 5 pork tenderloins

SAUCE:

2 tbsp. bourbon whiskey,
   cognac or rum
1 cup light soy sauce*
1 cup sugar
2 tsp. five spices powder
   (commercially prepared or
   homemade)*
3 tbsp. hoisin sauce*
4 tbsp. red bean curd sauce*
2 tbsp. bean sauce*
1 tbsp. sesame paste*
4 tbsp. or more dark soy
   sauce*
1½ cups white or dark corn
   syrup or honey

*Available in Chinese markets
   and by mail order.

Combine ingredients and spread all over meat pieces, work into meat a little. Baste occasionally during roasting. Roast at 350° uncovered until meat thermometer reaches 160°-175°, depending on individual preference.

PAULA TREHARNE

OVEN BARBEQUED PORK

1½ tsp. salt
1½ tbsp. sugar
2 cloves garlic (minced
   or mashed)
5 tbsp. soy sauce
3 tbsp. apple sauce
2 tbsp. sherry
2 lb. loin of pork (boned,
   butterflied and laid flat)

Combine salt, sugar, garlic, soy sauce, applesauce and sherry. Marinate meat in mixture for 2 to 3 hours. Place meat in roasting pan; pour in half of the marinade. Roast in a moderately hot oven (375°) for 1 hour or until tender. Baste occasionally with remaining marinade.

Serves 6-8.

MRS. BYRON FOREMAN

TWELFTH-NIGHT CROWN ROAST OF PORK

Allow 2 ribs per person
Crown roast of pork

FRUITED DRESSING

1 small box raisins
1 small box currants
   (2 cups or more)
3 tbsp. salad oil
¼ cup onion (finely
   chopped)
⅓ cup carrots (chopped)
1 cup celery (chopped)
2 tbsp. parsley (chopped)
1 cup boiled rice (or more
   to taste)
2 tsp. salt
1 tsp. pepper
1 tsp. paprika
¼ tsp. cloves
1 cup crushed pineapple
   (drained)
1 cup shelled pistachio nuts
2 cups dry bread crumbs
Grand Marnier Liqueur

CURRANT JELLY SAUCE

Currant jelly
Prepared mustard (or dry
   Coleman's mustard to
   taste)

Wipe roast with cloth; protect ends of bones by covering with foil. Bake in moderate oven 350°; allow 30-45 minutes to pound. Remove the roast before the last hour of cooking.

Fill the center with fruited dressing. Return to oven and complete the last hour of cooking. Season with salt and freshly ground pepper.

Remove foil covering from bones; garnish trim with paper frills, slice of pickle or a stuffed olive. Serve with currant jelly sauce.

Small whole par-boiled potatoes may be added to the pan for the last ½ hour or so of roasting. If there are insufficient drippings in pan, add a little fat. Because this is a rich and elegant entree, fresh green asparagus, cooked slightly crisp, makes a perfect accompaniment.

FRUITED DRESSING

Marinate raisins and currants in 4/5 quart Grand Marnier liqueur. Heat salad oil; brown onion in it lightly. Add and cook for 1 minute carrot, celery, chopped parsley, rice, salt, pepper, paprika and cloves. Add and mix well crushed pineapple, shelled pistachio nuts, marinated raisins and currants (strained of liqueur), and dry bread crumbs.

CURRANT JELLY SAUCE

Dissolve equal parts of currant jelly and prepared mustard over low heat.

★ JACK AND WALLACE ALBERTSON
JACK ALBERTSON: Actor, dancer, raconteur. Many theatre roles include THE SUBJECT WAS ROSES on Broadway (Tony Award 1965); film roles include film of the play, DAYS OF WINE AND ROSES and POSEIDON ADVENTURE; star of CHICO AND THE MAN and GRANDPA GOES TO WASHINGTON TV series.

SPICY PORK ROAST

4 to 5 lb. pork loin roast
1 tsp. salt
½ cup currant jelly
¼ cup honey
1 tbsp. lemon juice
1 tsp. prepared mustard
½ tsp. allspice
Red food coloring (optional)

Rub roast with salt. Place roast, fat side up, on rack in shallow, uncovered baking pan. Roast at 325° until fork tender (2¾ to 3 hours or until roast reaches an internal temperature of 170°).

Meanwhile, combine jelly, honey, lemon juice, mustard and allspice in a saucepan. Heat and stir until jelly is melted. Boil one minute. Add food coloring as needed to tint glaze an attractive red color.

Brush glaze over roast several times during last 30 minutes of roasting. Save remaining glaze to serve with roast.

Serves 6 to 8.

INGRID HEDBERG

SWEET AND SOUR SPARERIBS

3 lbs. (2 strips) lean spareribs
½ cup onion (finely diced)
¼ cup green pepper (diced)
2 small cans tomato sauce
1 tbsp. Worcestershire sauce
⅓ cup cider or wine vinegar
¼ cup brown sugar
½ tsp. dry mustard
1 #2 can pineapple tidbits and syrup

After every third rib, cut halfway down. Sprinkle with salt and pepper. Place in shallow roasting pan. Bake in 350° oven for 1¼ hours. Carefully drain off excess fat. While ribs are roasting, blend all other ingredients, let stand to blend flavors. Pour over ribs after 1¼ hours and bake 45 minutes longer. Serve with rice.

You can use the same sauce for chicken, bake for 30 minutes, add sauce and bake for another 25-30 minutes.

Serves 4 generously.

KATA WARREN

LAZY HELEN'S SWEET-SOUR RIBS

4 cloves garlic (minced or mashed)

⅓ cup honey

¼ cup soy sauce

½ cup catsup

1 can (about 14-oz.) regular beef broth

1 strip of pork rib or 4 lbs. beef short ribs (You'll need 2 ribs for each person)

4 tsp. cornstarch

4 tsp. water

In small saucepan mix the garlic, honey, soy sauce, catsup and broth. Bring to a boil and set aside.

Cut the ribs apart and arrange in a single layer in a large close-fitting baking dish. Pour on sauce; cover and marinate several hours or overnight in refrigerator. Turn occasionally.

Bake covered in a 350° oven for 1½ hours. Uncover and bake 30 to 60 minutes longer, until tender. Baste occasionally.

When the ribs are done lift from the sauce and set aside in a warm place. Skim fat from pan juices; bring juices to a rapid boil. Boil until reduced to about 1½ cups liquid. Blend cornstarch and water; stir into juices and cook, stirring, until mixture bubbles, turns clear and thickens slightly. Serve with ribs.

VARIATION: To barbeque, bake ribs for 45 minutes, drain off fat. Pour sauce over ribs, cover and marinate as above. Barbeque and baste-- hmm! good!

Serves 6.

MRS. ROBERT K. OSTENGAARD

The table is the only place
where a man is never bored
the first hour.
JEAN ANTHELME BRILLAT-SAVARIN

LEA'S SPICY PORK

This is my variation of a great Chinese dish, a particular favorite of our daughter, Linda, who intends to be a gourmet Chinese cook.

1 lb. very lean pork cut
  in small thin strips
1 tbsp. cornstarch
3 tbsp. soy sauce
1 tsp. oyster sauce
1 tsp. plum sauce
1 tsp. duck sauce
1 tsp. Hoisin sauce
1 tsp. red cooking wine
Dash salt and pepper
1 tsp. sugar
2 fresh red peppers (crushed)
1 cup vegetable oil
½ cup green onions
  (chopped)
¼ cup or more fresh
  mushrooms
4 tbsp. water
1 tbsp. ketchup
1 pkg. Chinese rice noodles
  or rice

Marinate meat in a mixture of 1½ tsp. cornstarch, 1 tbsp. soy sauce, ½ tsp. oyster sauce, 1 tsp. each plum, duck and Hoisin sauce, wine, salt and pepper, ½ tsp. sugar, ½ of the crushed peppers. (Marinate 1 hour, mixing periodically).

Bring oil to 400° in wok. Quickly fry onions and mushrooms. Remove. Then quick-fry meat (few pieces at a time).

Prepare a thickening sauce with 4 tbsp. water and remaining 1½ tsp. cornstarch, ½ tsp. oyster sauce, ½ tsp. sugar, and crushed red pepper, 2 tbsp. soy sauce and 1 tbsp. ketchup. Pour into wok with any remaining marinating sauce, stirring until smooth and thick. Add pork, onions and mushrooms. Stir and remove from heat.

Serve over rice noodles or in the middle of a bed of steamed rice.

Serves 4-6.

★ MRS. GREG MORRIS (LEA)
GREG MORRIS: Actor.
TV roles include co-star MISSION IMPOSSIBLE and VEGAS TV series.

*The pleasure of eating
is the only one which,
indulged in moderately,
is not followed by regret.*
        JEAN ANTHELME BRILLAT-SAVARIN

IRISH PORK TENDERLOIN

2 pork tenders
  (approximately 1½ lbs.
  each)
½ lb. finely chopped onion
1 bunch parsley (finely
  chopped)
Salt and pepper to taste
1 lb. fresh white breadcrumbs
8 tbsp. butter
1 tsp. EACH fresh chopped
  thyme and sage

Pork tenderloin is one of the most traditional cuts of meat in Ireland, which does not exist in English butchery. It is the filet of the pig and is absolutely lean and delicious.

Before stuffing they must be prepared as follows: the steaks are split along the length down the center, but not through. The two flaps are pulled gently so that the gap widens out. Then with a sharp knife it is scored down the length without cutting through the meat so when you finish it is a flattish rectangular shape. They are now ready for stuffing.

Mix the breadcrumbs with the onion, butter, parsley, salt and pepper and the herbs. Stuff the steaks, rub lightly with butter fitting one tenderloin over the other and then cover with foil to seal. Roast at 350° for about an hour. Potatoes may be roasted in the same pan. Serve with apple sauce.

Serves 6.

GERRI GILLILAND
Home Economist, Cooking Instructor

*Pray for peace and grace
and spiritual food,
For wisdom and guidance,
for all these are good,
But don't forget the potatoes.*

J. T. PETERS

HAM LOAF

1 lb. ham, ½ lb. beef,
 ½ lb. pork (ground
 together)
⅔ cup cracker crumbs
2 eggs
1 cup tomato sauce
½ cup milk
Dash of pepper

Mix all ingredients together and pack lightly in greased loaf pan. Pour small amount of hot water over top of loaf.

Bake 2 hours at 325°.

VARIATION: Serve with a sweet sour sauce.

Serves 6 to 8.

MRS. ROBERT L. HEMMINGS

UPSIDE-DOWN HAM LOAF

2 cups ham (ground
 and cooked)
1½ lb. fresh pork
 (ground)
2 eggs (slightly beaten)
1 cup cracker crumbs
1 cup milk
⅛ tsp. pepper
½ tsp. salt
¼ cup sugar
¾ cup brown sugar
1 tsp. dry mustard
½ tsp. vinegar
6 slices pineapple
10 maraschino cherries

Mix together ham, pork, eggs, crumbs, milk, pepper and salt.

Grease 2 5"x10"x3" loaf pans. Mix sugar, brown sugar, mustard and vinegar and pour over the bottoms of pans. On this base, press pineapple slices and cherries.

Spread meat mixture over the pineapple and pack into place.

Bake at 375° for 1½ hours. Drain fat off if necessary. Turn out on platter.

Serves 6.

GRACE H. McKNIGHT

*Promises and pie-crust
are made to be broken.*

JONATHAN SWIFT

HAM-SWISS CHEESE BAKE

SAUCE:

¼ cup butter
¼ cup flour
1 tsp. salt
1½ tsp. sugar
1 tsp. onion (grated)
2 cups sour cream
4 cups green beans (cooked)
½ lb. Swiss cheese (grated)
2 cups ham (cubed)
1 cup corn flakes
  (crushed)

Stir flour into melted butter, add salt, sugar, onion, sour cream and mix. In 3-qt. baking dish (9"x13") alternate layers of beans, cheese, ham and sauce in order given. Sprinkle corn flakes on top. Bake at 350° for 30 minutes.

VARIATION: Green peas and chicken may be used instead of the green beans and ham. One jar of chopped pimiento and 1 small can of drained sliced mushrooms may be added to the sauce. Optional: a dash of sherry wine, to flavor the sauce.

Serves 8.

MRS. ROBERT E. MITCHEL

HAM AND CHEESE FONDUE

3 cups French bread
  (cubed)
3 cups cooked ham (cubed)
½ lb. sharp cheddar
  cheese
4 eggs (separated)
3 tbsp. flour
1 tbsp. dry mustard
3 tbsp. butter (melted)
3 cups milk

Using buttered 10"x12" pan, make a layer of ham, bread and cheese mixture.

Mix flour and mustard; sprinkle over ham mix layer. Using half of the butter, drizzle over layer top; repeat for next half. Beat eggs separately and fold together; add milk and red pepper seasoning. Pour over mixture; cover; chill overnight.

Bake next day uncovered for one hour in 350° oven.

Serves 8.

FAY P. PETTIGREW

JUSTIN'S JAMBALAYA

3 mild Italian sausages
½ cup onions (chopped)
½ cup green pepper
  (chopped)
1 clove garlic (finely
  chopped)
½ lb. ham (diced)
½ lb. raw medium shrimp
  (shelled)
1 1-lb. 12-oz. can tomatoes
1 tsp. salt
½ tsp. Tabasco sauce
1½ cups cooked rice

Cut sausages into bite-size pieces and cook over low heat for 10 minutes. Add onions, green peppers and garlic and saute until lightly browned. Add ham and shrimp. Cook until ham is lightly browned and shrimp is pink. Cut tomatoes into fourths and add with salt and Tabasco sauce to mixture.

Cover and simmer for 5 minutes. Stir well, add rice and continue to simmer 5 minutes longer.

Serves 6.

MRS. R. JUSTIN DEDEAUX

HAM BALLS POLYNESIAN

2½ lbs. ham (ground)
1 lb. veal (ground)
½ lb. pork (ground)
½ cup onions or chives
  (chopped)
2 cups crackers (crumbled)
1 cup milk
4 eggs (well beaten)

POLYNESIAN SAUCE:

2 cans crushed pineapple
⅔ cup catsup
⅔ cup vinegar
¼ cup soy sauce
1 tbsp. ginger (ground)
¼ tsp. pepper
1 cup brown sugar

POPPYSEED NOODLES:

1 tbsp. poppyseed
2 8-oz. pkgs. noodles
Butter or margarine

Thoroughly mix the meats, then add the minced onion, cracker crumbs, milk and eggs. Mold into balls the size of an egg. Place close together in the bottom of a shallow casserole. Add Polynesian sauce. Bake, covered in a 325° oven for 1 hour. Uncover the last 15 minutes. Serve with poppyseed noodles.

POLYNESIAN SAUCE:

Mix everything together until well blended. It is better if it can stand for hour or two.

POPPYSEED NOODLES:

Boil noodles, following directions on package. Toss with enough melted butter, or margarine, to flavor well. Toss in poppyseeds.

Serves 12 or more.

MACKIE NASH

HAM ROLL-UPS

4 ham slices, ⅛" thick
  (cooked and warm)
¾ cup white rice (cooked)
2 eggs (beaten)
1 onion (minced and sauteed)
½ tsp. curry powder
½ tsp. salt
2 cans whole cranberry
  sauce
2 tbsp. brown sugar
2 tbsp. lemon juice
2 bananas (diced)
½ cup nuts (chopped)

Mix rice, eggs, onion, curry and salt for stuffing. Fill warm ham, roll up and fasten with toothpicks. Keep warm in 200° oven.

Mix cranberry sauce and brown sugar in pan and simmer. Pour lemon juice over bananas and add to sauce. Add nuts and heat. Serve ham with sauce.

NOTE: This entree is excellent served with broccoli, topped with a mayonnaise/mustard sauce. Add mustard to mayonnaise and serve over broccoli.

Serves 4

MRS. THOMAS V. BERNE

BURGUNDY-ORANGE HAM

1 10-15 lb. ham
Whole cloves
½ cup brown sugar
1 6-oz. can frozen orange
  juice (undiluted)
1 cup Burgundy
½ tsp. cinnamon
½ tsp. dry mustard

Bake ham according to package instructions. One hour before end of cooking time, remove ham. Drain excess fat; remove rind and score fat in diamond pattern. Center each square with clove.

Combine brown sugar, orange juice, Burgundy, cinnamon and mustard in saucepan. Simmer, stirring 5 minutes. Pour over ham and return to oven. Baste every 15 minutes until ham is done. Serve remaining sauce in gravy boat.

Serves 20.

MRS. JOHN ALCANTARA

GOLDEN GLAZED HAM WITH CHERRY SAUCE

1 5-lb. canned ham (or larger), or cooked boneless ham
1 10-oz. jar apple jelly or guava jelly
1 tbsp. prepared mustard
⅓ cup unsweetened pineapple juice
2 tbsp. dry white wine
1 1-lb. 5-oz. can cherry pie filling
½ cup light raisins

Place ham fat side up on rack in shallow pan. Heat as directed on can or at 325° for 1½ hours for a 5-lb. ham. Half an hour before end of heating time, remove ham from oven and score.

In medium saucepan combine jelly and mustard; stir in pineapple juice and wine. Cook and stir to boiling, simmer 2-3 minutes. Pour ⅓ of glaze over ham and return to oven. Spoon on remaining glaze at two 10 minute intervals.

In saucepan heat cherry pie filling and raisins to boiling, stirring occasionally. Remove ham to platter. Add glaze from baking pan to cherry sauce. Bring again to boiling. Spoon some over ham on platter; pass remainder in gravy boat. Makes 3 cups of sauce.

NOTE: This ham really looks beautiful at holiday time.

MARILYN SMITH

We can learn to be cooks,
but we must be born
knowing how to roast.
        JEAN ANTHELME BRILLAT-SAVARIN

DESSERTS

They dined on mince, and slices of quince
Which they ate with a runcible spoon;
And hand in hand, on the edge of the sand,
They danced by the light of the moon.

APPLE POPPINS

9 red or green apples
¼ cup water
½ tsp. cinnamon
½ tsp. nutmeg
3 tbsp. honey
1 gigantic tbsp. peanut
 butter
¼ cup walnuts (chopped)
1 cup All-Bran
Brandy to taste
Whipping cream (optional)

Slice tops off of 5 of the apples, try to keep the stems in, if possible, and put aside. Spoon out core and enough apple so that approx. ¼" of fruit is left with skin. Place apples and tops in baking dish. Add ¼ cup water to dish.

In a blender add 4 cut-up apples, skin and all, with cinnamon, nutmeg, honey, peanut butter and chopped walnuts. Blend. Remove ½ of the mixture to a sauce pan and set aside. To the remaining ½ add approximately 1 cup of All-Bran or enough to make a very thick mixture. Fill the apples with mixture very full. Put the filled apples with their tops back in the baking dish with ¼ cup of water. Cover with foil leaving the apples clear from touching the cover. Bake at 400° for 45 minutes to 1 hour.

Just before serving add brandy to taste to the ½ mixture you have put in sauce pan to heat. Carefully remove tops, pour sauce over apples, and then place the tops on. Of course, you could set the apples in a puddle of whipping cream.

Makes 5 servings.

★ JULIE ANDREWS
Actress, author, recording artist, singer.
Many roles in theatre musicals include co-star MY FAIR LADY on Broadway; films include star SOUND OF MUSIC and MARY POPPINS (Academy Award 1964); TV appearances include JULIE Special (Sylvania Award); several children's books.

BLUEBERRY NOVA SCOTIA

10 slices Pepperidge Farm
   thin sliced bread
1 cube butter
¾ cup granulated sugar
½ pt. whipping cream
Powdered sugar
Cinnamon
1 pt. blueberries or 1 pt.
   fresh peaches, (cut up)

Cut crusts off bread slices and cut into ¼" cubes. Melt butter and saute bread until golden and crisp.

Add granulated sugar and cook another minute.

Whip cream and season with powdered sugar and cinnamon to taste.

When ready to serve, add fruit to bread mixture and heat slightly so that fruit and bread are warm but not cooked.

Top generously with flavored whipped cream.

Serves 4 to 6.

MRS. ARTHUR ARMSTRONG

GRAPE BRULEE

2 lbs. white seedless grapes
1½ pts. sour cream
3 tbsp. cognac
Dark brown sugar

Pick over, wash and dry grapes. Fold into sour cream. Add the Cognac and lightly fold again. Put mixture into an 8" souffle or quiche dish. Smooth top with spatula and chill about three hours.

Just before serving, cover top of dish smoothly with about ½" of brown sugar. Place under broiler until sugar turns a nice brown. Let sit a few minutes before serving.

When serving, crack the carmelized top with a spoon and serve each person with pieces of glazed top; dig deep for the grapes and sour cream.

Serves 4 to 6.

MRS. FRANK L. WOLFSON

PEACHES SOUTH AFRICA

Peaches (fresh, sliced)
Lime juice
2 cups sour cream
¼ cup candied ginger
2-3 tbsp. brandy

Slice fresh peeled peaches and sprinkle with lime juice and sugar. Serve with 2 cups of sour cream mixed with ¼ cup chopped candied ginger and 2-3 tbsp. of brandy.

Serves 8.

MRS. PETER BERRINGTON

BAKED PINEAPPLE NATILLAS

1 large pineapple
¼ cup sugar
2 or 3 tbsp. rum or 1 tsp.
    rum flavoring
¼ cup butter

NATILLAS SAUCE:
1 pint half and half
¼ tsp. salt
¼ cup sugar
1 egg + 2 egg yolks
1 tsp. cornstarch
1 tsp. vanilla

Lay pineapple on its side and take off a thick slice that does not include the green top. Carefully scoop out the inside and cut into bite-sized pieces. Sweeten to taste. Flavor with rum. Put pineapple pieces back into pineapple shell. Dot the top with butter, cover with foil (including the leaves), and bake in a 350° oven for 20 minutes. Replace the top and bring to table on a warm plate. Top with Natillas Sauce.

Scald 1 pint half and half. Cool slightly. Add ¼ tsp. salt, ¼ cup sugar beaten with one egg and 2 egg yolks, 1 tsp. cornstarch and 1 tsp. vanilla. Cook over hot water, stirring constantly, until smooth and slightly thickened. Chill.

Serves 8.

GLENDA GRIBBEN

BRANDIED FRUITS

1 5-oz. can peaches (sliced)
1 5-oz. can cherries (red)
1 5-oz. can pineapple pieces
½ cup sultanas
½ cup raisins
½ cup prunes (stoned)
¾ cup sugar
¾ cup brandy
½ cup almonds (blanched)

Drain fruits in colander over saucepan, add dried fruits and sugar to liquid. Cook, stirring until syrup is fairly thick. Cool slightly, add brandy.

Arrange fruits in large screw top jar and pour syrup over. Keep in refrigerator for at least a month before serving with cream or ice cream.

MARY E. A. MOORE

Toorak, Victoria, Australia

COSTA DE ORO

1 cup fresh raspberries
1 cup sliced peaches
2 oz. Kirsch
3 oz. Triple Sec

Mix all ingredients together. Heat until the raspberries begin to lose their juice giving the liquors a light purple color. Now flame and serve a perfect ending to a lovely dinner.

★ MARY COSTA
Actress, recording artist, singer.
International concert artist, star of Metropolitan Opera, well-known for LA TRAVIATA role; many films; scholarship at University of Tennessee given by Magnavox in her name.

MOCHA TOFFEE DESSERT

8 to 12 ladyfingers, (split)
2 tbsp. instant coffee crystals
1 tbsp. boiling water
1 qt. vanilla ice cream, (softened)
⅓ lb. English Toffee, (crushed)
½ cup whipping cream
2 tbsp. white Creme de Cacao
Unsweetened chocolate curls

Line bottom and sides (2 inches up sides) of an 8" springform pan with the split ladyfingers.

Dissolve the coffee in the 1 tbsp. boiling water. Cool. Stir together coffee, ice cream and crushed candy. Spoon into springform pan; cover and freeze until firm.

Combine cream and Creme de Cacao; whip until soft peaks form. Spread over top of frozen ice cream. Garnish with unsweetened chocolate curls. It's a winner and easy too!

Serves 8.

EILEEN McCONNELL

OLD FASHIONED HOMEMADE ICE CREAM

Chancellor Young's Favorite Dessert

Regular milk
4 eggs (beaten)
1 qt. half and half
3 cans Eagle Brand sweetened condensed milk
4 tbsp. vanilla
Pinch salt

Pour regular milk into Old Fashioned ice cream freezer to ½ full line. Combine other ingredients into large mixing bowl. Pour this mixture into freezer and add milk necessary to bring up freezer to fill line. Put freezer lid in place and crank until firm. Follow directions for ice cream freezer regarding ice and salt.

★ MRS. CHARLES E. YOUNG (SUE)
CHARLES E. YOUNG: Administrator
Chancellor, University of California, Los Angeles; a Junior Chamber of Commerce Young Man of the Year 1962; Doctor of Humane Letters University of Judaism, Honorary Degree.

SIMPLE SIMON

2 cans sweetened condensed
  Bordens milk

Put in a large pot 2 cans of unopened milk. Cover cans with water and cover the pot. Boil gently two hours. Add water occasionally if necessary to keep cans covered. Remove and cool unopened cans. Open, whip and pour into champagne or wine glasses.

Serves 6.

PAT FISCHER

CREPES SUZETTE

CREPES:

1 cup milk
1 cup water
1½ cups flour (sifted)
4 eggs
½ tsp. salt
4 tbsp. butter

SUZETTE SAUCE:

4 lumps sugar
White part of orange rind
Thin orange part of rind
5 tbsp. sweet butter
Juice of 1 orange
Lemon juice
1 cup Grand Marnier

CREPES:

Blend all ingredients for crepes at least 2 hours before using. Makes 25 crepes.

SUZETTE SAUCE:

Rub lumps of sugar with white part of orange rind. Finely mince about an inch of thin orange part of rind. Crush 3 tbsp. of butter with above.

In chafing dish put 2 tbsp. butter, orange juice, few drops of lemon juice and Grand Marnier. When boiling, stir in other mixture.

Put in crepes. Fold. Add ½ cup hot Grand Marnier. Put a lighted match to the sauce; permit it to flame and serve crepes at once.

Sauce serves 4.

JANIE WILEY

CREPE TIVOLI

4 crepes
2 cups Creme Patissiere
2 tbsp. Curaçao
½ cup walnuts (finely
   chopped)
Kirsch
Small fresh strawberries
Melba Sauce

SAUCE

1½ cups milk
1 vanilla bean
½ cup sugar
4 egg yolks
¼ cup flour

SAUCE

¾ cup fresh strawberries
¾ cup fresh raspberries
Finely granulated sugar
   to taste
Kirsch to taste

Lay crepes flat. Flavor the pastry cream with the Curaçao. Add the nuts to flavored pastry cream and place a large dollop on each of the crepes. Fold crepes over filling. Warm some Kirsch and flame over crepes. Serve the crepes surrounded by tiny fresh strawberries and Melba Sauce.

CREME PATISSIERE

Scald milk with vanilla bean added. (If you use vanilla extract, add after cream is cooked.)

In a separate saucepan beat sugar and egg yolks with a wire whisk until mixture is thick and creamy and forms a ribbon when the whisk is removed. Sift flour into mixture and lightly blend. Stir in scalded milk very gradually until batter is smooth.

Cook mixture over low heat, stirring constantly with a whisk until it reaches a boil. Remove vanilla bean and strain through a fine sieve. Stir as the cream cools and add vanilla extract if you did not use the vanilla bean.

MELBA SAUCE

Force strawberries and raspberries through a very fine sieve. Add sugar and Kirsch to taste. Chill.

★ SCANDIA
West Hollywood
Bent Thomsen, Executive Chef

LEMON MOUSSE

5 eggs, (separated)
1½ cups sugar
6 tbsp. lemon juice
¾ tbsp. grated lemon rind
¾ pint whipping cream
Lemon or vanilla wafers

Beat the egg yolks well; beat the sugar into the yolks. Add lemon juice and rind. Cook in a double boiler about 7 minutes, stirring all the time.

When cooled, refrigerate until cold; add whipped cream. Fold in stiffly beaten egg whites. Pour into spring-form pan or pan with loose bottom. Cover with finely rolled lemon wafer crumbs.

Freeze, without stirring, at least 24 hours. When ready to serve, turn out and slice.

Serves 10 to 12.

MRS. JULIUS A. SAKAS
Escondido

RASPBERRY MOUSSE

1 envelope unflavored
   gelatin
¾ cup cold water
1 10-oz. jar black raspberry
   jelly (about 1 cup)
½ pt. heavy cream, (whipped)
3 tbsp. lemon juice
2 egg whites, (stiffly beaten)

Soften gelatin in cold water. Add jelly. Heat over low heat until jelly is melted and gelatin dissolved. Chill until firm. Beat gelatine mixture until light and fluffy. Fold in whipped cream and lemon juice. Fold in beaten egg whites. Pour into oiled 5-cup mold. Place in freezer to freeze solid. Unmold on serving plate. Return to freezer to keep firm. Serve plain or with more whipped cream.

Serves 8.

MISS LUISE HINES

L'ESCOFFIER CHOCOLATE MOUSSE

1½ lb. sweet chocolate
  (grated)
1 cup boiling water
10 eggs (separated)
1 cup sugar
1 pt. cream (whipped)

CHOCOLATE GANACHE
GLAZE

1 pt. whipping cream
1¼ lb. Zenda chocolate or
  bittersweet chocolate
Strawberries

Add the grated chocolate to the boiling water, melt, stir and cool. Add 10 egg yolks to the above. Whip 10 egg whites until stiff. Add 1 cup sugar slowly to egg whites, then fold into the chocolate mixture. Next fold in 1 pt. whipped cream. Fill glasses or molds; refrigerate several hours.

CHOCOLATE GANACHE:

Heat the cream in a double boiler at 125° until hot, not boiling; stir in chocolate pieces until melted. Cool, then it is ready for pouring over chocolate mousse molds. When ganache is set, decorate with whipped cream (bottom border, corners on top rosettes and diagonal strips, strawberries on 4 corners and 4 strawberries on top.)

★ L'ESCOFFIER ROOM
The Beverly Hilton
Beverly Hills
Monsieur Paul Quiaud, Chef De Cuisine

MOCHA MOUSSE

32 large marshmallows
  (not jet puffed)
1 cup strong hot coffee
½ pint whipping cream
  (whipped)
1 tsp. vanilla

Melt marshmallows in coffee and let cool. Add whipped cream and beat. Pour into mold and set in refrigerator for 3½ hours at least.

Serves 4-6.

SALLY GULICK

CHOCOLATE REFRIGERATOR PUDDING

1 German sweet chocolate
bar
4 Eggs, (separated)
¾ cup powdered sugar
1 cup cream (whipped)
¼ tsp. vanilla
½ lb. crushed vanilla wafers

Melt chocolate in double boiler. Add beaten egg yolks, sugar and whipped cream to melted chocolate. Add vanilla. Fold into mixture beaten egg whites. Place a layer of crushed wafers in bottom of pan. Pour half of mixture over wafers. Sprinkle wafers again. Add remaining mixture and top with remaining wafers. Freeze 1½ hours. Place in refrigerator.

Serves 6-8.

★ PAT CARSON (MRS. RICHARD CARSON)
RICHARD CARSON: Director
Director MERV GRIFFEN SHOW TV series.

HEAVENLY PUDDING

PUDDING:

2 cups bread (cut in
squares)
1 cup sugar
2 eggs (beaten)
½ cup butter (melted)
½ tsp. salt
½ tsp. cloves
½ tsp. cinnamon
½ tsp. nutmeg
1 tsp. soda (dissolved in
¼ cup water)
1 cup raisins
1 cup pecans (chopped)

SAUCE:

2 egg yolks
¾ cup powdered sugar
2 tbsp. Myers Rum (less
may be preferred)
½ pt. whipped cream

PUDDING:

Butter sides and bottom of the top of a double boiler. Mix together bread, sugar, eggs, butter, salt, cloves, cinnamon, nutmeg, soda, raisins and pecans. Pour into the buttered pan and steam for 2 hours.

SAUCE:

Beat egg yolks until thick. Add powdered sugar and mix well. Add rum, 1 tsp. at a time, until flavor is satisfactory to the taste. Fold in whipped cream.

Serves 8-12.

MRS. FRANK E. PICKETT

NOODLE PUDDING (KUGEL)

½ lb. wide noodles
1 stick (¼ lb.) butter or
  margarine
1½ cups milk
1 8-oz. pkg. Philadelphia
  Cream Cheese
4 eggs
½ cup sugar
Salt for seasoning
1 can mandarin oranges
  (or other fruit)
Cornflakes (crushed)
Cinnamon

Boil and drain noodles.

Melt and heat together margarine (butter), milk and cream cheese.

Beat eggs well. Add sugar and a little salt, and fruit. Blend everything together and place in a 2 qt. casserole. Sprinkle top with crushed cornflakes, cinnamon and sugar. Bake in 350° oven until brown for 1 hour.

Preferably mix the day before, and let stand 24 hours before baking for excellent blending of ingredients.

Serves 8.

★ MRS. KENNETH DAVIDSON (LYNNE)
Recording artist, singer
Featured regular on DON McNEILL'S radio BREAKFAST CLUB and GARRY MOORE'S CLUB MATINEE.

TRIFLE PUDDING

TRIFLE:
¼ lb. almond macaroons
¼ lb. lady fingers
¼ cup sherry wine
¼ cup brandy
½ cup raspberry jam

CUSTARD SAUCE:

3 tbsp. sugar
3 tbsp. egg yolks
2 cups milk
2 tbsp. cornstarch
3 tbsp. water
Maraschino cherries
1 pt. whipping cream
  (whipped)

Use a small glass bowl. Break macaroons and lady fingers in two and mix together. Line the bowl with part of jam. Add part of cakes to lining of bowl.

Add wine and brandy to custard sauce (all three whipped together). Add custard sauce to remainder of the cakes and fill bowl. Allow to set overnight. Just before serving decorate with Maraschino cherries and whipped cream.

CUSTARD SAUCE:

Heat milk in double boiler and stir in cornstarch. Beat together the sugar, egg yolks and water. Add to hot milk, stirring constantly. Cook for 5-10 minutes to a thin custard consistency.

Serves 4.

★ COCK 'N BULL RESTAURANT
West Hollywood

ROULADE AU CHOCOLAT

5 eggs (separated)
1 cup powdered sugar
¼ cup flour (sifted)
3 tbsp. cocoa
½ tsp. salt
1 tsp. vanilla

SAUCE:

1 cup butter
1⅓ cups sugar
10 tbsp. cocoa
1 cup whipping cream
Creme de Cocoa

Sift dry ingredients together 3 times. Beat egg yolks until thick. Fold in dry ingredients to yolks. In separate bowl beat egg whites until stiff, add vanilla, then fold egg yolks in with great care. Line a 10"x14" pan with wax paper. Spread batter evenly over pan. Bake at 400° for 15 minutes or until done. While cake bakes, dampen a linen towel. Turn cake out on towel quickly, peel off paper. Cut off any hard edges, roll up like jelly roll. Cool on rack. When cake is cold, unroll, spread with ice cream and roll again. Freeze until needed. Slice and serve with chocolate sauce.

Melt butter, gradually add sugar and cocoa, combining dry ingredients well. Slowly add cream, mix well, and allow to boil 1 minute. When sauce cools add liqueur. Can hold 1½ months.

Serves 8.

BONNIE WILKE

*The most indispensable quality
of a cook is promptness,
and it should be that
of the diner as well.*
JEAN ANTHELME BRILLAT-SAVARIN

CHOCOLATE SOUFFLE

3 oz. softened unsalted butter
2 heaping tbsp. all-purpose flour
2 cups hot milk with a few drops of vanilla
2 oz. bitter chocolate
1 pinch of salt
4 tbsp. sugar
6 egg yolks
8 egg whites (stiffly beaten)

Use a 1-qt. size souffle mold; buttered and sugared well; especially along rim. Over moderate heat in a saucepan, cook flour in the remaining butter for 1 minute or so. Stirring with a soft whip pour in hot milk and chocolate; add salt and remaining sugar. Stirring continuously bring gently to a boil and let cook for 2 minutes or so. Mixture must be very thick. Take pan off heat; mixing continuously stir in egg yolks, one at a time. Let stand. Beat egg whites until very stiff then fold them in carefully. This last operation should be done with a wooden spoon in 3 steps that should not take more than 2 minutes.

1st. One quarter of beaten egg whites should be mixed in very fast.

2nd. Another quarter should be folded in thoroughly.

3rd. The remainder of whites folded in, but very gently until no more trace of whites is noticeable.

Pour mixture into mold, forming center slightly higher than edge of dish. Bake in a preheated 350° to 375° oven for 25 minutes.

Optional: 1 or 2 tbsp. of dark rum may be added to the mixture before folding in egg whites.

Serve immediately.

Serves 4.

★ L'ESCOFFIER ROOM
The Beverly Hilton
Beverly Hills
Monsieur Paul Quiaud, Chef De Cuisine

SOUFFLE AUX FRAISES
(Cold Strawberry Souffle)

1 cup sugar
½ cup water
¼ tsp. cream of tartar
5 egg whites (well beaten)

STRAWBERRY PUREE:

1 pt. fresh strawberries
1½ cups sugar
5 egg yolks
3 cups heavy cream
6 egg yolks

Combine sugar, water and cream of tartar. Stir over moderate heat until sugar dissolves. Cook without stirring until syrup spins in long thread. Pour syrup gradually in thin stream into egg whites, beating continually with rotary beater until meringue stands in firm peaks. Set bowl in bowl of cracked ice to chill.

STRAWBERRY PUREE

Make strawberry puree by forcing fresh strawberries through fine sieve.

In top of double boiler cook puree with sugar and egg yolks, stirring constantly until custard thickens. Cook custard.

Whip heavy cream until stiff. Stir strawberry puree custard into cream. Fold in Italian meringue.

Butter souffle dish and tie standing collar of wax paper around edge. Turn cream in dish and chill in refrigerator until set. Remove paper collar and decorate top of souffle with whipped cream pressed through pastry bag fitted with fluted tube. Decorate with whole strawberries.

Serve chilled.

Serves 8.

EDIE HILTON
Home Economist, Caterer

FROZEN SOUFFLE AMARETTO

½ gal. vanilla ice cream
12 macaroons (crumbled)
6 tbsp. Amaretto
2 cups heavy cream
½ cup toasted almonds
(chopped)
Confectioners' sugar

HOT PEACH SAUCE:

6 peaches
5 tbsp. Amaretto

Soften ice cream slightly. Stir in crumbled macaroons and Amaretto. Whip cream until thick and fold into ice cream mixture. Spoon into bundt pan. Sprinkle top with almonds and a little powdered sugar. Cover with plastic wrap and freeze until firm, 4-6 hours or overnight. Unmold on a cold platter and return to freezer until serving time.

HOT PEACH SAUCE:

Mix sauce just before serving. Pare and slice peaches; simmer in saucepan until just soft, not mushy. Remove from heat; stir in liquor. Pass with souffle.

Serves 12-16.

ALPHA MacCORMACK

SOUFFLE GLACÉ

10 almond macaroons
(crumbled)
3 tbsp. orange juice
5 egg yolks
⅔ cup sugar
3 tbsp. Grand Marnier
1 tbsp. orange rind
(grated)
2 cups whipped cream
4 egg whites (stiffly beaten)

TOPPING:

Cocoa
Grand Marnier

Soak crumbled almond macaroons in orange juice. Mash mixture into paste. Set aside.

Beat egg yolks with sugar until light-colored and very thick. Stir in Grand Marnier and grated orange rind. Fold in whipped cream and stiffly beaten egg whites.

Fill 12 custard cups one-half full with batter. Divide macaroon paste into 12 balls. Place in center of cups. Fill with remaining batter. Freeze. Unmold. Sprinkle with cocoa and Grand Marnier.

Serves 12.

CAROLYN PATTERSON THEE

KIWI SOUFFLE A LA JIMMY'S

3 eggs yolks
⅓ cup brown sugar
⅓ cup flour
¾ cup milk
2 gelatin leaves
3 lime peelings (grated)
5 mashed Kiwis
1 tsp. Amaretto
5 snow white eggs
1 tsp. sugar

Heat milk over low flame. In a small bowl beat 3 egg yolks lightly. Add sugar and flour and mix well. Combine milk and cook over low heat until thickened.

In another saucepan melt 2 leaves gelatin in ½ cup of water. Mix in Kiwis and add 1 tsp. Amaretto. Beat egg whites stiff, but not dry. Fold egg whites into preparation.

Butter lining of 4 souffle molds (2½" diameter) and sprinkle with sugar. Pour souffle into molds filling ¾ of each container. Bake in preheated oven at 450° for 12 to 15 minutes. Serve with Parisienne Apricot Sauce and/or whipped cream.

Serves 4.

★ JIMMY'S RESTAURANT
Beverly Hills

FRESH PEACH SOUFFLE

1½ cups peaches (peeled and pitted)
¾ cup macaroon crumbs
3 tbsp. Amaretto di Saronno
½ cup butter
½ cup sugar
4 egg yolks
5 egg whites (stiffly beaten)

Crush peaches. Combine with macaroon crumbs soaked in Amaretto. Cream together butter and sugar. Add egg yolks one at a time, beating well after each addition. Combine egg and macaroon mixtures, fold in egg whites. Pour the mixture into a buttered and sugared souffle dish and bake in 350° oven for about 35 minutes, or until it is well puffed.

★ CAROL BURNETT
Actress, comedienne, dancer, singer.
Many TV appearances include GARRY MOORE SHOW and star CAROL BURNETT SHOW (countless Emmy Awards); theatre roles include ONCE UPON A MATTRESS on Broadway.

ORANGE MARMALADE SOUFFLE

5 egg whites
5 tbsp. granulated sugar
4 tbsp. Cross and Blackwell
   marmalade

SAUCE:

3 egg yolks
½ cup sugar
1 tsp. vanilla
2 tbsp. brandy
½ cup cream (whipped)

SOUFFLE:

Beat egg whites until fluffy. Add sugar gradually and beat until stiff. Fold in marmalade.

Pour into a greased 3-quart double boiler. Cook over simmering water until a silver knife inserted in the center comes out clean (about 1¼ or 1½ hours).

Cool to room temperature. Then turn it out on a platter and cover with sauce. Cut into pie-shaped wedges.

SAUCE:

Beat yolks, sugar, vanilla and brandy until lemon-colored. Add whipped cream. Pour over souffle.

Serves 8 to 10.

CHARLOTTE MITCHEL
Past President
Assistance League of Southern California

SOUFFLE TIA MARIA

1½ oz. flour
1½ oz. butter
1½ oz. sugar
8 oz. milk
4 egg yolks
2 oz. Tia Maria (liqueur)
5 egg whites
2 oz. sugar

Mix flour, butter and sugar well. Boil milk. Remove from stove and add to mixture. Blend well. Return to heat and cook for 2 minutes. Remove from stove, add yolks, blend well, add liqueur. Beat egg whites, add sugar and fold into mixture. Fill immediately in buttered and sugared molds. Bake at 400° for about 20 minutes in water bath. Serve immediately.

Serves 4.

MRS. GRAHAM POLK

VANILLA SOUFFLE WITH APRICOT SAUCE

3 tbsp. butter
2 tbsp. flour
1 cup milk
¼ tsp. salt
½ cup sugar
3 inch piece of vanilla bean
  or 1 tsp. vanilla extract
4 egg yolks
4 egg whites
Apricot sauce or any
  suitable fruit or dessert
  sauce

Melt 3 tbsp. butter in a sauce pan and blend with 2 tbsp. flour. Gradually add 1 cup milk, stirring constantly, and mix in ¼ tsp. salt, ½ tsp. sugar, and a 3-inch piece of vanilla bean (or 1 tsp. vanilla extract). When sauce is thick and smooth, remove from heat and cool. Remove the vanilla bean. Add 4 egg yolks and beat well.

Beat egg whites stiff and fold in yolk mixture. Butter a souffle dish, sprinkle it with sugar, and pour in the batter. Set the dish in a pan of hot water. Bake in 400° oven for 15 minutes. Reduce the heat to moderate (375°) and cook for 20 to 25 minutes longer.

Serve with apricot sauce or any suitable fruit or dessert sauce.

Serves 6 to 8.

★ MRS. BOB HOPE (DOLORES)
BOB HOPE: actor, author, comedian, dancer, raconteur, singer.
Top radio star including THE PEPSODENT HOUR; since 1950 star BOB HOPE TV SPECIALS; nearly 60 films include ROAD TO...series, SEVEN LITTLE FOYS, and BEAU JAMES; books include HAVE TUX WILL TRAVEL and ROAD TO HOLLYWOOD; given 5 Special Academy Awards, and almost every other award ever created.

Papa, potatoes, poultry, prunes, and prism,
are all very good words for the lips;
especially prunes and prism.
CHARLES DICKENS

APPLE STRUDEL

⅓ lb. (about 6 sheets) filo
  or strudel dough
½ cup butter (melted)
5 tart cooking apples (peeled
  and thinly sliced)
3 tbsp. sugar
1½ tsp. vanilla
2 tsp. cinnamon
¾ cup ground walnuts
¾ cup sugar
½ cup bread crumbs
Powdered sugar or
  whipped cream

Toss apples with 3 tbsp. sugar, vanilla and cinnamon. Set aside. Combine walnuts, ¾ cup sugar and ½ cup breadcrumbs.

Lay one sheet of filo on a clean dish towel; brush with butter and sprinkle with some of the crumb mixture. Continue to layer filo with butter and crumbs to about 6 sheets thick. Spread sliced apples on one-half of filo square. Begin rolling strudel, as for a jelly roll, from the end that has the apples on top. Gently roll until all filo is into strudel roll. Carefully lift onto a cookie sheet, seam side down. Brush roll with butter.

Bake at 350° for 45 minutes or until apples are tender and pastry is crisp. Cool slightly. Sift with powdered sugar over top or top with whipped cream.

This freezes beautifully before or after baking. To reheat, bake at 350° about 20 minutes.

NOTE: Strudel dough dries out very quickly. Cover the portion you are not using immediately with waxed paper and a damp towel.

Serves 10.

MRS. TERENCE C. McGAUGHEY

WIDOW MAKER

3 cups crushed macaroons
1 cup sugar
1 cup half and half
Pinch salt
3 cups whipping cream
  (whipped)
1 cup brandy

Combine macaroon crumbs, sugar, half and half and salt in large bowl. Gradually fold in brandy. Spoon into individual dishes such as pot de creme and place in freezer. About 15 minutes before serving, remove from freezer and let set at room temperature to partially thaw.
Serves 16 or more.

GLENDA GRIBBEN

BANANA NUT TORTE

1 cup granulated sugar
1 tsp. baking powder
3 large white eggs
¾ cup walnuts (chopped)
12 saltine crackers (finely chopped)
2 tsp. vanilla
2 or 3 bananas
1 cup whipping cream
2½ tsp. confectioner's sugar
½ cup walnuts (chopped)

Sift granulated sugar with baking powder. Beat egg whites until stiff. Add sugar mixture beating constantly. Fold in ¾ cup walnuts, saltines and 1 tsp. of the vanilla.

Spread evenly in a buttered 9" pie plate. Bake in a preheated 350° oven 20-25 minutes. The torte will not brown on top. Cool in pan on a wire rack.

When torte is cool, slice bananas generously over the top. Whip cream adding the confectioner's sugar and the remaining 1 tsp. vanilla. Spread cream over the bananas covering thoroughly. Sprinkle the ½ cup walnuts over the top. Put in the refrigerator until ready to serve.

NOTE: Other fresh fruit in season may be used in place of the bananas.

Serves 6-8.

MRS. PETER A. SNOWDEN

CHOCOLATE RUM TORTE

1 full-size angel food cake
8 tbsp. Jamaican rum
3 6-oz. pkgs. semisweet chocolate bits
6 eggs
2 tsp. vanilla
Dash of salt
2 pts. heavy cream
2 tbsp. sugar
¼ cup almonds (toasted and slivered)

Tear cake into small pieces; sprinkle with rum and toss lightly. Melt chocolate over very low heat. Turn melted chocolate into beater bowl and add eggs one at a time at medium speed. Beat in vanilla and salt.

Whip 1 pint of cream until frothy and add sugar. Whip until soft peaks form. Fold into chocolate mixture. Alternate layers of cake and chocolate into a greased 10" tube pan or an 8" springform pan.

Whip remaining 1 pint of cream; add a dash of rum or vanilla and frost cake. Garnish with the toasted almonds. Return to freezer.

About 30 minutes before serving, remove from freezer to soften. This may be refrozen.

Serves 10.

MRS. LEO POLLAKOFF

GRAHAM CRACKER DATE TORTE

This recipe is a creation of my mother's, Ruby Chaudoir, who lives in Sturgeon Bay, Wisconsin.

24 graham crackers
  (1 square each)
4 tbsp. butter (melted)
COOK (Pudding):
1 qt. milk
4 egg yolks (save whites)
1 cup sugar
4 tbsp. cornstarch
Salt
½ tsp. vanilla
  OR SUBSTITUTE
2 pkgs. vanilla pudding
FILLING:
¾ lb. dates
½ cup walnuts or pecans
  (chopped)

Roll graham crackers to crumbs. Mix with melted butter. Press half into bottom of 9"x12" baking pan. Pour pudding mixture into pan. Place layer of cut dates.

Beat 4 egg whites stiff and add sugar. Spread whites over dates, remaining crumbs over egg whites. Sprinkle walnuts or pecans on top. Bake at 350° for 15-20 minutes. Serve slightly warm.
Serves 12.

★ MRS. TONY TRABERT (EMERYL)
TONY TRABERT: Sportsman
U.S. Tennis Open Champion at Wimbledon, U.S. Davis Cup Captain (1976, 1977, 1978, 1979.)

HAZELNUT TORTE

1 lb. hazelnuts (finely
  ground in a nut machine)
10 eggs
1½ cup sugar
Rind of one lemon (grated)
1 tsp. vanilla
1 tsp. cream of wheat

Beat egg yolks, add sugar beating until fluffy. Add vanilla and lemon rind. Add nuts and cream of wheat and stir until mixed. Fold in slowly beaten egg whites.

Bake in an ungreased angel food tube pan at 350° for 40 to 45 minutes. Test with cake tester to see if done. Before serving, sprinkle with powdered sugar. Serve with whipped cream.

This is an old Christmas traditional. The secret is not to grind the juice out of the nuts while preparing them.
Serves 8.

HELEN TUPPAN

TORTILLA TORTE

2 11½-oz. pkgs. milk
  chocolate chips
6 cups sour cream
¾ cup powdered sugar
10 12-inch flour tortillas
Shaved bittersweet chocolate

Melt chocolate and mix with 4 cups sour cream. Mix sugar and remaining 2 cups sour cream and keep separate. On a plate large enough to hold tortillas layer 8 tortillas with chocolate mixture. It will take about ½ cup chocolate mixture to cover each tortilla. Add the ninth tortilla and cover with most of the sugar mixture. Add the last tortilla and spread remaining sugar mixture evenly over the top, covering all edges. Cover tortillas with a large bowl or other covering that does not touch surface. Refrigerate for at least 12 hours. Decorate with shaved chocolate and cut into small wedges to serve. Very rich!

Serves 20.

ILAMAY TALLAKSON

CHOCOLATE FUDGE SAUCE

½ lb. bitter chocolate
  (Bakers)
½ stick butter or margarine
3 cups sugar
3 heaping tbsp. cornstarch
⅒ tsp. salt
¼ cup light Karo syrup
1 lg. can evaporated milk
1 tsp. vanilla

Melt chocolate in double boiler; add butter and dry ingredients (which have been mixed or sifted together). Add other ingredients. Stir frequently; will be very thick.

Refrigerate. Will keep indefinitely. If you want it as fudge topping for ice cream, heat a second or two in microwave oven.

Makes about 2 cups.

MRS. A.E. KAISER

LEMON SAUCE FOR SHERBET, CAKE, ETC.

1 cup sugar
2 tbsp. butter
2 tbsp. cornstarch
2 cups boiling water
Grated rind of 1 lemon
Juice of 1 lemon

Mix sugar, butter and cornstarch; add boiling water gradually. Stir all the time with a wire whisk. Cook about 8 to 10 minutes over low heat. Add lemon rind and juice. Serve hot or cold. May be made the day before. Keeps a week in the refrigerator.

An "oldie" from a friend's grandmother's cook book.

Makes 2 cups.

MRS. HORACE E. MARTIN
Newport Beach, California
Past President
National Assistance League

PRALINE PARFAIT SAUCE

⅓ cup water
⅓ cup brown sugar
1 cup white Karo corn syrup
1 cup chopped pecans
½ tsp. vanilla

Bring water to boil; add the brown sugar and corn syrup. Cook slowly, stirring until mixture comes to a boil.

Remove from heat. Add pecans and vanilla. Pour into container and refrigerate. Mixture will thicken when cool.

Pour over ice cream and top with whipped cream.

Serves 6.

VICKI MAZZEI

CAKES

With weights and measures just,
Oven of even heat,
Well-buttered pans and quiet nerves,
Success will be complete.

ANONYMOUS

APPLE BRAN CAKE

1¾ cups flour
  (unsifted)
1½ tsp. baking powder
¾ tsp. baking soda
¼ tsp. salt
1½ cups sugar
1 tsp. cinnamon
⅛ tsp. ginger
¼ tsp. ground cloves
⅛ tsp. allspice
3 eggs
2 cups canned applesauce
½ cup oil
1½ cups All-Bran cereal
  or Bran-Buds cereal
¾ cup walnuts (coarsely
  chopped)
Powdered sugar

Stir together in medium size mixing bowl flour, baking powder, baking soda, salt, sugar, and spices. Set aside.

In large mixing bowl beat eggs until foamy. Add applesauce, oil and cereal. Mix well. Add dry ingredients except powdered sugar until combined. Stir in nuts. Pour into greased 13"x9"x2½" baking pan. Bake at 350° about 45 minutes or until toothpick inserted into center of cake comes out clean.

If using same size glass pan, bake only 35 minutes.

Cool in pan. Dust with powdered sugar just before serving. Cake may be frozen.

Serves 15.

BETTY WELBOURN

BRAN CRUNCH COFFEE CAKE

¼ cup butter (melted)
½ cup brown sugar
1 cup bran flakes
1 tsp. cinnamon
2 cups Bisquick (or
  prepared biscuit mix)
1 egg (slightly beaten)
¾ cup milk

Blend butter, brown sugar, bran flakes and cinnamon. Combine Bisquick, egg and milk and beat for 1 minute. Spread half the batter in a greased 8"x8" pan.

Sprinkle half the cereal mixture over top. Cover with remaining batter and top with remaining cereal. Bake at 375° for 20 minutes.

Serve warm.

INGRID HEDBERG

CRANBERRY NUT COFFEE CAKE

¼ cup brown sugar
¼ tsp. cinnamon
½ cup nuts (chopped)
2 cups Bisquick
2 tbsp. sugar
⅔ cup milk
1 egg
1 cup whole cranberry
   sauce

ICING:

1 cup powdered sugar
½ tsp. vanilla
1 tbsp. water

Heat oven to 400°. Grease 8" or 9" square pan.
   Mix sugar, cinnamon and nuts and set aside.
   Combine Bisquick, sugar, milk and eggs. Beat vigorously. Spread in pan. Sprinkle with nut mixture. Spoon cranberry sauce on top. Bake 20-25 minutes.
   While warm, spread with icing.

ICING:
Place all ingredients in bowl and mix.

Serves 10-12.

MRS. W. BERNARD MELONE

WALNUT SOUR CREAM COFFEE CAKE

½ lb. butter
¾ cup sugar
2 eggs
2 cups flour (sifted)
1 tsp. baking powder
1 tsp. soda
½ tsp. salt
1 cup sour cream
1 tsp. vanilla

FILLING:

⅓ cup brown sugar
⅓ cup white sugar
1 tsp. cinnamon
1 cup walnuts (chopped)

Cream butter and sugar until light and fluffy. Add eggs one at a time. Add flour, baking powder, soda and salt to creamed mixture alternately with sour cream and vanilla.
   Combine filling ingredients.
   Turn half of batter into greased 9"x13" pan; sprinkle filling over same. Pour remaining batter on top and sprinkle balance of filling over top. Bake at 350° for 35 minutes.
   Cut into diagonal strips, so as to make diamond-shaped pieces.

EVELYN SAMPSON

DOUBLE TOFFEE COFFEE CAKE

1½ cups brown sugar
1 cup nuts
1 tbsp. cinnamon
2 cups flour
1 cup sugar
¾ cup salad oil
2 tsp. baking powder
1 cup water
1 tsp. salt
1 tsp. vanilla
1 pkg. instant vanilla
   pudding
1 pkg. instant butterscotch
   pudding
4 eggs
2 tsp. cinnamon
2 tsp. sugar

Combine brown sugar, nuts and cinnamon and set aside.

Mix flour, sugar, salad oil, baking powder, water, salt, vanilla, both puddings and eggs together and beat at high speed for 2 minutes.

Grease and flour bundt pan. Mix cinnamon and sugar together and shake the mixture around the inside of the pan. Pour off excess.

Pour in ⅓ of batter, then ⅓ cinnamon-sugar-nut mixture. Continue layers until all mixtures are used.

Bake at 350° for 45 to 50 minutes. Cool 1 hour before removing coffee cake from the pan.

Serves 8.

KATHY BARTIZAL

ALMOND CAKE

2 cups unblanched almonds
   (shelled)
8 egg yolks
1½ cups granulated sugar
½ tsp. salt
1 tsp. vanilla
1 tsp. almond flavoring
3 tbsp. flour
½ tsp. cream of tartar
8 egg whites
7 minute or white icing

Grind almonds with finest blade of grinder. Beat yolks well and beat in sugar; add salt, vanilla and almond flavor, stir in ground almonds and flour.

Beat whites stiff with cream of tartar. Fold into yolk mixture.

Place in an angel food cake pan and tie a brown paper cover over pan. Bake 15 minutes in preheated 375° oven. Remove brown paper from pan and bake 30 minutes at 350°. Place pan bottom up to cool. Ice with 7-minute or your favorite white icing.

Serves 8-10.

CHARLOTTE MITCHEL
Past President
Assistance League of Southern California

APPLE HARVEST CAKE

FILLING:

1 dozen medium sized apples (Winesap or Jonathan)
2 tbsp. butter
6 tbsp. sugar
6 eggs
½ pint sour cream
1 tsp. vanilla

CRUST:

Pack of Zwieback
½ tsp. cinnamon
2 tbsp. butter (melted)
1 qt. vanilla ice cream

FILLING:

Peel and core apples. Cut into eighths. Combine apples, butter and sugar in a saucepan. Cover. Heat slowly over low heat until the apples soften. Cool.

In a separate bowl beat eggs until lemon-colored and thick. Add sour cream and apple mixture. Return to saucepan and cook 5 minutes. Add vanilla.

CRUST:

Roll whole package of Zwieback into crumbs. Add sugar, cinnamon and butter. Butter sides of a springform pan. Put ½ of the crumb mixture on the bottom. Add filling and top with remainder of the crumb mixture. Dot the top with chunks of butter and bake at 350° for 50 minutes.

Top apple cake with ice cream for a delicious treat.

This is a most unusual recipe and ideal for autumn entertaining.

Serves 8.

BUNNY FEUER

APPLE PIE CAKE

½ cup shortening
2 cups sugar
2 eggs
2 tsp. vanilla
2 cups flour
2 tsp. baking soda
2 tsp. nutmeg
2 tsp. cinnamon
½ tsp. salt
4 tbsp. hot water
5 cups apples (diced)
1 cup walnuts (chopped)
Whipped cream (optional)
Vanilla ice cream (optional)

Cream shortening and sugar together; stir in eggs and vanilla.

Sift together flour, baking soda, nutmeg, cinnamon and salt. Blend in one-half flour mixture. Add 4 tbsp. hot water and beat. Add balance of flour. Fold in apples and nuts.

Pour batter into two 9" round or 9"x9" square greased and floured pans and bake at 350° for 45-50 minutes.

Frost with white frosting, or eat unfrosted with whipped cream or vanilla ice cream.

Serves 12.

MRS. GEORGE B. SPEARS

BUTTERSCOTCH TOFFEE HEAVEN

1½ cups whipping cream
1 can (5½ oz.) butterscotch
  topping
½ tsp. vanilla extract
1 9½" unfrosted angel food
  cake
¾ lb. English Toffee
  (crushed)

Whip cream until it starts to thicken. Add butterscotch syrup and vanilla slowly and continue beating until thick.

Cut cake into 3 layers horizontally. Spread half of butterscotch mixture on layers and sprinkle each generously with crushed toffee. Put cake together and frost top and sides with remaining butterscotch mixture and sprinkle with remaining toffee.

Place cake in refrigerator and chill for a minimum of 6 hours.

Serves 12.

MRS. HAROLD DOUGHER

CARROT CAKE

1½ cups sugar
1 cup vegetable oil
3 eggs (separated)
½ tsp. soda in 2½ tsp.
  hot water
1½ cups flour
½ tsp. cinnamon
½ tsp. nutmeg
½ tsp. allspice
1 tsp. baking powder
1 cup grated carrots
  (or more)
1 cup nutmeats
Pinch salt

Mix oil and sugar. Add egg yolks one at a time. Add hot water. Sift dry ingredients. Beat into egg mixture. Add carrot and nuts. Beat egg whites until soft peaks form. Fold into carrot mixture.

Pour into greased and floured 10" tube pan. Bake 60-70 minutes at 350° or until knife comes out clean. Cool 15 minutes. Frost with cream cheese and powdered sugar frosting.

Serves 12-15.

★ LEE MERIWETHER
Actress.
Former Miss America; TV roles include co-star BARNABY JONES TV series.

BLUE FAIRY CHEESE CAKE

2 8-oz. pkgs. cream cheese
2 eggs
¾ cup sugar
1 tbsp. lemon juice
1 tsp. vanilla
Vanilla wafers
1 can cherry or blueberry pie filling. Dabs of different flavored jams can be used if preferred

Beat softened cream cheese with eggs, sugar, lemon juice and vanilla.

Put papers in muffin tins. Put a whole vanilla wafer in the bottom of each one. Fill each about ¾ full.

Bake at 375° for 15 to 20 minutes or until set. Top with pie filling or preserves and chill until ready to serve.

Serves 24.

NINE O'CLOCK PLAYERS
Pinocchio Cast Luncheon.

COINTREAU CHEESE CAKE

1¼ cups chocolate wafers (crushed) (20 round chocolate wafers)
⅓ cup butter (melted)
3 3-oz. pkgs. cream cheese
2 eggs
½ cup sugar
1 tbsp. Cointreau

TOPPING:

2 tbsp. sugar
½ pint sour cream
1 tbsp. Cointreau

Mix wafers and butter, press into an 8" pie pan. Chill while you do the next step.

Beat together cream cheese, eggs, sugar and Cointreau. Bake at 350° for 15-20 minutes. Filling should be partially set when you remove from oven. Let cool about 20 minutes before continuing with next step.

TOPPING:

Beat together all ingredients for topping. Pour on top of pie and bake at 350° for 5 minutes. Refrigerate at least 24 hours, 48 hours if possible.

Serves 8.

GLENDA GRIBBEN

CHEESECAKE
(Like Lindy's)

1 cup sifted flour
¼ cup sugar
1 tsp. grated lemon peel
½ tsp. vanilla
1 egg yolk
½ cup butter or margarine (softened)
Cheese filling

CHEESE FILLING:

5 8-oz. pkgs. cream cheese
1¾ cups sugar
3 tbsp. flour
¼ tsp. salt
1 tsp grated orange peel
½ tsp. grated lemon peel
5 medium eggs
2 egg yolks
¼ cup heavy cream

Combine flour, sugar, lemon peel and vanilla in a bowl. Make well in center, add egg yolk and butter. Work with tips of fingers until dough forms a ball and cleans sides of bowl. Wrap in waxed paper and chill for 1 hour. Roll ⅓ of dough between two pieces of waxed paper to fit bottom of a 9-inch springform pan. Place on bottom of pan. Bake at 400° 8-10 minutes or until barely golden. Cool. Grease sides of springform and fasten to base. Roll remaining dough into a 15"x4" rectangle, cut in half lengthwise. Carefully line sides of pan with dough strips, patch when necessary and press seams together. Pour cheese filling into crust and bake one hour longer. Let cool in place free from drafts. Remove sides of pan and chill 12-24 hours.

CHEESE FILLING:

Beat cheese until fluffy, combine sugar, flour, salt, lemon and orange peels and stir into cheese until smooth. Add eggs and egg yolks, one at a time, blending after each addition. Blend in cream.

Serves 12-16.

KATA WARREN

GRANDMA DURST'S POUND CAKE

1 cup shortening
1½ cups sugar
5 eggs
2 cups flour
1½ tsp. salt
½ tsp. mace
1 tsp. vanilla

Cream shortening and sugar. Add eggs one at a time beating after each addition. Add rest of ingredients beating thoroughly. Bake in loaf pan 60-80 minutes at 350°.

Makes 1 loaf

CAROL A. DURST

ITALIAN CREAM CAKE

1 stick butter
½ cup Crisco
2 cups sugar
5 egg yolks
2 cups flour
5 egg whites
  (beaten stiff)
1 cup black walnuts
  (chopped fine)
1 cup buttermilk
1 small can coconut
Vanilla

FROSTING:

1 8-oz. pkg. cream cheese
½ stick butter
1 box powdered sugar
Flavor with vanilla

Combine all ingredients, mix thoroughly. Bake in 2 layer pans at 350° for 25 minutes or until toothpick comes out clean. Mix frosting ingredients and frost.

Serves 8.

MRS. GEORGE B. SPEARS

CHOCOLATE NOUGAT CAKE

From 'THE PALATISTS' cookbook 1933

¼ cup butter
1½ cup powdered sugar
1 egg
1 cup milk
2 cups flour
3 tsp. baking powder
½ tsp. vanilla
2 squares chocolate (melted)
⅓ cup powdered sugar
⅔ cup almonds (blanched
  and chopped)
Whipped cream

Cream the butter, add sugar and the egg unbeaten. When well mixed, add ⅔ cup of milk, flour mixed and sifted with the baking powder, then the vanilla.

To the melted chocolate, add the powdered sugar and the rest of the milk and heat until smooth. Cool and add to cake mixture.

Bake in two layer cake pans in a 350° oven and when cool spread whipped cream between the layers and on top and sprinkle with chopped almonds.

★ CAROLE LOMBARD
Actress, comedienne
Many films include MY MAN GODFREY, NOTHING SACRED and TO BE OR NOT TO BE.

COINTREAU CHOCOLATE-ORANGE CAKE

1 1-lb. 3-oz. pkg. yellow
   cake mix
2 tsp. orange peel (grated)
CHOCOLATE
BUTTERCREAM:
¾ cup butter
1 cup sugar
4 oz. sweetened chocolate
   (melted and cooled)
2 tbsp. Cointreau
4 eggs
1 small container Cool Whip

Prepare package yellow butter-cake mix as package directs, adding grated orange peel to the batter. Grease and lightly flour four 9" cake pans. Divide batter among four pans. Bake in 350° oven for 15 minutes. Cool 5 minutes then turn out to cool.

BUTTERCREAM:

Cream butter, add sugar, chocolate and Cointreau and cream well. Add eggs, beat about 3 minutes until mixture is light in color, smooth and thick. Do not overbeat. Refrigerate or freeze until you need to use. After storing beat again if you want it lighter and fluffier.

Spread buttercream on each layer except top. Stack and refrigerate. Frost with Cool Whip before serving.

Serves 8.

BARBARA GALE

OLE KING COLE'S FUDGE CAKE

¼ lb. butter
2 squares unsweetened
   chocolate
2 eggs (slightly beaten)
1 cup sugar
½ cup sifted flour

Melt butter with chocolate. Add remaining ingredients and mix. Pack into greased 8" pie or cake pan. Bake at 350° for 30 minutes. Cut into wedge shapes.

This is like a fudgy brownie cake wedge and very rich. A little goes a long way. If desired, serve with puff of whipped cream.

Serves 6.

MRS. BERNARD RAMOS

SOUR CREAM CHOCOLATE CAKE

1½ cups flour (sifted)
1 cup sugar
½ tsp. salt
½ tsp. baking powder
½ cup Ghirardelli chocolate/
  cocoa (may substitute other
  cocoa)
½ cup sour cream
1 cup walnuts or pecans
  (chopped)
1 cube butter or margarine
  (melted)
½ cup hot water
1 egg
1 tsp. vanilla

FROSTING:

1½ oz. baking chocolate,
  semi-sweet
1½ tbsp. butter
1 tsp. vanilla
½ cup sour cream
1 box powdered sugar
¼ cup walnuts or pecans
  (chopped)

Mix all ingredients together in large bowl. Beat by hand two minutes. Pour into greased and floured glass baking pan. Bake 30-45 minutes at 350°. Cool in baking pan and frost top.

FROSTING:

Melt together chocolate and butter. Stir in vanilla and sour cream. Add powdered sugar to spreading consistency and beat until light. Frost top of cake and decorate with chopped nuts.
NOTE: This cake is very moist and keeps well if refrigerated. "Chocoholics" delight!

JEANNE ROUSSELOT

The Queen of Hearts, she made some tarts,
All on a summer day:
The Knave of Hearts, he stole those tarts,
and took them quite away!
  LEWIS CARROLL, 'ALICE IN WONDERLAND'

BART STARR'S FAVORITE COCONUT PECAN CAKE

½ cup each margarine and shortening
2 cups sugar
5 eggs (separated)
1 tsp. vanilla
2 cups all-purpose flour (sifted)
1 tsp. soda
½ tsp. salt
1 cup buttermilk
1 can (3½ oz.) coconut (flaked)
1 cup pecans (chopped)

Cream margarine and shortening until light and fluffy. Add 1½ cups sugar gradually; beat again until light and fluffy. Add egg yolks and vanilla; beat thoroughly. Add flour sifted with soda and salt in thirds alternately with buttermilk, beating until smooth after each addition.

Turn batter into a 3-quart mixing bowl.

Beat egg whites until stiff but not dry; beat remaining ½ cup sugar in gradually. Fold egg whites into batter gently but thoroughly. Fold in coconut and pecans. Spread batter in 3 greased, wax paper-lined and again greased 9" cake pans.

Bake at 375° for about 25 minutes or until brown.

Fill and frost as you wish. We use a boiled icing with additional coconut. Whipped cream also would be good.

★ CHERRY STARR (MRS. BART STARR)
BART STARR: Sportsman.
Coach for Green Bay Packers football team; All-Pro Football quarterback; awarded Jim Thorpe Trophy, Player of the Year 1966; Super Bowl Most Valuable Player 1967 and 1968; in Major League Hall of Fame and Professional Football Hall of Fame.

FRUIT CAKE

From THE PALATISTS Cookbook. 1933

2 lbs. currants (picked, washed and dried)
2 lbs. raisins (cut)
1 lb. crystallized ginger (cut in small pieces, or 2 tsp. ground ginger)
1 lb. citron (thinly sliced)
1 lb. blanched almonds (chopped)
4 tsp. nutmeg
2 tsp. mace
1½ tumblers of brandy
20 eggs
2 cups butter
4 cups sugar
6 cups flour
1 tsp. soda
1 tsp. salt

Cream the butter well and add the sugar gradually, beating until light and fluffy. Beat eggs until creamy and add alternately with the flour which has been browned in the oven and sifted with the soda, salt and spices. Stir in the brandy and lastly, the fruit, which has been thoroughly dried and dredged with enough flour to keep it from sticking. Bake very slowly.

MRS. HANCOCK BANNING
Founder President
Assistance League of Southern California

FRUIT NUT TORTE

From our list of most-requested recipes

1 egg
¾ cup sugar
1 cup fruit cocktail (undrained)
1 cup flour
1 tsp. soda
¼ tsp. salt
½ cup walnuts (chopped)
¼ cup brown sugar
¾ cup sugar
½ cup milk (evaporated)
⅓ cup butter or margarine
½ tsp. vanilla extract

Beat egg well. Add ¾ cup sugar and fruit cocktail. Stir in flour, soda and salt and mix thoroughly. Pour into greased 9" round pan. Combine walnuts and brown sugar and sprinkle evenly over top of batter. Bake at 350° for 30 minutes.

Eight minutes before cake is done, begin to prepare icing. Combine ¾ cup sugar, evaporated milk and butter. Bring to a boil and boil three minutes, stirring constantly. Remove from heat. Add vanilla. Pour hot icing over cake as it comes out of oven. Serve with whipped cream.

Serves 8.

★ CLIFTON'S CAFETERIAS
Southern California
Mrs. Ronald C. Roeschlaub
(Jean Clinton Roeschlaub)

KAHLUA CAKE

1 cup butter (softened)
2 cups powdered sugar
5 egg yolks
½ cup Kahlua
1 cup almonds (toasted, slivered)
Angel Food cake (1 lb. size, round)

FROSTING:

1 pt. heavy whipping cream
¼ cup Kahlua
½ tsp. vanilla
3 tbsp. powdered sugar

Blend butter and sugar; beat until fluffy. Blend in egg yolks one at a time beating well. Blend in Kahlua and almonds. (If mixture is too runny, chill until stiff enough to spread).

Line a mixing bowl with wax paper.

Slice angel food cake horizontally in ½" thick slices. (This should make 4 slices.) Layer cake with mixture in the bowl, ending with cake layer.

Cover well and refrigerate overnight.

When ready to frost, lift cake out of bowl onto a cake dish.

FROSTING:

Whip cream until stiff. Fold in remaining ingredients and frost cake.

This is a very rich and delicious cake. If a less sweet frosting is desired, Kahlua in the frosting may be deleted.

Serves 10-12.

FRAN ARMSTRONG

MAYONNAISE CAKE

1 cup mayonnaise (scant)
1½ cups sugar
2 egg yolks
1 tsp. baking soda
¼ tsp. salt
1 cup dates (chopped)
1 cup walnuts (chopped)
1 cup boiling water
2 cups flour
1 tsp. cinnamon
1 tsp. cloves
1 tbsp. baking powder
White icing

Cream mayonnaise, sugar and egg together, then add salt, dates, walnuts and water. Cool the mixture and then add flour, cinnamon, cloves and baking powder. Mix all ingredients together and put in two 8" round pans and bake at 350° until toothpick comes out clean. Frost with white icing.

RUTH SHIRLEY

PRUNE CAKE

1½ cups sugar
1 cup shortening
3 eggs
2 cups flour
1 tsp. baking soda
1 tsp. baking powder
1 tsp. salt
1 tsp. cinnamon
1 tsp. nutmeg
½ tsp. allspice
1 cup soured buttermilk
1 cup cooked prunes
  (chopped)

Cream sugar and shortening. Add eggs. Mix and add dry ingredients alternately with buttermilk. Add prunes. Mix again and bake in three 8" layers at 350°.

LENA MARIE GARNER

PUMPKIN PIE CAKE

1 pkg. Yellow Cake Mix
¾ cup butter
3 eggs
1 cup pumpkin
2½ tsp. pumpkin pie spice
½ cup brown sugar
⅔ cup milk
½ cup sugar
1 tsp. cinnamon

Reserving one cup of cake mix for later use, combine cake mix with ½ cup butter and 1 egg. Pat into a 9"x13" pan.

Combine pumpkin, pumpkin pie spice, brown sugar, 2 eggs, and ⅔ cup milk. Spread on mix in the pan.

Combine reserved cake mix with sugar, cinnamon and ¼ cup butter. Sprinkle over top of other two layers.

Bake for 45 minutes to 1 hour at 350°. Serve with whipped cream or ice cream.

DOROTHEA HEITZ

RUSSIAN ROLL

1 tbsp. gelatin
2 cups milk (scalded)
3 egg yolks
½ cup sugar
¼ tsp. salt
1 tsp. vanilla
1 cup whipping cream
1 cup chopped nuts
½ cup maraschino cherries
  (chopped)
1 large Angel food cake

Soak gelatin in 2 tbsp. cold water for 5 minutes. Scald milk in double boiler. Beat egg yolks. Add sugar and salt. Mix gelatin in with egg mixture. Pour scalded milk over eggs, then pour back into double-boiler. Stir constantly until slightly thickened. Cool. Add vanilla. Chill until it begins to thicken, then add cream, whipped (fold it in). Fold in drained cherries and chopped nuts. Split large angel food cake into three layers. Put filling between and over top and sides of cake.

NOTE: The gelatin custard mixture may be chilled until firm, then beaten with egg beater before adding whipped cream.

MRS. MARVIN J. McCONNELL

SUNSHINE CAKE

1½ cups sugar
½ cup water
6 eggs (beaten separately)
1 cup flour
½ tsp. cream of tartar
1 tsp. flavoring

Place sugar in saucepan. Add water and boil until it threads when dropped from the end of a spoon. Pour gradually in a fine stream on the stiffly beaten whites of eggs, beating until cool. Add the egg yolks well beaten.

Sift the flour with the cream of tartar and fold in gradually. Place in a large ungreased tube pan and bake about 50 minutes in a 325° oven, covering cake with heavy paper during the first 15 minutes. Invert to cool, then remove from pan.

★ RABBI EDGAR F. MAGNIN, D.D.
Author, clergyman, columnist, lecturer.
Senior Rabbi of Wilshire Boulevard Temple of Los Angeles; star of inspirational TV series; book HOW TO LIVE A RICHER, FULLER LIFE.

SHEATH CAKE

2 cups flour
2 cups sugar
1 tsp. soda
½ tsp. salt
¼ tsp. cinnamon
2 sticks margarine
4 tsp. cocoa
1 cup water
2 eggs
½ cup buttermilk (or sour cream)
½ cup nuts
1 tsp. vanilla

Combine flour, sugar, soda, salt and cinnamon. Set aside.

Melt margarine, cocoa and water in pan and bring to boil. Add to flour mixture and blend. Add 2 eggs and remaining ingredients.

Bake in pan 10"x15½" for 20 minutes at 400°. If larger pan is used, bake 15 minutes.

★ MRS. JERRY LEWIS (PATTI)
JERRY LEWIS: Actor, author, comedian, director, producer, singer, volunteer.
Top nightclub headliner; many TV appearances include JERRY LEWIS SHOW TV series and annual MUSCULAR DYSTROPHY TELETHON; many films include THE NUTTY PROFESSOR and THE BIG MOUTH; volunteer chairman for 28 years Muscular Dystrophy Association; National Association of Producers and Exhibitors Award of Year 1978; awarded Best Director of Year 8 times since 1960 in Italy, Netherlands, Belgium, Germany, Spain and 3 times in France.

STRAWBERRY CAKE

¼ cup water, boiling
1 sm. pkg. strawberry gelatin
¾ cup cooking oil
1 pkg. white cake mix
4 eggs
½ pkg. frozen strawberries and juice, thawed
FROSTING:
¼ lb. butter or margarine
1 lb. powdered sugar
½ pkg. frozen strawberries, thawed

Mix water and gelatin, add oil and cake mix. Beat one minute. Add eggs, strawberries and juice. Beat 2 minutes. Pour into 3 greased and floured 8" cake pans or two 9" pans and bake at 350°.
FROSTING:
Cream butter and sugar, add strawberries slowly, being careful not to get mixture too thin. Fill between layers and cover cake.

Serves 12.

LORRAINE WOOD

STRAWBERRY HEAVEN ANGEL CAKE

1 pkg. angel food cake mix
1 pt. frozen strawberries
  (in syrup)
1 can lemon icing
1 lemon
Fresh peach slices
  (peeled and dipped in
  lemon juice)
Fresh or whole frozen
  strawberries (cut in half)

Thaw and drain all juices from frozen berries, reserving juices.

Mix cake batter according to directions, EXCEPT substitute juice for water, to make 1 cup. Very gently fold well-mashed thawed berries into batter.

Now banish all small children, large dogs, and large husbands from kitchen and bake as directed. Cool cake for 2 hours before removing from pan.

Add 4 drops lemon juice to icing and heat in pan till warm. Pour over cake, letting it drizzle down sides and in center. Overlap peach slices on top of cake and stud sides and rest of top with as many strawberry halves as possible.

Serves 12.

★ LOLA ALBRIGHT
Actress, singer.
Many TV roles include co-star PETER GUNN TV series; films include A COLD WIND IN AUGUST and co-star LORD LOVE A DUCK (Berlin Film Festival Best Actress Award).

The cook was a good cook, as cooks go;
and as cooks go, she went.
                    HECTOR HUGH MUNRO

THREE LAYER DESSERT

CAKE:

1½ cups flour
1 rounded tsp. sugar
1⅓ cubes margarine
¾ cup nuts (chopped)

MIDDLE LAYER:

1 8-oz. pkg. cream cheese (softened)
⅔ cup powdered sugar
1 tsp. vanilla
¼ of a 12-oz. size of Cool Whip

TOP LAYER:

1 pkg. Jello Instant Chocolate Pudding (5½ oz.)
2¾ cups whole milk
1 tsp. vanilla
¼ cup walnuts (chopped)
¾ of a 12-oz. size of Cool Whip

CAKE:

Preheat oven to 350°. Mix all ingredients. Place in a 9"x13" pan and spread evenly. Press with a flat pancake turner. Bake 30 minutes at 350°. Cool on wire rack.

MIDDLE LAYER:

Blend ingredients well and spread on cooked cake crust.

TOP LAYER:

Mix all ingredients except nuts and Cool Whip. Whip until thickened. Spread evenly over middle layer in pan. Frost with remaining Cool Whip. Sprinkle with nuts. Refrigerate for several hours.
    Cut into squares when chilled.

HINT: Cool Whip must be used.

Serves 14-16.

MRS. JOHN McCLURE

Qu'ils mangent de la brioche.
Let them eat cake.

MARIE ANTOINETTE
A WELL-KNOWN SAYING, ROUSSEAU

VIENNA CAKE

1 sponge cake

VANILLA MOCHA FILLING:

⅓ cup sugar
⅓ cup flour
¼ tsp. salt
2 cups milk (scalded)
1 cup butter
1 tsp. vanilla

CHOCOLATE MOCHA FILLING:

1 oz. sweet chocolate (melted)

NUT BRITTLE:

½ cup pecans or blanched almonds
⅓ cup granulated sugar

VANILLA MOCHA FILLING:

Mix together sugar, flour and salt. Add gradually to scalded milk, cook over low heat, stirring constantly about 15 minutes or until thick and smooth. Add butter and vanilla, mixing well. Remove ⅓ of filling to a bowl. Set remaining filling aside to cool.

CHOCOLATE MOCHA FILLING:

To the ⅓ mocha filling, add melted sweet chocolate. Mix well, cool.

NUT BRITTLE:

Chop pecans or blanched almonds. Melt granulated sugar in frying pan over low heat. When melted, add nuts and pour into buttered shallow pan to cool.

Bake any good sponge cake in a tube pan. When cold, cut crosswise into four layers of equal width. Place bottom layer on cake plate, spread with chocolate mocha filling. Place next layer on top, spread with vanilla mocha filling. Add third layer and spread with remaining chocolate mocha filling. Add last layer and frost top and sides with remaining vanilla mocha filling. Grind the nut brittle and sprinkle over cake.

DON AMENT

PIES

What moistens the lip,
And what brightens the eye,
What calls back the past
Like rich pumpkin pie.

JOHN GREENLEAF WHITTIER

AVOCADO PIE

1 can Eagle Brand sweetened
condensed milk
½ cup lemon juice
¼ tsp. lemon rind (grated)
¾ cup avocado (strained)
1 8"-pan lined with graham
cracker crust (baked)

SOUR CREAM TOPPING:

½ pint sour cream
1 tsp. vanilla
1 tsp. sugar

Combine all main ingredients and pour into pie
shell. Cover with sour cream topping. Sprinkle
some graham cracker crumbs over the topping
and put in oven for 5 minutes at 325°.

JANICE VOGEL ACKLES

DREAMY CREAMY BANANA PIE

6 tbsp. cake flour
⅔ cup sugar
¼ tsp. salt
1¾ cups milk
2 egg yolks
1 tsp. vanilla
½ cup heavy cream
(whipped)
2 or 3 bananas
1 9-inch pie shell (baked)

Sift together the flour, salt and sugar into the top
of a double-boiler. Add milk and cook over hot
water stirring constantly until mixture thickens.
Cook 20 minutes longer, stirring occasionally
and covering lightly between stirs.

Beat egg yolks till foamy. Put a small amount of
cooked mixture into the egg yolks; blend well and
pour into the mixture in the double boiler. Cook
two minutes, stirring enough to blend. Remove
from heat.

Place a piece of plastic wrap or waxed paper on
top of mixture to prevent over-thickening of top.
Cool. Add vanilla and half (more or less) of the
whipped cream. Spread a layer of mixture on
bottom of pie shell, then alternate layers with
sliced bananas. Decorate top with remainder of
whipping cream. May be served as a pudding.

MRS. LOGAN G. WILSHIRE

BLACK BOTTOM PIE

GINGERSNAP CRUST:
35 gingersnaps
¼ lb. butter (melted)
1 tbsp. confectioners
    sugar

CHOCOLATE LAYER:
1 tbsp. unflavored gelatin
4 tbsp. cold water
1 tbsp. cornstarch
4 egg yolks (beaten)
1 tsp. vanilla
½ cup sugar
2 cups milk
¼ tsp. salt
2 oz. (2 squares) chocolate
    (unsweetened and melted)

CREAM LAYER:
4 egg whites
1 tbsp. rum
1 tbsp. shaved unsweetened
    chocolate
⅛ tsp. cream of tartar
1 tsp. sherry
½ cup sugar
¾ cup heavy cream

With rolling pin crush snaps to fine crumbs. Add melted butter and sugar, mix well. Press firmly into 9" pie tin. Bake at 300° 5 minutes.

Soften gelatin in cold water. Scald milk in double boiler. Mix sugar, cornstarch, salt and stir slowly into milk, cook until thick. Add gradually to beaten egg yolks. Return to double boiler and cook 3 minutes longer. Stir in gelatin, dissolved. Divide in half; add melted chocolate and vanilla to half of mixture. Pour carefully into gingersnap crust.

Beat egg-whites until frothy; add cream of tartar, continue beating to a soft peak. Gradually add sugar. Fold meringue into cool custard. Add flavorings. Pour carefully over chocolate layer. Chill in refrigerator until set. When ready to serve spread whipped cream on top of pie, sprinkle with shaved chocolate.

★★ GENA ROWLANDS CASSAVETES AND JOHN CASSAVETES
Actress — Actor, director, writer
Her films include WOMAN UNDER THE IN-FLUENCE (Golden Globe Award Best Actress 1976) — His many TV and film roles include ROSEMARY'S BABY and DIRTY DOZEN. Writing and directing OPENING NIGHT and WOMAN UNDER THE INFLUENCE. (One of only three artists ever to be nominated for an Oscar in the three categories of acting, directing and writing.)

BAVARIAN CREAM PIE

CRUST:

1½ cup graham crackers (crushed) (approximately 11 double crackers)
⅓ cup powdered sugar
⅓ cup margarine (melted)

CREAM FILLING:

1 tbsp. gelatin
¼ cup water
2 eggs (separated)
½ cup sugar
¾ cup milk
⅛ tsp. salt
Hershey almond bar

CRUST:

Mix crumbs with powdered sugar and add melted margarine. Press in bottom and sides of 8" or 9" pie plate. Bake 5 minutes at 325°. Cool. Enough for 2 pies.

CREAM FILLING:

Dissolve gelatin in water. Mix and cook separated yolks, water, sugar, milk and salt in top of double boiler, stirring constantly until slightly thickened. Add gelatin and stir until dissolved. Cool until it begins to jell. Add vanilla, beaten egg whites and 1 cup whipped cream, folding in gently. Pour into crust and chill. Grate Hershey almond bar over top.

(If custard gets too thick before folding in other ingredients, beat with mixer and proceed quickly.)

MRS. MILES W. NEWBY, JR.
Newport Beach, California
President, National Assistance League

CHESS PIE

1 cup raisins
3 tbsp. water
½ cup butter
3 egg yolks (slightly beaten)
½ cup sugar
3 tbsp. milk
1 tsp. vanilla
½ cup walnuts (chopped)
3 egg whites (beaten)
3 tbsp. sugar

Simmer raisins in water until puffy and water is nearly gone. Add butter and let melt.

Mix egg yolks, milk and sugar. Add egg mixture to raisin mixture and cook until slightly thickened. Add vanilla and walnuts.

Put mixture in baked pie crust. Put meringue made of egg whites and sugar on pie and brown slightly.

FLORENCE B. SCHANKE

BEAU CATCHER CHOCOLATE PIE

18 graham crackers
6 tbsp. butter (melted)
4 squares bittersweet
   chocolate
½ lb. butter
1½ cups sugar
4 tsp. vanilla
4 eggs
1 pint whipped cream
   (sweetened)
Confectioner's sugar
2 tbsp. butter
1 pkg. almonds (slivered)

Make pie crust using 18 graham crackers crushed fine and mixed with 6 tbsp. melted butter. Pat into a large 10" pie plate (Pyrex). Set aside to cool.

Melt chocolate, set aside to cool. In a mixer put butter and sugar, beat thoroughly, add 2 tsp. vanilla and cooled chocolate. Continue mixing. Then add 2 whole eggs and beat for 3 minutes, then add 2 more whole eggs and beat another 3-4 minutes. Put this mixture into cooled pie crust. Put in refrigerator for at least 2 hours.

Whip 1 pint of whipping cream, add powdered sugar to taste and 1 tsp. vanilla. Spoon over chocolate pie.

Fry until golden 1 pkg. slivered almonds in 2 tbsp. butter, drain and dry thoroughly. Place almonds in a ring around edge of whipping cream top. Grate semisweet chocolate for center (optional).

VARIATION:

Recipe can be cut in half for use in an 8" pie plate.

This can also be made as individual tarts using foil cup cake liners and patting a tbsp. of the crust mixture at the bottom of each liner. Makes 24, which stretches the recipe considerably and is much easier to serve a group.

Serves 10.

PAT ALCANTARA

CHOCOLATE CHIP PIE

30 marshmallows
½ cup milk
½ pint whipping cream
  (whipped)
1 6-oz. pkg. chocolate chips
  (Nestle's REAL Semi-
  Sweet)
1 tsp. vanilla
CRUST:
15 graham crackers
  (crushed)
¼ cup butter (melted)
Save ½ cup for top.

Melt butter. Add crumbs and line a pie pan. Reserve ½ cup for top. (I use a glass cake dish if it is to be frozen any length of time. Also easier to divide to serve more people.) Place marsh-mallows and milk in double boiler. Melt thoroughly. Beat well and set aside to cool. When thick and cold, beat with electric mixer. Add whipped cream, mix until smooth, pour into lined pan. Sprinkle ½ cup cracker crumbs over top. Garnish with nuts. Freeze. Important to use real chocolate chips.

Serves 8.

MRS. NORRIS J. ROBERTS (NORA)

CRUSTLESS APPLE PIE

8 large cooking apples
  (peeled)
½ cup water
½ tsp. cinnamon
½ cup butter
1 cup brown sugar
½ cup flour
¼ tsp. salt
1 cup Grape Nuts

Fill 8" square pyrex dish with thin-sliced apples. Cover apples with water; sprinkle cinnamon on top. Mix together: butter, brown sugar, flour, salt and Grape Nuts. Spread above mixture over apples.
  Bake one hour at 350°.
HINT: Serve with whipped cream or ice cream. Pie can be baked in morning and reheated for 20 minutes at 350° at dinner time.

Serves 8.

MRS. ERNEST ACH

ICE CREAM PIE

15 Oreo chocolate cookies
1 pint vanilla ice cream
1 pint dark coffee ice cream
½ pint whipping cream
   (flavor with 1 tsp. instant
   coffee, vanilla and 1 tsp.
   sugar)
1 square bitter Hershey
   chocolate

Butter 9" or 10" pie tin lightly. Roll out cookies. Press cookie crumbs around sides and bottom of pie tin.

Take ice cream out of freezer long enough to get a little soft. Spread pie crust with vanilla, then top with coffee ice cream. Cover with whipped cream.

Shave bitter chocolate on top. Freeze 24 hours. Take out of freezer 10 minutes before serving. Wonderful!!

ANNETTE TUTHILL

FROZEN LEMON PIE

1¾ cups crushed vanilla
   wafers
¼ cup + margarine
1½ cups sugar
9 tbsp. lemon juice
   (fresh lemons)
3 cups whipping cream
6 eggs (separated)
¼ tsp. salt

Dissolve sugar in lemon juice in large bowl. Whip cream and set aside. Beat egg yolks with salt until creamy. Add egg yolks to lemon juice mixture and beat well. Beat egg whites until very stiff. Fold cream into egg yolk mixture and then fold in egg whites.

Pour over crust in 9"x13"x2" Pyrex pan. Freeze. Decorate as desired at serving (crumbs sprinkled over top - whipped cream - or crushed sour lemon balls sprinkled over the top).

CRUST:

Melt butter and pour over crumbs in Pyrex pan. Mix thoroughly. Press crust on bottom of pan.

Serves 9-12.

FORNIA HORSLEY

MAUI CREAM PIE

⅔ cup sugar
1 envelope unflavored gelatin
3 tbsp. arrowroot
Pinch of salt
3 oz. pkg. cream cheese (softened)
1¾ cups light cream
6 tbsp. sour cream
1 cup macadamia nuts
2 eggs, separated
1 cup heavy cream, whipped
1 9" pie shell (baked)

Blend first 7 ingredients in blender. Pour into top of double boiler and cook over medium heat until thick (approximately 10 min.) Mix a spoonful of hot sauce into egg yolks and then add yolks to sauce. Cook 2-3 minutes more. Remove and cool.

Beat egg whites until stiff then fold into sauce.

Chill 30-40 minutes. Add whip cream and ½ cup nuts. Pour into baked pie shell. Sprinkle rest of nuts on top.

Refrigerate 4-5 hours before serving.

JEAN MALONEY

MOCHA MOUSSE PIE

FILLING:
3 cubes butter
2 cups sugar
6 squares (1 oz. ea.) unsweetened chocolate
2 squares (1 oz. ea.) semi-sweet chocolate
8 tsp. instant coffee powder
6 eggs

CRUST:
1 pkg. Nabisco wafers (crushed)
1 cube butter
1 tbsp. sugar

TOPPING:
2 cartons heavy cream (whipped)

In a large bowl cream butter and sugar. Melt chocolate and blend in coffee powder until dissolved. Add to sugar and butter; mix thoroughly. Add 1 egg at a time, blending until very smooth each time. Pour into crust, refrigerate 4 hours and top with whipped cream (2 cartons).

CRUST:

Add melted butter and sugar to crumbled cookies. Pat into 10½" spring form pan. Bake at 350° for 8 minutes. Cool and fill.

Serves 12.

MRS. J. O. YUNGFLEISCH (MARY)

PEANUT CREAM PIE

1 graham cracker pie
  shell

FILLING:

½ cup nutty peanut
  butter
½ cup apricot and
  pineapple jam
½ cup milk
1 8-oz. non-milk Whipping
  cream (whipped)

Mix peanut butter, jam and milk together. Fold in whipped cream. Pour into pie shell. Top with whipped cream and a sifting of ground peanuts. Keep cool in refrigerator.

ROMAINE H. PAULEY

PUMPKIN PIE ROBERT

(From THE PALATISTS cookbook 1933)

1½ cups prepared pumpkin
1 cup brown sugar
1 tsp. cinnamon
½ tsp. cloves
2 tsp. ginger
1 tsp. salt
2 eggs
2 cups milk
1 glass of brandy
1 pkg. Pabst-ette Cheese
½ cup heavy cream

Scald the milk. Combine the sugar, spices and salt; beat the eggs until light and cream with the sugar mixture. Pour scalded milk over the egg mixture beating constantly, then combine with the pumpkin. Lastly, add the brandy.

Turn into unbaked pie shell; bake in hot oven 450° for 10 minutes then reduce to 325° and bake 30 to 40 minutes until a knife comes out clean. Decorate with 1 package Pabst-ett cheese into which ½ cup of heavy cream has been blended.

★ MAE WEST
Actress, author.
Many films include SHE DONE HIM WRONG, GO WEST, YOUNG MAN and MYRA BRECKEN-RIDGE; guest MR. ED TV series; book GOODNESS HAD NOTHING TO DO WITH IT.

CREAM CHEESE PEACH PIE

CRUST:
16 graham crackers
¼ cup sugar
½ tsp. cinnamon
¼ cube butter (melted)

FILLING:
3 or 4 peaches (large)
1 8-oz. pkg. cream cheese
2 eggs
⅓ cup sugar
1 tsp. vanilla

CRUST:
Crush graham crackers, mix all ingredients except filling and bake in 9" pie shell for 10 minutes at 350°.

FILLING:
Slice peaches into pie shell and sprinkle with sugar. Cream together cheese, eggs, sugar and vanilla. Pour over peaches in graham cracker shell. Bake at 350° for 40 minutes. Will come from oven puffy, but will settle as it cools. Refrigerate before serving.

Serves 6-8.

MRS. THOMAS A. MITCHELL, JR.

CHOCOLATE PECAN PIE

2 1-oz. squares unsweetened chocolate
3 tbsp. butter
1 cup light corn syrup
¾ cup granulated sugar
½ tsp. salt
3 eggs (slightly beaten)
1 tsp. vanilla
1½ cups chopped pecans
1 unbaked 9" pie crust
Pecan halves
Whipped cream or ice cream

Preheat oven to 375°.

In a double boiler melt chocolate and butter together.

In separate pan, combine corn syrup and sugar and simmer 2 minutes. Add chocolate mixture and cool. Add salt to slightly beaten eggs.

Slowly dribble syrup mixture into eggs, stirring constantly. Blend in vanilla and nuts; pour into pie crust and place halves of pecans on top. Bake for 35 minutes.

Serve with whipped cream or ice cream.

Serves 8.

MRS. CHARLES J. BROSKA

NEW ORLEANS PECAN TARTLETS

¼ lb. butter
1 3-oz. pkg. cream cheese
1 cup flour (sifted)
1 cup pecans (chopped)
2 eggs
1 cup light brown sugar
2 tbsp. butter (soft)
1 tsp. vanilla
⅛ tsp. salt

Cream stick of butter and cream cheese then blend in flour. Form dough into a ball and refrigerate 1 hour.

Divide dough in half and form each ball into 12 small balls. Place balls into ungreased 1¾" muffin pans, press into tartlets using fingers over bottom and sides of pan.

In a bowl beat eggs, sugar, butter, vanilla and salt until smooth.

Place 2 tsp. of pecans in each tartlet, spoon egg mixture over pecans. Bake in 325° oven for 25 minutes or until set. Cool. Remove from pans.

Alternative baking: 350° for 15 to 20 minutes. The dough may also be rolled out and cut to fit pans. NOTE: In doubling the recipe, use ½ cup more flour and 1 more egg.

Makes 24 tartlets.

MRS. ANNETTE LIVINGSTON

SUSAN'S TEXAS PECAN PIE

9" inch pie crust (uncooked)
3 eggs
Pinch of salt
1 cup sugar
1 heaping tsp. flour
1 cup light Karo syrup
1 tsp. vanilla
Large whole pecan halves

Mix all ingredients until smooth. Pour into pie crust. Top with large whole pecan halves and bake in preheated 350° oven for 1 hour or till filling is almost set. It should jiggle a little. Cool completely before cutting.

Serve with generous amounts of whipped cream.

★ SUSAN HOWARD
Actress.
Many films and TV roles include PAPER CHASE TV series.

STRAWBERRY-KIWI-PEACH TART

TART SHELL

1 cup sifted all-purpose
  flour
2 tbsp. powdered sugar
½ cup butter or margarine

FILLING

3 egg yolks
½ cup granulated sugar
¼ cup water
½ cup butter
1 3-oz. pkg. cream cheese
⅛ tsp. almond extract
½ cup peach jam
1 large peach
2 Kiwis
15 strawberries

Sift flour with powdered sugar. Cut in ½ cup butter until mixture forms fine crumbs. Press dough into 10" spring mold pan. Bake at 425° for 8 to 10 minutes. Cool.

FILLING:

Beat 3 egg yolks until pale yellow. In a small pan combine ½ cup sugar and ¼ cup water. Bring to a boil. Boil 2 minutes to soft ball stage (236° on candy thermometer). Gradually pour syrup into egg yolks in mixer at medium speed. Beat until mixture is lukewarm. Continue beating while adding in small pieces butter and cream cheese. Add ⅛ tsp. almond extract. Beat until smooth. Spread in cooled baked tart shell. Chill.

Heat peach jam; strain and cool to lukewarm. Peel and slice peach and Kiwis. Arrange slices artistically over chilled filling. Fill center with 15 large strawberries, stem ends down. Brush fruit with jam. This is a spectacular desert. Beautiful enough to impress an in-law!

Serves 8.

JAN STEIGER

THELMA'S IMPOSSIBLE PIE

4 eggs
1 cup coconut (shredded)
½ cup margarine or
  butter (soft)
1 cup sugar
½ cup flour
Pinch of salt
2 tbsp. vanilla

Put ingredients in blender, blend well.

Pour into large pie pan, greased or buttered. Cook in 325° oven approximately 1 hour or until browned. Coconut forms top crust and flour forms lower crust.

Serves 6-8.

JANE SUMPTER

COOKIES

The British call it biscuit
And it's koekje with the Dutch
But no matter how you say it
All cookies please us much.

ANONYMOUS

APRICOT BARS

⅔ cup dried apricots
½ cup soft margarine
  or butter
¼ cup granulated sugar
1⅓ cups flour
  (sifted)
½ tsp. baking powder
¼ tsp. salt
1 cup brown sugar
  (packed)
2 eggs (well beaten)
¾ tsp. vanilla
½ cup nuts (chopped)
Confectioners' sugar

Rinse apricots; cover with water; boil 10 minutes. Drain, cool and chop. Heat oven to 350°. Grease 8"x8"x2" pan.

Mix margarine, sugar and 1 cup of flour until crumbly. Pack into pan and bake 25 to 30 minutes or until lightly brown.

Sift ⅓ cup flour, baking powder, salt and set aside.

In a separate large bowl, beat brown sugar into eggs. (Be sure to mix well.) Mix in flour mixture, then vanilla.

Stir in nuts and apricots. Spread over baked layer. Bake 30 to 40 minutes or until testing with toothpick indicates bars are done. Cool in pan. Cut into bars. Roll bars in confectioners' sugar.

Makes 32 2"x1" bars.

MRS. ROBERT G. GRAW, JR.
Davidsonville, Maryland

APRICOT DAINTIES

3 tbsp. soft butter
  or margarine
⅓ cup sugar
¼ tsp. vanilla
1 egg yolk (unbeaten)
1 cup flour
  (sifted)
¼ tsp. salt
½ tsp. baking powder
½ cup apricot jam

MERINGUE TOPPING:

1 egg white
¼ cup sugar
¼ tsp. almond or
  vanilla extract
⅔ cup fine coconut
1 tbsp. soft butter

Mix butter and sugar until well blended; add egg yolk and vanilla; beat well. Add flour sifted with baking powder and salt. Press this crumbly mixture into bottom of well greased 8"x8" pan. Spread jam over mixture.

TOPPING

Beat egg white until stiff; add sugar and remaining ingredients. Spread carefully over jam topping to make a thin meringue. Bake all at 325° for 40 minutes. Cool; cut into squares or bars.

Makes 24 bars.

ALMA ENGER

BUTTERSCOTCH SQUARES

½ cup brown sugar
½ cup butter
2 eggs
1 tsp. vanilla
1 cup flour
1½ tsp. baking powder

Dissolve sugar in butter over low flame. Cool.

Beat eggs well, add butter-sugar mixture and vanilla. Stir in flour and baking powder.

In 10" square, buttered pan place wax liner. Pour mix into pan and bake 25 minutes at 350°.

Turn onto board and remove wax paper. Dust with powdered sugar.

Makes 24 squares.

MYNA ROSS

CARAMEL BARS

(more like candy than a bar)

2 cups flour
½ tsp. salt
½ tsp. soda
1 cup brown sugar
1½ cups oatmeal
1 cup butter
6 oz. chocolate chips
1 jar caramel topping
4 tbsp. flour

Mix first 6 ingredients. Spread half of mixture in 9"x13" pan and bake at 350° for 10 minutes. Combine 1 jar caramel topping and 4 tbsp. flour. Heat. Pour over bottom crust. Sprinkle with chocolate chips. Spread with remaining flour mixture. Bake at 350° for 20 minutes. Cut into small squares.

ILAMAY TALLAKSON

CHEERI-CHOC QUICKIES

2 squares Hershey's chocolate (unsweetened)
1 stick margarine
2 cups granulated white sugar
½ tsp. salt
2 eggs
1 cup white flour
½ cup Cheerios
½ cup Grape Nuts cereal

In a 2 qt. saucepan melt chocolate with margarine. While it is melting, grease and flour an 8"x8" baking pan. Preheat oven to 375°.

Add granulated sugar, salt and eggs. Mix well. Add flour, Cheerios and Grape Nuts cereal. Pour into baking pan.

Bake for 25 minutes. It may not look set, but cool a few minutes and score into 36 squares. They harden as they cool.

Makes 36 cookies.

PAT YEOMANS

CARROT COOKIES

½ cup shortening
½ cup butter or
  margarine
1 cup carrots (cooked
  and mashed)
¾ cup sugar
2 eggs
2 cups all-purpose flour
2 tsp. baking powder
1 tsp. cinnamon
½ tsp. nutmeg
½ tsp. salt
¾ cup coconut
  (shredded)

FROSTING:

2½ tbsp. soft butter
1½ cups powdered sugar
  (sifted)
1½ tbsp. orange juice
2 tsp. orange rind

Cream shortening and butter with sugar. Add eggs and carrots and continue with creaming. Sift dry ingredients together and blend into shortening mix. Add coconut. Drop dough by teaspoonfuls about 2" apart on lightly greased baking sheet. Bake in a 400° oven for 8 to 10 minutes, or until no imprint remains when touched lightly. Cool, then frost.

FROSTING:

Blend together butter and sugar. Stir in orange juice and rind. Mix well.

Makes 4 dozen.

ANNA MAE DE WEERDT

CHOCOLATE WALNUT SQUARES

½ cup shortening
¼ cup white sugar
¾ cup brown sugar
1 egg yolk
½ tsp. vanilla
½ cup rolled oats
  (quick)
½ cup flour
⅛ tsp. salt
4 small Hershey bars
1 tsp. butter
Walnuts (chopped)

Mix ingredients in order given, except for Hershey bars, butter and walnuts. Spread in 7"x11" pan and bake 20 minutes at 350°. Melt Hershey bars with butter.

When cookies have cooled 10 minutes, spread with chocolate mixture and sprinkle with finely chopped walnuts.

Cut into 1" squares while partially warm.

INGRID HEDBERG

CHOCOLATE CRANBERRY BARS

BARS:

1 4-oz. pkg. sweet cooking chocolate
2 cups cake flour (unsifted)
½ tsp. baking soda
¾ tsp. cinnamon
½ tsp. cloves
1 cup butter or margarine
1½ cups granulated sugar
2 eggs
1 tsp. vanilla
1 cup whole cranberry sauce
½ cup buttermilk
Confectioners' Sugar

MEXICAN CHOCOLATE ICING:

1 stick margarine
2 squares unsweetened chocolate
6 tbsp. milk (or 4 tbsp. milk and 2 tbsp. rum)
1 1-lb. pkg. Confectioners' sugar
1 tsp. vanilla extract
½ cup chopped pecans (or walnuts)

Melt chocolate in sauce pan over very low heat, stirring constantly. Cool.

Mix flour with baking soda and spices.

Cream butter; gradually add sugar creaming well after each addition. Add eggs one at a time, beating well. Blend in melted chocolate, vanilla and cranberry sauce. Add flour mixture alternately with buttermilk, beating after each addition until smooth. Pour into greased and floured 13"x9" pan. Bake at 350° for about 40 minutes or until cake just begins to pull away from sides of pan; then remove from pan. Sprinkle with confectioners' sugar. Cut into bars. I prefer to use Mexican Chocolate Icing instead of the easy confectioners' sugar.

Combine margarine, chocolate and milk in a saucepan and heat until bubbles form around the edge. Remove from heat. Add confectioners' sugar, vanilla and pecans; beat. Ice cake while still warm. I use 4 tbsp. of milk and 2 of rum... if needed add more of either... I prefer walnuts to the pecans or if one wishes they need use neither.

Makes 30 bars.

★ MRS. LEROY PRINZ (BETTY)
LEROY PRINZ: Choreographer, director, producer.

Many films include MURDERS IN THE RUE MORGUE, GUS KAHN STORY, HELEN MORGAN STORY and SAYONARA.

CHOCOLATE COOKIES

3 cups sugar
1½ cups milk
⅔ cups cocoa
4½ tbsp. butter (melted)
Pinch of salt
1 pkg. graham cracker
  crumbs
Vanilla

Mix first five ingredients. Bring to a boil for three minutes or until soft ball forms and holds together when dropped in cold water. Beat until cool and mix begins to thicken. Add vanilla and one package graham cracker crumbs. Mix well. Drop cookies by spoonful on wax paper. Cool.
Makes 2½ dozen.

VALLIE BOWMAN

CALIFORNIA DATE BARS

¾ cup flour (sifted)
½ cup butter or
  margarine
2 eggs
1 cup brown sugar
  (packed)
¾ cup dates (chopped)
¾ cup walnuts (chopped)
¼ tsp. baking powder
1 tsp. vanilla
1 tsp. lemon peel
  (grated)
2-3 tbsp. lemon juice
1 cup powdered sugar

Mix flour and butter as for pastry. Sprinkle in 8" square pan. Bake at 350 ° for 10 minutes.

Beat eggs, blend in brown sugar, dates, nuts, baking powder and vanilla. Spread over crust in pan and bake 20 minutes.

Stir lemon juice and peel into powdered sugar and spread over hot mixture as it comes from oven. Cool. Cut into squares or bars.

GERI BUTTKE

SAHARA DATE SQUARES

1 cup sugar
3 eggs
1 cup all-purpose flour
  (sifted)
1 tsp. salt
½ tsp. baking powder
⅛ tsp. cloves
¼ tsp. cinnamon
1 tsp. vanilla
1 cup walnut or pecan
  meats (broken)
2 cups dates (chopped)

Beat eggs until light. Add sugar gradually. Resift flour with baking powder and salt. Add cloves and cinnamon. Add sifted ingredients to the egg mixture with the vanilla. Blend until ingredients are well mixed. Add dates and nuts. Mix light. Pour into greased and floured 9x12" pan. Bake 25 minutes at 325°. May be rolled in powdered sugar or left plain.

Delicious for any occasion.
Makes about 50 squares.

JACKIE BROWN

". . . LIFE IS JUST A BOWL OF CHERRIES
SO LIVE AND LAUGH AT IT ALL."

— 1931

Lyrics by LEW BROWN
Music by RAY HENDERSON
Copyright © 1931 by DeSylva, Brown & Henderson, Inc.
Copyright Renewed, Assigned to Chappell & Co., Inc.
International Copyright Secured
All Rights Reserved
Used by Permission

Photography by
PAUL CURRIER
Dallas, Texas

HEALTH COOKIES

¾ cup currants or
  raisins
1 stick margarine
½ cup water
¾ cup flour (sifted)
½ tsp. baking soda
½ tsp. salt
½ tsp. allspice
1 cup dark brown sugar
  (packed)
1½ cups quick oats
½ cup chocolate chips
  (mini ones if possible)
½ cup coconut flakes
½ cup walnuts
  (chopped)
1 tsp. vanilla

Heat water and margarine in saucepan. Add currants and let cool. Sift together the flour, salt, soda and all spices. Add the brown sugar and oatmeal, mixing well. Add the vanilla to the liquid mixture and combine with the dry ingredients. Stir in the chocolate bits, coconut, and nuts. Chill well in the refrigerator, overnight if you like.

Place in walnut-size chunks on greased cookie sheet, leaving space for them to spread. Bake at 350° for 12-15 minutes until a medium brown. Cookies are limp when taken from the oven, but become crisp when cooled.

Makes 5-6 dozen two-inch cookies.

MRS. LOGAN G. WILSHIRE

LEBKUCHEN

3 eggs (beaten slightly)
  then add
1 lb. brown sugar
3 heaping tbsp. Ghiradelli
  Chocolate
2 tsp. cinnamon
1 tsp. cloves
½ tsp. baking soda
2 tbsp. honey
3 cups flour
¼ lb. citron and orange
  peel (candied)
½ lb. almonds (blanched)
(Put above 2 items through
  meat grinder - second
  knife)

Mix all together, make one long roll, then cut into ½" pieces and pat them into little round cookies. Bake about 10-15 minutes at 350°. Ice while warm with a mixture of powdered sugar and lemon juice. May put ½ blanched almond in center of cookie before baking.

This is an old German Christmas family recipe.

Makes 4 dozen.

HELEN TUPPAN

LACE COOKIES

1 cube butter
1½ cups oatmeal
  (quick-cooking)
¾ cup sugar
1 tsp. baking powder
1 tsp. flour
½ tsp. salt
1 egg
2 tsp. vanilla
½ cup pecans, macadamia or
  other nuts (chopped
  coarsely)

Melt butter and pour over quick-cooking oatmeal. Mix with sugar, baking powder, flour and salt. Beat egg with vanilla and mix with above. Add nuts.

Drop small amount on tin-foil lined cookie sheet. (They spread.) Bake until done (about 5 minutes) in a 350° oven. Let stand on cookie sheet 5 to 10 minutes.

Makes 6 dozen.

ALPHA MacCORMACK

NO BAKE COOKIES

2 cups sugar
⅓ cup cocoa
½ cup milk
½ cup butter
2½ cups quick cooking
  oatmeal
½ cup peanut butter
1 tsp. vanilla

Mix sugar, cocoa, milk and butter. Cook 2 minutes at medium heat until boiling. Turn down heat, simmer and cook 2 minutes. Add oatmeal, peanut butter and vanilla. Stir and drop by spoonful onto wax paper to cool - then store.

CLAIRE STORM

OATMEAL COOKIES

2 cups Crisco
2 cups sugar
4 eggs (slightly
  beaten)
1 tsp. cinnamon
1 tsp. each cloves
  and allspice
¾ tsp. salt
4 cups flour
2⅔ tsp. soda
⅓ cup buttermilk
3 tbsp. molasses
2 cups currants, raisins
  and nuts
4 cups oatmeal

Cream Crisco and sugar until very light. Add eggs. Sift spices and salt with flour. Add soda to buttermilk. Add molasses to creamed Crisco and sugar. Add flour mixture, fruit and nuts. Add oatmeal last.

Drop dough by small spoonfuls on floured and greased cookie sheet. Bake at 400° for 8 minutes.

Makes 8-10 dozen.

MILDRED M. POWERS

PEANUT COOKIES

½ cup shortening
1 cup brown sugar
1 egg
½ tsp. soda
½ tsp. baking powder
⅓ tsp. salt
1 cup flour
1 cup quick cooking oatmeal
½ cup cornflakes (crushed)
⅔ cup salted peanuts

Cream shortening and sugar until the mixture is light and fluffy. Add egg and beat well.

Add soda, baking powder and salt to flour and sift together three times. Add to creamed mixture then blend in oatmeal and cornflakes. Fold in salted peanuts.

Drop dough by tablespoon 2 inches apart onto greased cookie sheet. Flatten lightly with fork. Bake in a 375° oven about 12 minutes or until set.

Makes about 3 dozen.

INGRID HEDBERG

PEANUT BUTTER NUGGETS

1 18-oz. jar peanut butter (if you prefer crunch, use nutty peanut butter)
6 oz. butter (or margarine)
1 lb. graham crackers (crushed)
1 pkg. chocolate bits
1 lb. pkg. powdered sugar
Enough cream or milk to moisten lightly

Blend peanut butter and butter. Crush graham crackers and add to above mixture. Add chocolate bits and powdered sugar (save small amount of sugar for "dusting" the cookies). Mix well. Add enough liquid to blend ingredients (keep on dry side).

Form into balls, dust with powdered sugar and refrigerate or freeze.

Makes several dozen depending on size.

MRS. THOMAS C. LEAHY

PECAN TURTLE BARS

CRUST:

2 cups all-purpose flour
1 cup brown sugar
  (firmly packed)
½ cup butter or
  margarine
1 cup whole pecan halves
  (not chopped)

CARAMEL LAYER:

½ cup brown sugar
  (firmly packed)
⅔ cup butter or
  margarine
1 cup chocolate chips
  (semi-sweet)

Preheat oven to 350°. Mix crust ingredients until particles are fine. Pat firmly into greased 9"x13" baking pan. Sprinkle pecans evenly over the bottom of the unbaked crust.

In a heavy 1-qt. saucepan combine brown sugar and butter. Cook over medium heat stirring constantly until entire surface is bubbly; then boil ½ to 1 minute, stirring constantly. Pour evenly over pecans.

Bake in 350° oven for 18 to 22 minutes or until bubbly and light golden brown. Remove from oven and immediately sprinkle with chocolate chips. Let chips melt slightly (2 to 3 minutes) then lightly swirl as they melt. Do not spread chips. Cool completely. Cut into bars or squares.

Makes 3 to 4 dozen, depending on size desired.

MRS. FRANK L. WOLFSON

PERSIMMON COOKIES

½ cup shortening
1½ cups brown sugar
1 egg (beaten)
1 cup persimmon pulp
2 cups flour
1 tsp. soda
½ tsp. cinnamon
½ tsp. ground allspice or
  cloves
½ tsp. salt
1 cup raisins (ground)
1 cup walnuts (chopped)

Cream shortening and sugar. Add egg and persimmon pulp. Sift together flour, soda, cinnamon, allspice and salt. Add sifted dry ingredients, then raisins and nuts.

Drop by spoonfuls on greased cookie sheet. Bake at 350° for 10 to 15 minutes.

Makes 3 dozen.

MRS. GEORGE B. SPEARS

SHORTBREAD

½ lb. butter
2 cups flour
¼ cup cornstarch
½ cup sugar
½ tsp. salt
Nutmeg

Cream butter and sugar well. Add remaining ingredients. Roll out on well floured board to ¼" or ⅓". Cut with cookie cutters and bake in a slow oven (325°) for 15 minutes. Cool on cake rack.

Makes 4 dozen.

BETTY BERRINGTON

SUNFLOWER SEED COOKIES

1 cup butter or
   shortening
1 cup sugar
1 cup brown sugar
   (firmly packed)
2 eggs
1 tsp. vanilla
1½ cups flour
   (unsifted)
1 tsp. soda
½ tsp. salt
3 cups quick cooking
   oats
1 cup salted sunflower
   seeds (shelled)

Cream butter and 2 sugars. Add eggs and vanilla. Beat. Add flour, soda, salt and oatmeal. Mix thoroughly. Gently blend in sunflower seeds. Form on long rods about 1½ inches in diameter. Chill thoroughly. Slice ¼ inch thick. Put on ungreased cookie sheet. Bake 350° for 10 minutes. Cool on wire rack. Store.

Makes 9 dozen.

MRS. W. BERNARD MELONE

Coleridge holds that a man
cannot have a pure mind
who refuses apple-dumplings.
I am not certain but he is right.

CHARLES LAMB

SWEDISH COOKIES

¼ lb. butter
½ white sugar
½ cup brown sugar
1 egg
½ cup flour
½ tsp. baking powder
½ tsp. salt
½ tsp. soda
1 tsp. vanilla
1 cup coconut
1 cup oats (for
    quick cooking oatmeal)
1 cup almonds
    (chopped)

Have butter at room temperature. Cream butter and sugars. Add egg.

Sift dry ingredients and add to butter and mix. Add vanilla, coconut, oats and almonds.

Mix well, drop by teaspoonfuls on ungreased cookie sheet.

Bake 12 minutes at 350°.

These are better frozen. Eat directly from freezer.

Makes 4 dozen crisp, lacy cookies.

MRS. W. BERNARD MELONE

TORTILLA COOKIES

2 tsp. cinnamon
½ cup sugar
12 flour tortillas
Vegetable oil for frying

Mix together cinnamon and sugar.

Fry 1 tortilla at a time until golden brown. Turn, repeat. Remove tortilla to paper towel and sprinkle with 1 or 2 teaspoons cinnamon mixture. Cut into wedges and serve warm.

Wonderful for breakfast.

Serves 12.

MRS. ALI SAR

CANDY AND NUTS

Between almonds and fudge
I cannot judge,
But it makes me wince
If you forget the mints.

ANONYMOUS

ALMOND BUTTER CRUNCH

(Important: Must have candy thermometer)

1½ cups butter
1½ cups sugar
1 tsp. corn syrup
1 cup almonds (unblanched)
6 oz. semi-sweet chocolate
½ cup blanched almonds
   (slivered)

Melt butter in skillet. Add sugar and corn syrup, bring mixture to a boil, stirring with a wooden spoon. Set a candy thermometer at slant and cook mixture over medium heat, stirring constantly, until the thermometer reaches 270°, stir in blanched almonds and continue to boil, stirring constantly, until 290°. (Butter and sugar will not blend until temperature is 250°; if heat is not maintained they will separate so keep mixture bubbling. If they do separate, add 1 tbsp. cold water and continue cooking until temperature reaches 290°).

Remove from skillet and pour on 12"x15" cookie sheet lined with waxed paper. Let cool and set. Melt 3 oz. chocolate and spread over surface when hardened. Sprinkle half of unblanched almonds over chocolate surface. Let dry. Turn candy sheet over and repeat process. When cooled and set break into pieces and serve.

BETTY JONES

BUTTER CARAMELS

(Must have candy thermometer)

My great grandmother's recipe from Scotland.

1 cup butter
½ cups Karo (light)
1¼ cups whipping cream
½ cup milk
2 cups sugar
1 cup walnuts (diced)
1 tsp. vanilla
½ tsp. salt

Check candy thermometer by plunging into boiling water. Adjust according to above or below boiling point or 212° at sea level. Subtract 1° for every 500 feet above sea level.

Mix ingredients in large pot. Cook to 244-248°. Pour into 8"x8" or 9"x9" pan greased with butter. Let set until slightly firm, then score for cubes. When totally firm, remove from pan, cut and wrap with waxed paper.

BETTY JONES

CHOCOLATE CANDY ROLL

1 12-oz. pkg. chocolate chips
½ cup margarine (1 stick)
2 tsp. vanilla
1 cup nuts (chopped)
1 pkg. miniature
   marshmallows (colored
   preferred)
7-8-oz. pkg. shredded
   coconut

Melt chocolate chips and butter in a double boiler and blend. Remove from heat, add nuts, marshmallows and vanilla.

Place about 1/5 of coconut and 1/5 of chocolate mixture on large sheet of wax paper about 18" long and gently roll into a roll 15" long. Makes 5 rolls, each about 1" diameter. Place in refrigerator until ready to use. Slice into 1" pieces. Can be prepared in advance. Freezes well.

Makes 80 pieces.

PAULINE SIMON

CHOCOLATE ORANGE BALLS

6 oz. chocolate chips
½ cup sugar
¼ cup light corn syrup
2½ cups vanilla wafers
   (crushed) (1 pkg.
   Sunshine cookies)
1 cup nuts (chopped)
1 tsp. orange extract
Roll in red or green sugar

Melt chocolate chips over hot water, remove and stir in sugar and syrup. Blend in water (about ¼ cup). Combine wafers, nuts and add chocolate with orange extract. Mix well. Form in 1" balls. Roll in decoration. Let ripen in covered container for at least several days. Will keep 3 or 4 weeks.

Makes 4½ dozen candies.

MRS. WILLIAM J. REA

CHOCOLATE WALNUT BUTTER CRUNCH

1 cup butter or margarine
1⅓ cups granulated sugar
1 tsp. light corn syrup
2 tbsp. water
1 cup walnuts (coarsely
   chopped)
4 4½-oz. bars milk chocolate
   (melted)
1 cup walnuts (finely
   chopped)

Melt butter in heavy 2-qt. saucepan. Add sugar, syrup and water. Cook, stirring often, to hardcrack stage (300°). Take off burner at 280°.

Quickly stir in coarsely chopped nuts; spread in well-greased 13"x9"x2" pan. Cool.

Turn out on waxed paper. Spread top with half the chocolate and sprinkle with half the chopped nuts; cover with waxed paper; invert and repeat chocolate and nuts. Chill to firm. Break before it gets too firm.

KAREN MARSHALL

MICROWAVE FUDGE

1 lb. powdered sugar
½ cup unsweetened Hershey cocoa
¼ cup milk (add 1 tbsp. if using marshmallows)
¼ lb. butter or margarine
1 tbsp. vanilla
1 cup walnuts (chopped)
½ cup miniature marshmallows (optional)

Blend sugar, cocoa, milk and butter in non-metallic mixing bowl. Cook for 2 minutes. Remove bowl, mix with spoon to completely blend. Add nuts and marshmallows and quickly pour into greased dish and allow to cool in refrigerator before serving.

SALLY GULICK

SOUR CREAM WHITE FUDGE

2 tbsp. butter
2 cups sugar
½ tsp. salt
1 cup sour cream
½ cup nuts (chopped)

Combine sugar, salt, sour cream. Boil until temperature reaches soft ball. Stir constantly. Add 2 tbsp. butter. Cool to room temperature. Beat until gloss disappears. Add ½ cup chopped nuts. Pour into 8"x8" dish.

MARILYN SMITH

PEANUT BUTTER BON BONS

1 cup chunk peanut butter
¼ cup soft butter
2 cups powdered sugar
1 cup salted peanuts (chopped)
1 lg. pkg. chocolate chips
1 tbsp. paraffin (melted)

Mix and chill all ingredients. Form mixture into small balls. Melt 1 large package chocolate chips over very hot water. Add 1 tbsp. melted paraffin into the chocolate. Dip balls into chocolate. Chill.

PATT DALEY

PANUCHA

1 lb. brown sugar
Few grains of salt
1 tbsp. light corn syrup
1 tbsp. butter
¾ cup evaporated milk
1 tsp. vanilla
⅔ cup nuts (chopped)

Mix thoroughly all ingredients, except nuts. Cook over medium heat to soft ball stage, stirring constantly. Turn into buttered pan. Cut into squares when cool.

NANCY POLIMER

CREAMY PRALINES

3 cups light brown sugar
  (firmly packed)
1 cup heavy cream
¼ lb. butter
⅛ tsp. cinnamon
1½ cups nuts (pecans or
  walnuts) (chopped)

Combine sugar, cream, butter. Bring to boil, to soft ball stage. Stir occasionally. Remove from heat. Stir in cinnamon and nuts. Beat candy until it begins to thicken. Drop on wax paper by the spoonful. Cool until firm.

Makes 3 dozen.

GLENDA GRIBBEN

ENGLISH TOFFEE

1 cup sugar
1 cup pecans (chopped)
1 cube butter
Milk or semi-sweet chocolate
  bar for coating
Powdered sugar for coating

Stir sugar, pecans and butter over low heat in saucepan until butterscotch color (just past fat separation stage). Pour quickly, patting smoothly, in buttered pie tin which has been covered with grated sweet or semi-sweet chocolate. Immediately rub with more sweet chocolate. Cool. Break into pieces and dust with powdered sugar.

RUTH H. WILT

PRISSY PECANS

1 lb. pecan halves (shelled)
½ cup butter (melted)
¼ cup sugar
3 tbsp. sherry (I use cream sherry)
1 tsp. grated nutmeg
Dash of salt

Put pecans in shallow baking pan and roast in 325° oven for 20 minutes, turning frequently with a fork. Melt butter and combine with sugar, sherry, nutmeg and salt.

Pour over pecans; return to oven for 20 minutes, again turning with fork. When nuts have absorbed most of the butter mixture, turn out on paper towels and dry.

Makes 1 quart.

MRS. CHARLES J. BROSKA

SOUR CREAM NUTS

1 cup brown sugar (packed firm)
½ cup white sugar
½ cup sour cream
1 tsp. vanilla
2½ cups nuts (large, broken pieces)

Dissolve first four ingredients over low heat, stirring constantly until firmer than soft ball stage. (240° on candy thermometer.)

Stir in nuts, coating thoroughly. Spread on waxed paper to cool. Break apart into serving pieces.

EDIE BARTLETT

SPICED PECANS

1 egg white
¼ tsp. water
1 lb. pecan meats (large and whole)
½ cup sugar
¾ tsp. cinnamon
½ tsp. salt

Whip egg white and water until frothy but not stiff. Put nuts in egg whites and stir until coated. Mix sugar, cinnamon and salt; add to nuts and stir until coated with sugar. Place on buttered cookie sheet. Spread out evenly. Bake at 250° for 1 hour. Turn every 15 minutes with spatula. Spread nuts as much as possible so they won't cluster.

EMMA L. KELLOGG

MORE PIZAZZ

Peter Piper picked a peck of pickled peppers,
A peck of pickled peppers Peter Piper picked;
If Peter Piper picked a peck of pickled peppers
Where's the peck of pickled peppers Peter Piper picked?

NURSERY RHYMES 1819

CURRIED FRUIT BAKE

1 can peaches
1 can pears
1 can apricots
1 can pineapple chunks
1 stick butter
1 cup light brown sugar
3 tbsp. curry powder
Sprinkle of cinnamon

Mix first 7 ingredients, add juice of any of the fruits to cover. Sprinkle cinnamon on top. Bake at 350° for 1 hour.

Serves 8.

MRS. HORACE L. MARTIN
Newport Beach, California
Past President,
National Assistance League

PEACHES IN WINTER

1 lug fresh peaches in the fall (or as many as you have the time and energy to work with when the price is right and the quality high)
Gallon-size zip lock bags
1 plastic straw

Work with just a few peaches at a time. Peel; halve and remove pits.

Arrange in zip-lock bags in single layer, flat rows. Fill bag; close bag, except to insert straw. Remove extra air in bag by sucking on straw and snap shut.

Immediately freeze in flat layers (may use cookie sheet). Keeps beautifully all year.

HINTS. Marvelous for a quick tart; just remove as many peaches as required. Also nice for a bag lunch. Remove one peach half and put over ½ carton cottage cheese; keeps cheese cool as it thaws. Best used when partially frozen.

MRS. BRIAN L. COCHRAN

OYSTER DRESSING

⅛ lb. butter
¼ lg. green pepper
3 lg. stalks celery
1 lg. onion
1 lg. can water chestnuts
1 qt. oysters (cooked or canned)
½ cup oyster liquor
1 box dry prepared bread dressing
½ tsp. marjoram
½ tsp. summer savory
1 tsp. celery salt

Chop vegetables, water chestnuts and oysters very fine. Saute vegetables and chestnuts in butter. Combine with dry bread dressing, add oysters and oyster liquor. Season.

Stuff turkey or butter the inside of a casserole and bake, covered, in a 350° oven for about 1 hour.

If baked in casserole, it is desirable to add a little chicken broth to the mixture to keep it moist.

Stuffs up to 14 lb. turkey.

Serves 12.

LORRAINE WOOD

VEGETABLE DRESSING

4 onions
1 full stalk of celery (leaves also)
1 bunch of carrots
½ bunch of parsley
1 tsp. thyme (ground) (2 tsp. fresh)
2 tsp. poultry seasoning
Salt & pepper to taste
2 tbsp. butter
2 cans of chicken broth

Chop all vegetables to ½ inch squares-approximately. Saute in butter to tender, do not brown. Add seasoning and broth, simmer for ½ hour and serve as a vegetable or after cooking, cool and stuff chicken or veal.

★ MRS. DAVID ROSE
DAVID ROSE: Arranger, composer, conductor, pianist, recording artist.
Music Director, M-G-M; songs include HOLIDAY FOR STRINGS and THE STRIPPER; film scores include OPERATION PETTICOAT and NEVER TOO LATE; TV scores include FRED ASTAIRE SPECIALS (Emmy Award 1959), RED SKELTON SHOW and BONANZA.

YORKSHIRE PUDDING

3 cups milk
2 oz. butter (softened)
4 tbsp. flour
4 eggs
Salt

Mix flour with small amount of cold milk. Heat remainder of milk and pour into flour mixture, stirring well. Add softened butter, eggs and salt. Beat well. Pour into buttered pie plate. Cook 30 to 40 minutes in oven with roast.

Cut in squares and serve around roast beef.

GRACE SEMER

PINK GRAPEFRUIT JAM

8 large grapefruit
7 cups sugar
1 pkg. Certo (Certo now
    comes in foil envelopes,
    2 to a package)
Red vegetable dye

Peel and cut grapefruit in 2" sections, removing seeds. Steam in a pressure cooker for 10 minutes at 5 pounds pressure. Then force fruit through a colander using a tablespoon to force some of pulp through. You should get 3½ cups.

Mix grapefruit and sugar in a large pan, stir occasionally and bring to a rolling boil. Turn off heat and add the Certo, stirring well.

Add red vegetable dye to get proper pinkish color. Let cool 5 minutes, then seal in jam jars.

PAUL MARSH

GENEVIEVE'S FROZEN STRAWBERRY JAM

3½-oz. package powdered
    pectin
1 cup white corn syrup
4 cups strawberries (crushed)
5½ cups sugar
¼ cup lemon juice

Slowly sift pectin into crushed berries. Set aside 30 minutes, stirring occasionally. Gradually add corn syrup, stir well. Gradually add sugar. When dissolved, add lemon juice.

Pour into covered containers and freeze 24 hours at least. May be stored a month in the refrigerator or indefinitely in the freezer.

JANICE VOGEL ACKLES

WHOLE STRAWBERRY PRESERVES

4 boxes whole strawberries
(washed and stemmed)
6 cups sugar
1 tbsp. lemon juice

Place berries in a large bowl, cover with boiling water for 3 minutes. Put in a colander and drain until the water starts to run red. Put into a large kettle (4 to 6 quarts), bring to a boil and boil for 3 minutes. Watch sticking, stir with a wooden spoon. After the 3 minute boil, add 3 cups sugar and bring to a boil and boil for 5 minutes. After the 5 minute boil add 3 more cups sugar and boil to 220° on a candy thermometer, skimming when necessary. Remove from fire, add 1 tbsp. lemon juice, stir and cool in pan. Shake pan frequently and vigorously during cooling process to plump berries. When cool, put in sterilized jars and seal with paraffin.

Yield 2½ pints.

JOAN O. ST. CLAIR

CORN RELISH

4 cups sugar
4 cups vinegar
1 tbsp. salt
1 tbsp. celery seed
1 tbsp. turmeric
4 cups onions (chopped fine)
4 cups tomatoes (chopped fine)
4 cups cabbage (chopped fine)
4 cups cucumber (chopped fine)
4 cups corn

Heat sugar, vinegar and spices to boiling, add vegetables and cook uncovered 25 minutes.

Pack in pint jars, seal well and refrigerate well before serving.

Makes 5 quarts.

MRS. GEORGE B. SPEARS

PINEAPPLE CRANBERRY RELISH

1 lb. cranberries
2 whole oranges
2 apples
1 small can crushed
   pineapple (well drained)
2 cups sugar
1 envelope gelatin
   (optional)

Grind together cranberries, whole oranges and apples. Add crushed pineapple and sugar. If too juicy, add 1 envelope of Knox unflavored Gelatin. May be made way ahead of time.

Makes 3 cups

DOROTHEA HEITZ

DOYNE'S SPICED CRANBERRIES

2 cups sugar
2 cups water
½ tsp. salt
½ tsp. ground cloves
½ tsp. ground mace
¼ tsp. lemon peel
1 tsp. cinnamon and 1
   cinnamon stick
½ tsp. allspice
Juice of 1 lemon
½ cup cider vinegar
   (add toward last)
8 cups cranberries

Use 6 quart container. Boil for at least 20 minutes the first 10 ingredients. Let the syrup string.

Wash cranberries thoroughly and add to container. Let simmer 6-10 minutes or until berry skins pop.

Can be stored in refrigerator for several months.

Makes 2 quarts.

DOYNE WOOD

SWEET PICKLES

1 quart whole dill pickles
   (not kosher)
½ cup vinegar
1 tbsp. celery seed
1 tbsp. mustard seed
1" cinnamon stick
3½ cups sugar

Drain, rinse and cut pickles into thick slices. Put into glass or plastic bowl that has lid. Combine next 4 ingredients and pour over pickles. On top of this pour the 3½ cups sugar. Do not stir the sugar into the brine. It will dissolve in a few days. Cover and let stand in refrigerator 10 days before using.

Makes 1 quart.

MRS. THOMAS O. BROWN

SAUERKRAUT RELISH
(Old German Recipe)

2 onions (sliced in
   rings)
4 pieces bacon (cut in
   small pieces)
1 large can sauerkraut
3 apples (peeled & quartered)
1 tsp. caraway seed
1 tbsp. flour
Dash of white wine

May be served hot or cold--keeps a week in refrigerator--nice with chicken, ham and most especially turkey.

Braise onions, add bacon and cook (not crisp); add sauerkraut and apples and one cup water. Add caraway seed, simmer covered 1½ hours. If more liquid is needed, add more water. Just before serving stir in flour and a nice dash of white wine.

MRS. ROBERT L. HICKS

ZUCCHINI RELISH

10 zucchini (ground) (can use
   very large squash. Discard
   seeds from these, takes
   about 5-6 lbs. squash)
4 cups onion (ground)
2 tbsp. salt (sea or
   pickling)
2 red bell peppers (ground)
2 green bell peppers,
   (ground)
2¼ cups cider vinegar
4 cups sugar
2 tsp. each celery seed and
   black pepper
1 tsp. each nutmeg, turmeric,
   dry mustard and
   cornstarch

Combine zucchini, ground onion and salt. Let stand in refrigerator overnight.

In the morning cover with cold water, let stand one hour, drain, add bell peppers (green and red).

Combine cider vinegar, sugar, celery seed, black pepper, nutmeg, turmeric, dry mustard and cornstarch. Heat and stir until sugar is dissolved then add squash, onion, peppers. Boil gently for 30 minutes. Seal in sterile jars.

Makes 1 quart

ESTER D. McGINNIE
Portland, Oregon

APPLE SAUCE

8 Roman Beauty apples
   (peeled, cored and sliced)
¼ lb. butter
1 cup brown sugar
1 tbsp. cinnamon

Place ingredients in covered saucepan over low heat, stirring often and cook until its consistency is soft.

Serves 6.

★ MRS. ROBERT VINTON (DOLLY)
BOBBY VINTON: Singer.
Nightclub headliner, known as THE POLISH SINGER.

BARBEQUE SAUCE

2 tbsp. butter
1 onion (sliced)
¾ cup sugar
½ cup chili sauce
2 tsp. Worcestershire Sauce
½ cup celery (chopped)
2 tsp. vinegar or wine
1 tsp. horseradish mustard
1 clove garlic
1 tsp. garlic salt or salt
2 tsp. lemon juice
½ cup catsup
2 tbsp. brown sugar
½ tsp. pepper

Melt butter and brown onions. Add remaining ingredients and cook 20 minutes.

Makes 2 cups

MRS. MILES W. NEWBY, JR.
Newport Beach, California
President
National Assistance League

*The critical period in matrimony
is breakfast-time.*
   SIR ALAN PATRICK HERBERT, "UNCOMMON LAW"

CHILI SALSA

1 large clove garlic (minced)
½ cup onion (chopped)
2 tbsp. olive or corn oil
1 tbsp. flour
¼ cup chili powder (or as
  desired)
½ tsp. dried oregano leaves
½ tsp. dried cumin
  (if desired)
1 tsp. salt
1 cup tomato puree (or more)
1 cup water or bouillon
1 or 2 fresh medium sized
  tomatoes (chopped)

Cook onion and garlic in shortening until limp (about 8 minutes). Stir in flour, heat to boiling, stirring. Add all remaining ingredients. Heat to boiling and simmer 20 to 30 minutes.

Any leftover salsa may be frozen for future use in spaghetti sauce or to pour over chicken and bake.

Freezes well.

Makes 2½ cups

VIOLETTA FOSS MOORE

MY UNCLE JIM'S HOT SAUCE

1 large and 1 small can solid
  packed tomatoes (drain off
  excess water)
3 pinches oregano
1 tsp. cumin
3 cloves garlic
1 bunch green onions or 2
  leeks (chopped fine)
4 oz. La Victoria brand
  yellow chili peppers
  (pickled)
2 tbsp. Accent (optional)
Paprika to color

Grind tomatoes, garlic and leeks together. Add oregano, cumin and Accent. Add chili peppers to grinder. Drain off excess juice. If too hot can be cooled down by using more tomatoes.

Excellent as a dip with tortilla chips, served with fish or Mexican food.

GLORIA ARNETT

MUSTARD SAUCE

¼ cup butter (melted)
1 tbsp. flour
½ cup boiling water
½ cup vinegar
½ cup French's prepared
  mustard
1¼ cups sugar
2 egg yolks

Mix butter and flour. Stir the butter-flour mixture with water, vinegar and mustard. Beat in blender one minute. Add the sugar and beaten egg yolks. Add to the hot mixture slowly. Cook until thick. Do not boil. At first bubble remove from heat. Very good with ham.

Makes 1½ cups.

MRS. ROBERT C. SCHMIDT

SHRIMP SAUCE

24 oz. mayonnaise
12 oz. cocktail sauce
1 tbsp. dry mustard
½ tsp. black pepper
¼ tsp. cayenne
3 tsp. curry powder
2 tsp. dried tarragon
2 tsp. dried parsley
1 tsp. dried basil
2 tbsp. dehydrated
  horseradish
1 tsp.Tabasco sauce
1 tbsp. Worcestershire
  sauce
1 tsp. capers (chopped and
  drained)

Mix all ingredients together and store in glass jar in refrigerator. Will keep for months.

MRS. ARNOLD BERG

*He was a bold man
that first ate an oyster.*

JONATHAN SWIFT

HOT CRAB SANDWICH

6 slices of bread or
  English muffins
Anchovy paste
1 3-oz. pkg. cream cheese
1 tbsp. milk
4 hard-boiled eggs (chopped)
¼ cup mayonnaise
1 7-oz. can of crabmeat
¾ cup black olive wedges
½ cup mayonnaise
1 tbsp. lemon juice

Spread bread (or English muffins) with anchovy paste. Soften cream cheese in milk; fold in hard-boiled eggs, mayonnaise, crabmeat and black olive wedges. Spread mixture on bread or muffins and seal with ½ cup mayonnaise mixed with lemon juice. Place in 400°-425° oven on cookie sheet until bubbly and tinged with brown.

Serves 6.

MRS. EDWARD L. SMITH

OUT OF THIS WORLD SANDWICH

4 large slices sour
  dough bread
1 can Ortega chilis (peeled
  and sliced)
8 slices tomato
8 slices bacon
8 slices sharp cheddar
  cheese
1 large avocado
Soft butter

Spread four slices of bread lightly with butter, add chilis, 2 slices bacon, 2 slices cheese, 2 slices tomato. Broil in broiler until bacon is crisp and cheese is melted. Just before serving, slice ¼ of an avocado on each.

HINT: Brown the bacon first to reduce fat splatters in the oven during broiling.

Serves 4.

JACKIE MARQUARDT

TWENTY-FOUR HOUR SANDWICHES

2 cans tuna
4 eggs (hard cooked and
  chopped)
2 small jars Old English
  sharp cheese
2 eggs
½ cup ripe olives (sliced)
⅔ cup mayonnaise
1 cup butter or margarine
  (softened)
14 slices bread

Combine tuna, olives, eggs and mayonnaise.

Cut crusts from bread and spread half of slices with tuna mixture. Cover with remaining slices to make sandwiches. Cut sandwiches diagonally at corners to divide three ways.

Combine Old English cheese, butter and eggs. Beat until thoroughly mixed. Frost individual sandwiches and place on greased cookie sheet. Cover and refrigerate 24 hours.

Bake 8 to 10 minutes in 425° oven. Garnish with parsley.

BOBBI McCORMICK

HOROSCOPE
HOSPITALITY

ARIES
MARCH 21 — APRIL 20

An energetic, restless Aries guest of honor might enjoy a patio barbeque, with tables covered in bright red cloths, copper bowls of geraniums and honeysuckle. Lots of hurricane lamps or torches will ensure a warm, cheery background. A sun-sign gift would include a diamond.

SUGGESTED MENU

John's Spinach Salad
(Recipe on Page 104)

Barbequed "Butterfly" Lamb
(Recipe on Page 256)

Rita's Honey Onions
(Recipe on Page 143)

Strawberry Heaven Angel Cake
(Recipe on Page 320)

TAURUS
APRIL 21 — MAY 20

A charming, unpretentious Taurus guest of honor might enjoy an early dinner in the garden with a soft pink or pale blue cloth centered with an arrangement of roses, violets and foxgloves. Provide comfortable seating in a relaxed atmosphere. A sun-sign gift would include a sapphire.

SUGGESTED MENU

Abalone Cocktail
(Recipe on Page 40)

Veal Piccata
(Recipe on Page 252)

Spinach Stuffed Zucchini
(Recipe on Page 150)

Fresh Peach Souffle
(Recipe on Page 295)

GEMINI
MAY 21 — JUNE 21

A lively, youthful Gemini guest of honor might enjoy a buffet dinner in the game room with bright yellow cloths and yellow tulips. Good friends, bright conversation, charades or pool will make the evening a happy one. A sun-sign gift would be made of agate.

SUGGESTED MENU

Avocado Mushroom Salad
(Recipe on Page 90)
Tiny Meatballs
(Recipe on Page 56)
Pasta Primavera
(Recipe on Page 165)
Lemon Mousse
(Recipe on Page 287)

CANCER
JUNE 22 — JULY 22

A sensitive, imaginative Cancer guest of honor might enjoy a luncheon in the atrium with pale green or gray cloths, baskets of daisies and wild flowers, and lots of delicate green plants. Close members of the family will help provide a warm, loving atmosphere. A sun-sign gift would contain a pearl or be made of silver.

SUGGESTED MENU

Broccoli Salad
(Recipe on Page 90)
Crabmeat Soufflé
(Recipe on Page 178)
Tangy Baked Tomatoes
(Recipe on Page 148)
Coconut Pecan Cake
(Recipe on Page 314)

LEO
JULY 23 — AUGUST 22

An enthusiastic, dramatic Leo guest of honor might enjoy a formal dinner served with your best silver and crystal on a cream damask cloth centered with a large arrangement of golden chrysanthemums, marigolds, and gladiolas. Invite the boss or business associates and set the stage to let your Leo shine. A sun-sign gift would contain a ruby or be made of gold.

SUGGESTED MENU

Caesar Salad
(Recipe on Page 91)

Beef Wellington
(Recipe on Page 223)

Cointreau Carrots
(Recipe on Page 137)

Trifle Pudding
(Recipe on Page 290)

VIRGO
AUGUST 23 — SEPTEMBER 22

An energetic, health-conscious Virgo guest of honor might enjoy a colorful South-of-the-Border luncheon with cloths of dark blue striped with yellow and brown. Little clay bowls of brightly colored phlox, poppies, or portulaca might display individual place cards. Put on some guitar records or bring in a small Mariachi group to accompany the meal. A sun-sign gift would be made of sardonyx.

SUGGESTED MENU

Chilled Avocado Soup
(Recipe on Page 85)

Mexican Salad Bowl
(Recipe on Page 97)

Venezuelan Chicken
(Recipe on Page 211)

Souffle Tia Maria
(Recipe on Page 296)

LIBRA
SEPTEMBER 23 — OCTOBER 23

An attractive, affable Libra guest of honor might enjoy a brunch with crystal bowls of cabbage roses on dust rose cloths or pots of hyacinths on powder blue. Old friends and a relaxed opportunity to be sociable will guarantee a successful day. A sun-sign gift would contain a sapphire.

SUGGESTED MENU

Frozen Waldorf Salad
(Recipe on Page 114)
Scrambled Eggs with Shrimp & Cheese
(Recipe on Page 158)
Scottsdale Potatoes
(Recipe on Page 144)
Orange Nut Bread
(Recipe on Page 123)

SCORPIO
OCTOBER 24 — NOVEMBER 22

A cool, magnetic Scorpio guest of honor might enjoy a midnight supper by candlelight with American Beauty roses or dark red anthurium on burgundy mats. Wine and classical music in the background will assist the romantic mood. A sun-sign gift would contain an opal.

SUGGESTED MENU

Caviar Mold
(Recipe on Page 43)
Rigatoni Alla Gorgonzola
(Recipe on Page 164)
Baked Steak
(Recipe on Page 238)
L'Escoffier Chocolate Mousse
(Recipe on Page 288)

SAGITTARIUS
NOVEMBER 23 — DECEMBER 21

An independent, exciting Sagittarius guest of honor might enjoy a light buffet brunch on the tennis court. An arrangement of iris, epiphelia and ferns on a purple cloth will provide a dramatic setting for an informal gathering after tennis. A sun-sign gift would contain a topaz.

SUGGESTED MENU

Cheesey-Gritty Casserole
(Recipe on Page 155)
Tongue Mold
(Recipe on Page 113)
Dilly Casserole Bread
(Recipe on Page 121)
Apple Poppins
(Recipe on Page 280)

CAPRICORN
DECEMBER 22 — JANUARY 19

A conservative but humorous Capricorn guest of honor might enjoy a dinner traditionally served but done with a light touch. A dark brown or gray cloth with white china and candles centered with a pewter bowl of ivy will provide a comfortable setting to entertain business partners or club members. A sun-sign gift would contain a turquoise.

SUGGESTED MENU

Peanut Soup
(Recipe on Page 81)
Phyllis Diller's Chicken Charisma
(Recipe on Page 198)
Gateau de Carrotes
(Recipe on Page 136)
Chess Pie
(Recipe on Page 326)

AQUARIUS
JANUARY 20 — FEBRUARY 18

A friendly, unpredictable Aquarius guest of honor might enjoy a late buffet supper set on electric blue mats with a large loose arrangement of delphinium, orchid or fruit blossom sprays. Plump cushions spread about for informal seating and some favorite records playing in the background will create a compatible atmosphere. A sun-sign gift would contain an amethyst or uranium.

SUGGESTED MENU

Apricot Salad Mold
(Recipe on Page 105)
Celery Bread
(Recipe on Page 119)
Natural Lamb Stew
(Recipe on Page 266)
Crustless Apple Pie
(Recipe on Page 328)

PISCES
FEBRUARY 19 — MARCH 20

An empathetic, sentimental Pisces guest of honor might enjoy a light luncheon by the pool with water lilies or lotus floating in a flat bowl on an aqua cloth. Tell the guests to bring their swim-suits and stay the afternoon. A sun-sign gift would include a moonstone or bloodstone.

SUGGESTED MENU

Cucumber Sesame Salad
(Recipe on Page 96)
Salmon Steak Teriyaki
(Recipe on Page 187)
California Cauliflower Casserole
(Recipe on Page 138)
Mocha Toffee Dessert
(Recipe on Page 284)

Looking north up Vine Street from Sunset Boulevard in the Heart of Hollywood. N.B.C. Studios on the right, A.B.C. Studios at left-center, C.B.S. Studios off-camera to the right about two blocks. The sign above the famous Brown Derby Restaurant is visible at center-right.

Circa 1950

"HOORAY FOR HOLLYWOOD!
THAT SCREWY, BALLYHOOEY HOLLYWOOD . . ."

— 1937

INDEX

★ INDEX

RECIPES INDEX